Dreams and Spiritual Growth: A Judeo-Christian Way of Dreamwork

Dreams and Spiritual Growth: A Judeo-Christian Way of Dreamwork

◆

With More Than 35 Dreamwork Techniques

by
Louis M. Savary
Patricia H. Berne
Strephon Kaplan Williams

Paulist Press, Mahwah

Book design and art by Gloria C. Ortíz

Cover Concept by Dorothy Valakos

Library of Congress
Catalog Card Number: 84-60566

ISBN: 0-8091-2629-X

Published by Paulist Press
997 Macarthur Boulevard
Mahwah, New Jersey 07430

Printed and bound in the United States of America

Contents

FRONTISPIECE

"How much there is in the Bible about dreams! There are, I think, some sixteen chapters in the Old Testament and four or five in the New in which dreams are mentioned; and there are many other passages scattered throughout the book which refer to visions. If we believe the Bible, we must accept the fact that, in the old days, God and his angels came to humans in their sleep and made themselves known in dreams."[1]

Abraham Lincoln

---

[1]Reported in Lloyd Lewis, *Myths after Lincoln* (New York: Grosset & Dunlap, 1957) p. 294. The story is told by Ward Hill Lamon, Lincoln's bodyguard and, later, biographer.

Introduction:
Our Purpose and Perspective

◆

Dreamwork: Ancient Traditions, New Methods

In the early Church, many Christians followed their dreams to find God's will and to understand how God was working in their lives. Dreamwork was commonly and openly practiced. In time, however, this reverential attitude toward the dream fell into disrepute. Dreamwork as a Christian tradition was practically lost for many centuries.

Recently this tradition was rediscovered and promoted by John Sanford and Morton Kelsey. Today, thanks to the pioneering research of these two priest-therapists, it is not unusual in Christian contexts for spiritual directors and retreat directors, as well as counselors and therapists, to ask clients to observe their dreams.

Colleges, universities and study groups are offering courses on dreams and dreamwork. New books on dreams and the Christian spiritual tradition are being published. Yet, many courses and books on dreams talk about dreamwork but do not explain adequately how to do it.

Our Purpose

In writing this book, our purpose is to present a comprehensive method for using your dreams to connect you with God, yourself, and the believing community. It is a new approach which applies much of the research and wisdom of modern psychology to the Judaeo-Christian dreamwork tradition.

We present more than thirty-five dreamwork tools and techniques that have been tried and tested by public and professionals alike. We show you how to use these techniques to begin finding meaning in your own dreams. We believe you can do dreamwork on your own; in fact, we feel you are probably the best one to discover the meaning of your own dreams.

We do not present ourselves as dream interpreters, but as dreamwork technicians. If you were to come to us, recount a dream you had, and ask us to tell you what the dream is saying, we would not try to interpret it for you. Rather, we would help you select appropriate dreamwork techniques and encourage you to search, through dreamwork, to discover for yourself the dream's various levels of meaning.

In doing your own dreamwork, you learn to work directly with spiritual energy and the language of symbols. This effort is exciting and rewarding because it allows you to develop your own relationship to God and to assume responsibility for your own spiritual practice and life. By the time you complete the final chapter you will be familiar with a comprehensive dreamwork methodology.

While our approach does not demand the help of a professional counselor, therapist, or spiritual director, we suggest clear ways that psychological and spiritual professionals can enhance dreamwork done by a client. (See especially Chapters 14 and 15.)

Our Perspective

Our perspective on dreamwork is four-dimensional: psychological, spiritual, historical, and theological.

Psychologically, we view dreamwork as a holistic process leading toward personality transformation. For this reason, we integrated into our approach an understanding of dreams and certain dreamwork techniques developed by modern psychology.

Spiritually, we view dreamwork as an arena of relationship between you and God, and as a helpful resource on the journey toward holiness as well as wholeness. Specifically, dreamwork is a way to foster practical connections between inner and outer life, between symbolic process and daily choices, between personal intuitions and decisions which affect others.

Historically, we hope to reconnect with, develop, and help carry on the vital Judaeo-Christian dreamwork tradition which functioned in the Church from the time of the Old Testament patriarchs until about the fifth century A.D. We hope to create a basis for Christians doing dreamwork today. We support a renewal of dreamwork as an accepted and important spiritual practice, along with meditation, prayer, spiritual reading, liturgy, service to others, and so on.

Theologically, we view the dream as an ever-present call to holiness and wholeness, and see dreamwork as a way of fostering relation to our souls and to God. We want to show how dreams and dreamwork can benefit the believing community, and our hope is that dreamwork will become an integral resource for the Christian community in understanding itself and seeking its divine purposes.

Dreamwork and Non-Christians

Dreamwork is not only for Christians. Dreams are given to everyone. As such, they are a continual reminder to all persons of the universal call toward holiness and wholeness. How persons *respond* to their dreams is the issue. From ancient times, people of all religions have shown reverence for dreams and sought to understand their meaning. The God of Israel often directed the history of the chosen people by means of dreams given to non-Hebrew people as well. For example, in the Book of Genesis such dreams were given to Hagar, Abraham's Egyptian maid (Gen 16:7; 21:17), King Abimelech (Gen 20:3), Laban, Jacob's father-in-law (Gen 31:24), and the Pharoah in Egypt (Gen 41:1).

In writing this book our intention is not to exclude non-Christian readers, but primarily to reconnect Christians with the powerful dreamwork tradition that is their heritage. Although we present stories and examples of dreamwork from a Christian perspective, the dreamwork techniques in this book are ecumenical and may be used equally well by all people. The procedures will prove helpful to anyone who accepts the premise that dreams come from a source other than one's own conscious ego and are given to strengthen and guide us on our spiritual path.

Some Contrasts

Taking a Christian perspective enriched by the insights of contemporary psychology has taught us to look upon the dream in fresh ways.

While many people look to a dream to find an *answer* to their problems, we have discovered that a dream is more helpful when viewed as a *question*. So, instead of seeking to discover what a dream is telling us to do, we suggest looking for the central question that a dream may be asking us to reflect or focus upon.

Again, while many people see a dream as something with a *hidden meaning*, we discover that once people begin doing dreamwork regularly they can learn to feel at home with a dream's *clear, but symbolic, language,* and become familiar with spiritual energy.

Third, while many treat a dream as *a piece of information* to be conceptually grasped, we have found, in contrast, that a dream is more helpfully viewed as an *invitation to relationship.* What if we experienced our dreams as an invitation given by the Source of our life and destiny calling us to a spiritual journey toward greater consciousness, and to a relationship with the divine?

Again, while some may view dreams as *something useless and worthless,* we find it helpful to view a dream as a *gift* and to value it as an important addition to our life. When appropriate dreamwork is done upon a dream, it can become an experience which heals, comforts, guides, and warns us. It inspires new perspectives on life and calls us to live our waking hours in enriched and more vital ways.

Finally, while some view a dream as something *uniquely personal only,* we have discovered again and again, as the early Christians did, that a dream is a gift not only to the individual but also to the *community.* A dream may offer meaning, insight, and energy to others as well as to the dreamer. If we work toward wholeness simply in personal terms, we may miss the fact that we are developing ourselves for service in the community. Our individual work, and the community itself, can be a vehicle of grace for a larger totality than our personal self-actualization.

What Is a Dream?

A night dream is a spontaneous symbolic experience lived out in the inner world during sleep. Such dreams are composed of a series of images, actions, thoughts, words, and feelings over which we seem to have little or no conscious control. The people, places, and things of our dreams can sometimes be related to remembered life experiences or images that remain in our memory, but often they seem to come from sources to which we have little or no conscious access.

Whatever the source and content of our dreams, sleep researchers inform us, we usually dream about five times during an ordinary night's sleep. Periods of dreaming may be less than a minute or as long as an hour.

People who claim not to dream, researchers say, simply do not recall dream content. Most people remember only their final dream before waking, and even that dream may be lost if it is not recorded in written or spoken form immediately upon awakening. With practice, we can learn to wake ourselves after dreaming periods and so record at least one if not several dreams each night.

It has been observed that each of the dreams of a single night may relate to a similar issue, but they are presented from a number of different perspectives. It is traditionally believed that the final dreaming period of the night, just before waking, is the most important one, and perhaps even summarizes the wisdom of the other dreams.

The dreamwork techniques presented throughout this book may be used with any and all dreams. However, you will realize as soon as you begin doing dreamwork that you will not have time to reflect upon every dream. You will need to make choices how to spend your dreamwork time.

What Is Dreamwork?

"A dream unexamined is like a letter unopened," wrote a Jewish sage. Another way of saying this is that a dream is often incomplete without dreamwork. Dreamwork is a conscious, intentional response to a dream. It usually involves using techniques designed to find in the dream ways to further the process of our call to holiness and wholeness, and to deepen our relationship with God.

If a dream is indeed like a letter, then there is someone who sent it. Receiving a dream implies there is a relationship between us and the one who sent the dream. To do dreamwork is to carry on that relationship. Dreamwork is like opening the letter, reading it, and responding to it. Dreamwork becomes one way of consciously getting in touch with God's will for us and cooperating with it. Using the dreamwork techniques in this book will allow you to revivify your dreams, begin to understand them, and find ways to cooperate with them in becoming who you are called and meant to be.

For example, a woman recently separated from her husband woke up after a dream feeling disoriented and uncomfortable. "In my dream," she explained, "I was driving my two teenaged children with all their 'junk' from my house to the house where their father was living. I awoke without peace in the relationship with my children. In recalling the dream I felt a sense of loss." This was clearly an unwelcome dream for her. Her immediate reaction was she was giving up her children, but after doing dreamwork she discovered that her relationship with her daughters was fine, even though they were moving in with their father. The dream was simply asking her if she was ready to give up the role of being "keeper of her daughters' junk." When she realized the insight and invitation the dream was making, her body felt the truth of it. After doing dreamwork, her peace returned because the dream was resolved. In fact, the dream helped her change her attitude toward certain issues involving her daughters. They were now moving into a closer relationship with their father: she would let them work out the details (junk) of structuring this relationship for themselves. As she began letting go of some of her usual mother role, she felt at peace in seeking other creative avenues for her fulfillment.

After doing our own dreamwork, we usually experience our dreams more meaningfully and clearly than we did originally. As the woman learned, dreamwork helps a dream come alive in new and different ways, and shows us how to integrate its wisdom into our personality, our daily lives, and our relation to God.

When we approach a dream as a gift, we give it a loving response. The work of love is attention. Dreamwork is a process of attention to a dream; therefore it is also a process of gratitude and love: gratitude for the gift of the dream, and love for God the Source of the dream.

What would it mean to really live life in this spirit, to offer gratitude for things revealed to us because we have asked and have been truly receptive?

Doing Dreamwork Yourself

Many current and ancient approachs to dreams use a dream as a way of providing an opportunity for a professional to suggest insights and interpretations about the dreamer's life and behavior. Our approach goes beyond this by creating useful avenues for dreamers themselves to work with their dream material and to respond to the invitation to wholeness which it brings.

Many books about dreams focus on people's fascinating dream experiences and ways dreams have changed their lives. While other books may inspire you with the possibilities of dreamwork, our main intent is to show you *how to do dreamwork* in ways that will help guide your personal and spiritual growth. We want to give you the tools to transform the inspiration of your dreams into energy applied to your own life and your relation to God.

Dreamwork as an Art

Doing dreamwork may be viewed as an art. The cultural arts—painting, poetry, sculpture, and the like—deal with values and events symbolically. So does dreamwork. In this book we offer a broad range of dreamwork techniques to foster your creativity in understanding what your dreams are asking of you and saying to you. The techniques in this book will help you practice making your dreamworld and waking life come more alive spiritually and psychologically. Regularly practicing them—alone, with a dreamwork partner or with a dreamwork group—will develop your proficiency and confidence in them.

We hope you will try each of the dreamwork techniques at least once. Then, by experimenting, you will gradually discover those that seem to work best for you. Like any art or life skill, practice will help dreamwork develop for you as you move forward and deepen your process.

A basic level of commitment to dreamwork usually involves keeping a dreamwork journal in which you write your dreams as they come to you and record the dreamwork you do. Newcomers to dreamwork usually work on one dream each week, even though they may routinely record a number of dreams in a week.

The actual dreamwork is usually done alone in the quiet of your own solitude, but this may often be followed by sharing your dream and dreamwork with a friend, a therapist, a spiritual counselor or in a dream group. Dream-group sharing has the advantage of providing support and feedback in the dreamwork process, especially if the group members are all using a similar approach to dreamwork. At times you may feel the need to seek professional help if material coming up in your dreams or in your life seems potentially overwhelming. In doing dreamwork, you will also be acknowledging that God is communicating with you directly and personally through dreams.

Dreamwork as Prayer and Healing

In treating a dream and its divine Source with reverence, the time of dreamwork becomes a time of prayer and worship. We acknowledge that God has given energy to our soul. In return, by doing dreamwork we consciously present to God the dream's gift of our life energy. We offer back to the Source ourselves transformed by the energy, or grace, coming to us through the dream. We are graced in receiving the dream, and our dreamwork returns the dream, now transformed, as an offering to God.

When Jesus cured the ten lepers, all ten were healed in his presence, but only one returned to give thanks. Certainly all ten experienced healing and felt grateful. Why did Jesus find this one man so different? The one who returned acknowledged his gratitude by honoring the

Source of his healing and establishing a conscious relationship to that Source.

Establishing *relationship* to God is a keynote of the Western spiritual tradition. In doing dreamwork we are acknowledging the Source of our healing and wholeness, and we are also building a relationship to that Source. In dreamwork, as in meditation and contemplation, we are strengthening our relationship to God.

Doing dreamwork in a religious context also seems to create in people a greater likelihood of having healing experiences. Many of life's conflicts and challenges are so powerful that most people have difficulty dealing with them using merely their own conscious values and willpower. However, a religious perspective introduces a transcendent power for healing and wholeness working in every situation in our lives. It makes a difference how actively we choose to relate to the Source of this power. Healing of wounds, psychological and spiritual, or achieving new growth does not necessarily happen just because we *will* it to. Any therapeutic process really begins to move forward when we choose to work with God as an active force in our life helping to bring about our destiny and wholeness. This sense of actively cooperating with the divine Source is frequently experienced during dreamwork or in the reflection upon dreamwork.

Can we say that through dreams, as well as certain events in our lives, God answers our prayers daily? Certainly we can respond to God's dream-gifts by our dreamwork through which we live changed and meaningful lives.

What Is Spiritual Growth?

Spirituality may be defined as our way of responding to God, or our style of living in relation to God. More generally, our spirituality might be defined as our pattern of being and acting in the world in light of our ultimate values.

One of the tasks of the spiritual path is to become conscious of the values in which our lives are rooted. Values are the context of our lives and choices. We live our lives in the light of ultimate values, whether we are conscious of them or not. One of the first signs of spiritual growth is becoming conscious of our ultimate values by discovering what it is which deep down motivates our choices and actions.

Whether we affirm it or not, we are continually in a growth process—physically, psychologically, spiritually, socially, culturally. Growth means not only adding something new to our life but also often letting go of something old and no longer useful. Birthdays are celebrations of growth that symbolize both an adding to life as well as a leave-taking from that which has already been lived.

Spiritual growth calls us consciously to choose to work toward wholeness—our own wholeness and, whenever possible, the wholeness of our intimates and the larger community.

Following our dreams and doing dreamwork helps us grow familiar with a world larger than our waking life. It can take us on a spiritual journey and put us directly in touch with the energies of God. Through dreams God inspires us to become whole and holy.

Part I

Relating to God Through Dreams and Dreamwork

◆

Chapter 1

Dreamwork in Old Testament Times: Relating to God Through Dreams and Visions

◆

The Voice of God

Where is the voice of God in our day? Where has it been found in times past?

What better place to begin our exploration of dreams and the spiritual life than to go back to Old Testament times? In doing this, we are placing ourselves at the original site and experience which initiated the historical development of the Judaeo-Christian religion. And since dreams themselves are very much original experience, it will not be surprising to discover the central place dreams held in the lives of the Hebrew prophets, leaders, and people.

What approach did the ancient Hebrews take toward the dream? How did they value dreams? What was the tradition of dreams and dreamwork found in the Old Testament? How are dreams and visions related to each other in the Bible? What did the Hebrews look for in their dreams? These are some of the questions to which we seek answers.

Jacob's Dream

Today we live in a world of material wealth and technological convenience, with little emphasis placed on God's revelation through inner experiences such as dreams, images, and primary intuitions of spiritual truth. In a spirit of openness to certain eternal spiritual images and what they might evoke for us personally, let us explore freshly the account of Jacob's ladder dream as recounted in Genesis 28:10–22.[1]

JACOB PREPARING FOR THE DREAM (vv. 10–11)
Jacob left Beer-sheba and set out for Haran. He came upon a certain place[2] and stopped there for the night, since the sun had set. Taking one of the stones from that place, he put it under his head and lay down on that spot.

JACOB'S DREAM (vv. 12–15)
He had a dream: a ladder (or stairway)[3] was set on the ground, with its top reaching to the sky; and the angels of God were going up and down on it.
And there was Yahweh standing beside him and saying:
"I Yahweh am the God of your forefather Abraham and the God of Isaac; the ground on which you are resting I will give to you and to your offspring. Your offspring shall be as plentiful as the dust on the ground, and you shall spread out west and east, north and south; and all the communities of the earth shall bless themselves by you and your off-spring. Remember, I am with you; I will protect you wherever you go, and bring you back to this land; nor will I leave you until I have done what I promised you."

JACOB'S RESPONSE TO THE DREAM (vv. 16–22)
Jacob awoke from his sleep and said, "Truly, Yahweh abides in this site, but I was not aware!" Shaken, he exclaimed, "How awesome is this place! This is none other than the abode of God and the gateway to heaven!"

14

Early next morning, Jacob took the stone that he had put under his head, set it up as a pillar, and poured oil on its top. He named that site Bethel, whereas the former name of that town had been Luz.

Jacob then made a vow, saying, "If God remains with me, protecting me on this journey that I am taking, and giving me bread to eat and clothing to wear, and I come back safe to my father's house, Yahweh shall be my God. This stone that I have set up as a pillar shall be God's abode; and of all that you shall grant me, I will always set aside a tenth for you."

Jacob's Dreamwork

Through a dream Jacob has seen angels and heard the voice of God. What relationship to God is being conveyed to Jacob in the dream itself, and how does he respond to it? Does Jacob really understand the meaning of his dream? Can we tell by the dream itself and his response? What specifically are his reactions?

Jacob is awakened by his dream and deeply moved. He recognizes that he has been visited by God and that the place where he slept is sacred. It is a gateway to heaven, the world of divine energy. Jacob recognizes also that he was unaware—we might say unconscious—of the place's significance. Jacob then does several things which we in our contemporary approach would call dream tasks, that is, specific actions in response to a dream.

Jacob creates an altar, or sacred place, by setting up the stone and anointing it. Then he renames the place Bethel, which means "house of God." Jacob's third response, his commitment to Yahweh, is interesting since it is conditional. Because of the dream, Jacob knows that God is present to him and has offered to protect him and his people. But Jacob will only choose Yahweh to be his God if Yahweh really carries out his promise to protect him. Jacob spells out even further than in the original dream what God must do. Fourth, Jacob states that he will give a tenth of all that he receives from God back to him.

What can we conclude from Jacob's response to his dream? Can we say that he sees the covenant between God and himself as a mutual or two-way agreement? In the dream, God made an offer. Jacob responds by making the offer more specific and then puts a condition on the entire relationship. He will accept Yahweh as his God if God fulfills the promises. Can we not view our dreams and our responses to them as a kind of dialogue with God?

In the history of the Hebrew people, Jacob is a crucial link. He is not merely a runaway who has taken the birthright and blessing that by tradition would belong to his brother Esau. He receives the covenant which defines the relationship between God and the chosen people, and he is to be the parent of a community that will cover the earth. This important communication comes through the dream at Bethel.

God Makes Contact
Through Dreams and Visions

A number of Old Testament attitudes toward dreams and relating to God are evident from Jacob's dream. First, through his dream Jacob was convinced that God had made direct contact with him. We have here, then, the belief that God speaks through dreams and, as seen elsewhere in the Old Testament, through visions also.

In the Old Testament, both dreams and visions seem to possess equal spiritual authority. In fact, in Hebrew and Greek, the words for dream and vision are related to the same prophetic root experience. Further, dreams and visions were often spoken of in the same breath, for example, "If anyone among you is a prophet, I will make myself known to him in a vision, I will speak to him in a dream" (Num 12:6). Or, speaking through Joel, one of the later prophets, God says,

> I will pour out my spirit on all mankind. Your sons and daughters shall prophesy, your old men shall dream dreams, and your young men shall see visions. Even on the slaves, men and women, will I pour out my spirit in those days (Jl 2:28–29).

On the day of Pentecost, the first words of Peter's speech to the assembled crowds were those very words from Joel (Acts 2:17–18).

Thus, a basic principle of biblical dream theory is that *God makes direct contact with people through dreams and visions.* God is interested in establishing relationship, and does it through such inner experiences. This basic principle is taken up by Christians in the first centuries, and remains the foundation stone of the contemporary theory of dreams and dreamwork presented in this book.

Both dreams and visions seem to come from the same source in the inner world. The difference is that dreams appear to us during sleep, while visions are experiences of intense imagery, sound and feeling occurring during the waking state. Most commonly, visions happen to people during prayer, but also in periods of major stress and transition points. One woman who was staying day and night by her dying son's bedside had extremely intense visions of the Virgin Mary, which gave the woman support and a deeply religious perspective in dealing with her son's dying.

We note also that in biblical times God spoke through dreams and visions not only to individuals but to the community as well.[4] This is certainly true of Jacob's dream at Bethel, for the message in the dream was meant not only for Jacob but for his family and his descendants. For example, the prophet Hosea felt that Jacob's dream was the property of the entire Hebrew community. In commenting on Jacob's dream, the Greek translation has Hosea saying, "God met Jacob at Bethel and spoke to him." In the original Hebrew, however, the text reads, "God met Jacob at Bethel and spoke to us" (Hos 12:5).

The Symbolic and Literal Content of Dreams

Jacob's dream contains both literal and symbolic material. Yahweh's words (vv. 13–15) seem to be a clear and direct communication to Jacob, and may be considered the literal or manifest content of the dream. But what are we to make of the symbolic images in this famous dream? The ladder? The angels? Note that Jacob does not seem to deal directly with the imagery. It is simply there—perhaps as an added sign that God is really present in the dream and in the place where he is sleeping.

In the Old Testament, there seem to be different ways of dealing with symbolic imagery in dreams. One way is Jacob's, who seems inspired by the images of his dream, but does not attempt to interpret them. Jacob's son Joseph, who deals with symbols in another way, becomes a direct interpreter of dream images. He tends to find messages in the symbols.

Symbolism is a universal language. Symbolic images, such as those which happen in dreams and visions, are more primary and more universal than concepts, usually communicated in a dream by specific words; these words, of course, may have symbolic as well as literal meaning.

A symbol is an image or cluster of images with more than one possible meaning. Dreams speak to us largely in images because, in consciousness, image is prior and more primary than concept. We can see this difference between image and concept as one of the major differences in emphasis between the Catholic and Protestant churches. Catholicism has kept the ancient tradition of relating to images in order to experience the mystery behind the image. Protestantism, on the other hand, developed in reaction to what it considered an overemphasis on the symbolic, and it emphasized, instead, rational thought and a theology of consciousness. Today, there seems to be a growing need to integrate both the symbolic and the literal into balanced forms for expressing the religious experiences of humankind.

This balanced dynamic of the word accompanying the image is clearly seen in Jacob's dream. In later chapters, we will be presenting dreamwork techniques which both enhance the power of images and change imagery into usable concepts for everyday living and direction in life.

It may be that in dreams and visions the symbolic experience acts as a sign of or prologue to a dialogue with God. For example, Moses saw the symbol of the burning bush before God began to speak with him (Ex 3:1–6). And Ezekiel had an image of a valley full of dry bones before God began a dialogue (Ez 37:1–10). Moses, like Jacob, does not seem curious about the meaning of the symbol. He simply experiences it directly. In contrast, interpretation basically means changing image into concept or symbol into meaning. Jacob's son Joseph and Daniel are perhaps the most famous dream interpreters in the Old Testament. It is interesting that both Joseph and Daniel seem mostly to interpret the symbolic dreams of non-Jews (see Gen 40—41, and the Book of Daniel), perhaps implying that the Jewish patriarchs and prophets experienced the meaning of their own dream symbols directly.

Our position as dreamwork practitioners is not to interpret dreams for others, but to help others learn how to experience their own dreams as revelatory. We encourage people to be more like Moses and Jacob, to work with their own dreams and symbolic experiences.

Actualizing Dreams

The result of Jacob's direct experience of his dream, and therefore of God, was action. He acted on his dream in a number of significant ways. In this, he was doing what we call actualizing a dream. It is our fundamental premise that we gain more from dreams by doing things in response to them than we do from simply interpreting them. As we mentioned before, after his dream Jacob actualizes it in a number of ways: he makes sacred the place where he slept by changing its name from Luz to Bethel, he anoints the stone on which his head rested and sets it up as a monument, he agrees to accept Yahweh as his God if he and his people prosper, and he agrees to tithe to the service of God a tenth part of all he gains. Notice that Jacob's actualizations are directly related to the dream and yet are not simply a literal carrying out of something spoken or enacted in the dream. Clearly, Jacob has somehow worked with the dream material and responded to it in a way that is important to him and his growth as a person and as a leader of his tribe. Many of the dream-work techniques we suggest throughout the book are ways of actualizing dreams.

Joseph, too, was a dream actualizer. Even though he interprets the pharaoh's dream, he does not let his insight remain within the realms of concepts and thoughts. He acts upon the dream, and the pharaoh acts with him. The dream interpreter is also considered a wise man of action, and so the pharaoh appoints Joseph as his minister for organizing the country against the coming famine (see Gen 41:33–43) predicted in the pharaoh's dream.

In contrast to this approach of actualizing symbolic dream experience in the everyday world, some later, rather skeptical, Old Testament writers believed that dreams were of no consequence—for example, in Sir 34:1–8 or in Eccl 5:7. The words in Ecclesiastes are: "For in a multitude of dreams there is futility, and ruin in a flood of words." We agree with this observation in the sense that a multitude of dreams or words remains unproductive if not worked with, organized, and integrated.

The *Encyclopedia Judaica* reports a prayer from the Talmud related to dreams that is recited during the priestly benediction:

> Sovereign of the Universe, I am thine and my dreams are thine. I have dreamt a dream and do not know what it is. Whether I have dreamt about myself, or my companions have dreamt about me, or I have dreamt about others—if they are good dreams, confirm and reinforce them like the dreams of Joseph. If they require a remedy, heal them. . . . As Thou didst turn the curse of the wicked Balaam into a blessing, so turn all my dreams into something beneficial for me.[5]

This ancient prayer provides some striking insights. Its central motif seems to be that not only the person but his or her dreams belong to God; also that some dreams need understanding and some dreams need healing and transforming. The transforming is evoked by the person and done by God. This prayer echoes our dreamwork approach in that we utilize dreams to relate to God, and that we also work to resolve and transform dreams that seem frightening or unresolved. Also, as the prayer intimates, we feel it is important to actualize dreams by discovering their practical application to our own and others' lives.

The Prophet Daniel and Dreams

The Old Testament story of Daniel and his relation to dreams is a powerful and revealing one. Briefly, young Daniel, in captivity with his fellow Hebrews under the Babylonians, is chosen and educated by them for King Nebuchadnezzar's service. One night the king has a very disturbing dream that he does not understand. He is so demanding of his wise men that he insists they also read his mind and tell him what he has dreamed, as well as give him the dream's correct meaning. The Babylonian seers fail, and all are to be executed, including Daniel who had not even been told of the challenge. Under shadow of imminent death, Daniel consults the God of the Jews, the king's dream is revealed to him as well as its interpretation, and Daniel saves himself and the rest of the wise men.

The dream's message is that the king is growing completely unreasonable because of his enormous power and will have a mental breakdown that can be healed only if the king acknowledges God, and not himself, as the supreme ruler. Nebuchadnezzar does indeed go through this sequence of events and experiences a transformation before his death. Daniel is given ministerial power in the kingdom, he interprets dreams and visions for the succeeding king, and he has powerful dreams and visions of his own.

Daniel remains an excellent example of how to use and relate to dreams within the context of relating to God. Daniel's image of God is of one who reveals that which is vitally important, one who responds when evoked through devotion; he calls God "the revealer of mysteries" (Dan 2:29, 47). Daniel, unlike the king, does not claim to be the source of his own gift for understanding dreams, but acknowledges that such wisdom and power come from God, from sources other than merely human.

It is our position, then, as with Daniel, that dreams, because of their power and possibility for evoking change, are best worked with within a spiritual framework, a framework that acknowledges that we are only one of the factors in the dream and dreamwork process.

We may not have dreams of Jacob's or Daniel's magnitude, but certainly all of us have extremely intense and significant dreams during our lifetimes. Our attitude toward such dreams, and our commitment and ability to work with them, can make a decisive difference in our lives.

In seeking the meaning of a dream, Daniel prayed, opened himself to God, and affirmed God as dream source. He acknowledged that both the dream content and the understanding of the dream did not come from his own ego or intellect, but from a Source wiser than his own conscious knowledge and beliefs.

Daniel does dreamwork and God gives dreams in order that he should learn what the dream means and understand his innermost thoughts. In this book we take a similar perspective. Dreams are given to us so that we may grow in wisdom and understand ourselves better.

Dreamwork Technique 1:
The Dream Report

Writing down your dream, or whatever of it you can recall immediately upon waking, is a first and essential step in dreamwork. Writing a dream report makes the dream more available to work with in using various other dreamwork practices. As you write, you will often recall other details, and the dream may grow more vivid. By committing yourself to recording your dreams, you are in effect saying they have value to you in your waking life. You are also practicing recall of thoughts and feelings which are barely conscious, and thus learning how to tune into your inner resources.

For those who have blocks to writing down dreams, we suggest that you at least make a few notes, and perhaps do some other activity such as drawing an image from the dream, telling the dream into a tape recorder, or sharing it with a friend.

Dreamwork Technique 1
The Dream Report

Procedure:
1. Just before falling asleep, prepare your consciousness for dreaming and for remembering your dream upon waking. Consider important moments of the past day or the coming day, and think of any issues about which you would like to have a dream. Fall asleep saying to yourself, "I will wake up remembering my dream." Have by your bedside a light, a journal, and a pen for recording your dreams.

2. If possible, let yourself awaken to the memory of your dream before the alarm clock goes off. In any case, as soon as you awaken, write down your dream or the thoughts in your head, without censoring or editing. Include images, actions, reactions, thoughts,

attitudes, feelings, conversations, choices, character descriptions—anything you can recall happening in the dream. Describe things in sensory details such as colors, sounds, tastes, movements, sensations, etc. Write quickly without concern for grammar, spelling or punctuation. Then, when finished writing and recalling the dream, go over what you have written, making the writing and context clearer.

3. Next, beneath the dream, write the subheading "Comments," and write after it any feelings or thoughts that come to you. These are immediate reactions. Do not analyze or depart too far from the dream. Simply record your mood and the questions, associations and images which naturally come to you. These may help clarify the meaning and context of the dream. Now you are ready for dreamwork. But even if you do nothing further with this dream, you have honored it and the divine Source from which it came.

Dreamwork Technique 2: Title, Theme, Affect, Question (TTAQ)

As soon as you finish writing your Dream Report, do the TTAQ technique. It is perhaps the most universally helpful short technique in dreamwork, and provides a good first step toward understanding your dream when you have very little time to devote to dreamwork.

First, give your dream a *title.* Letting a title come to you helps focus on the dream's essence and gives you an easy way to refer to the dream later on. The title may be one word or a series of words. It can be a question, a feeling statement, an action sentence, or a primary image and the dreamer's interaction with that image. For example, Jacob might have titled his dream, "The Ladder and the Angels," "My Destiny Dream," "Making a Covenant with God," "God with Me," and so on. More than one title may come to you, in which case you may choose the one that seems more primary, or include both. You might feel a need to create separate titles for distinct parts of your dream. One way to focus yourself in doing this technique is to ask: "What title does this dream want itself to have?"

Next, beneath the title, write the dream's main *theme or major issue.* If there are a number of themes, list them in the sequence in which they appeared in the dream. We can't know for certain what theme Jacob felt was most important; perhaps he might have considered issues such as "my relationship to God," "the connection between earth and heaven," "the future of my family and tribe," or "the faithfulness of God." Naming a theme requires that you stand back and see the dream in an overview. In discovering and naming the major theme or issue for yourself, you are beginning to find the dream's meaning for you and your life. You are learning what the dream considers important for you, but you are also beginning to take your own stance in directly relating to the dream. If you feel overwhelmed or confused by the dream, perhaps because of its complexity or magnitude, deal with pieces of the dream one at a time, finding a theme for each one.

At this stage of dreamwork, you are reflecting your present conscious perspective on the dream. It is a place from which to start. Further dreamwork may alter your perspective. A dream theme you first thought of as "my relationship with friends" may, after more dreamwork, turn out to be "my insecurity." That's all right, because dreamwork is always a process, and in a process some things invariably change.

Third, next to the word Affect, write down the *feelings and emotional states* in the sequence in which they were experienced during the dream. We relate to dream experiences not only by conceptualizing them, as in stating the major theme and issues, but also through our emotional responses such as feelings, moods, anxieties, etc. The question to ask yourself here is: "How did I feel about the dream and what was happening in the dream while the dream was occurring? And how did I feel about the dream after it was all over?" These questions may point to different experiences. Feelings include such states as fear, joy, enthusiasm, insecurity, delight, comfortableness, pleasure, frustration, anxiety, curiosity, anger, and so forth. Although we are not told of Jacob's feeling responses during the dream—only he could know those—we are told of his sense of wonder, awe, reverence, surprise, and readiness to make a covenant with God upon awakening.

Fourth, Q stands for *question:* not *"What question would you ask of this dream?"* (which is Dreamwork Technique 3), but *"What question does this dream seem to be asking of you?"* This fourth step suggests you listen to the dream as if it were a friend asking you a meaningful question.

As we mentioned in the Introduction, a dream is better viewed as a question rather than an answer. If we begin to look in a dream for questions rather than answers, we begin actively relating to the dream. We open ourselves to new possibilities and meaning. We begin establishing a relationship between the dream and our spiritual life. There is a need for answers. We do not deny that. But the deepest answers come not out of the dream, nor out of our own ego consciousness, but out of the *active relationship* between ourselves and the Source of the dream.

Rather than give us answers, dreams may put us in touch with options, alternatives, choices, possibilities, patterns in our lifestyles, situations needing resolution, relationships needing attention, potentials needing activation.

With regard to dreams, and even life itself, perhaps it is better not to seek for answers, but to focus instead on our *responses.* A response usually produces an interaction between two beings. It usually also produces a shift in our awareness, an increase in consciousness. As Jacob began to respond to his dream, he became aware of God's presence and power in his life in ways he had never been conscious of before. Responses open us up to fuller possibilities, while answers tend to close us down to narrow and absolute definitions of things. At times, of course, a very specific answer is appropriate to a situation. But, in general, thinking in terms of responses guards against seeing symbolic dream material as literal messages or commandments to do this or that, or as promises that a specific thing will surely happen.

Dreamwork Technique 2
Title, Theme, Affect, Question
TTAQ

Procedure:

1. TITLE. Give your dream a title. Let it come to you spontaneously, or ask yourself, "What title does this dream want itself to have?"

2. THEME. State the major theme or issues which surfaced in the dream. If there are more than one, note them in sequence.

3. AFFECT. What was the dominant feeling or emotional energy experienced during the dream? If there was a sequence of feelings, state them in sequence.

4. QUESTION. What question is the dream asking of me? What is the dream trying to help me become conscious of?

Notes to Chapter 1
Dreamwork in Old Testament Times
1. The significance of Jacob's dream episode as a foundation stone of the Hebrew nation and religion was sensed very early in the shaping of the Book of Genesis, for both the

Elohist and Yahwist sources contain the story. And instead of parallel accounts of it separately presented, as is usually the case, e.g., the creation stories, in this passage is found "a composite version intricately blended," according to the Old Testament scholar E.A. Speiser, whose translation of the passage we follow: E.A. Speiser, *Genesis: The Anchor Bible* (New York, Doubleday, 1964), p. 219.

2. The story implies that Jacob was hoping God would communicate with him. It is, therefore, not unlikely that the "certain place" where Jacob decided to sleep was a religious sanctuary. Such a place, probably belonging to the Canaanites, would contain small stone pillars of the kind Jacob placed under his head. Using a symbolic stone for a pillow was a common practice in the dream sanctuaries of that time.

3. E.A. Speiser says the Hebrew word here suggests, not a ladder, but rather a ramp or solid stairway. Archeologically, the Mesopotamian temple towers, or ziggurats, were equipped with flights of stairs leading up to the summit where the deity would supposedly visit and communicate with mortals. During his journey to Mesopotamia, Jacob would have been familiar with these "gateways to heaven." *Op. cit.* p. 219.

4. Some Old Testament dreams intended for the benefit of the community include: Gen 20:3; 31:10–24; 37:5–9; 40; 41, Jgs 7:13, 1 Kgs 3:5–15; Dan 2; 4.

5. *Encyclopedia Judaica* (New York: Macmillan, 1971), Vol. 6, pp. 209–10.

Chapter 2

Dreamwork in New Testament Times: God's Guidance Through Dreams

◆

The roots of the Christian religion lie in the religion of the Hebrew people. But with the birth and teaching of Jesus, and later of the Christian founders, a new element entered the consciousness of humanity. What was this element, and what was its relation to God who speaks through dreams and visions?

Inner Experience

Perhaps the crucial turning point in the evolution from the Old to the New Testament which Jesus brought into the world was that he taught a religion one of whose foundations was *inner experience.* Not only do we have such statements as "The Kingdom of God is within," but we have all the parables which emphasize inner experience, as well as Jesus' own example of relating to God as Abba, a personal Father. Could Jesus have been suggesting that God not only works in history, the outer events and the religious community, as was the dominant Jewish belief of the times, but that God also works through inner experience, not just in the prophets, but in everyone? This is relevant to our exploration of one of the most central experiences of the inner world, the dream, its meaning and significance.

In the New Testament books, dreams are mentioned most frequently in the Gospel of Matthew, the Acts of the Apostles, and the Letters of Paul. Visions and other spiritual visitations, which possess an authority similar to dreams, are mentioned in all the Synoptic Gospels, as well as in John's Gospel and in the Apocalypse.[1]

Stories around the birth of Jesus contain much dream and vision material. According to some biblical scholars, the infancy narratives, at least as written documents, are to be dated after the time of the apostles.[2] In any case, they may be treated as religious statements from early Christianity. Thus, these infancy narratives are informative, for they reveal attitudes toward dreams and visions, and the uses of these inner experiences in religious teaching and practice during the first centuries of the Church. Joseph's dream to marry Mary is a good example of this.

Joseph's Dream (Mt 1:18–25)

BACKGROUND OF THE DREAM (vv.18–19)
This is how Jesus Christ came to be born.
His mother Mary was betrothed to Joseph; but before they came to live together, she was found to be with child through the Holy Spirit. Her husband, Joseph, being a man of honor and wanting to spare her publicity, decided to divorce her informally.

JOSEPH'S DREAM (vv. 20–21)
He had made up his mind to do this when the angel of the Lord appeared to him in a dream and said:
"Joseph, son of David, do not be afraid to take Mary home as your wife, because she has conceived what is in her by the Holy Spirit. She will give birth to a son and you must name him Jesus, because he is the one who is to save his people from their sins."

EVANGELIST'S COMMENT (vv. 22–23)

Now all this took place to fulfill the words spoken by the Lord through the prophet: "The virgin will conceive and give birth to a son and they will call him Emmanuel, a name which means 'God-is-with-us.' "

JOSEPH'S RESPONSE TO THE DREAM (vv. 24–25)

When Joseph woke, he did what the angel of the Lord had told him to do: he took his wife to his home and, though he had not had intercourse with her, she gave birth to a son; and he named him Jesus.

Joseph's Attitudes Toward the Dream

First of all, Joseph listens to his dream. He does not dismiss it but, rather, pays attention to it and values it.

Moreover, he presumes that he can be in direct contact with the spiritual world, and that a dream can be a way for such contact to happen. He presumes that a dream can offer him wisdom that he does not possess on his own.

Perhaps the most striking attitude of Joseph is his willingness to follow the direction of the dream rather than Jewish custom or law. According to customs of the time, Joseph had only two alternatives when he discovered Mary pregnant with a baby not his own: to have her publicly stoned to death or to send her away from the community to have her baby (and, of course, not marry her). The dream offers him a third choice—to take Mary to live in his home and thus declare to the community that he is choosing to be her husband despite the apparent adultery. Joseph follows the (Christian) principles of love, forgiveness, and acceptance, and responds to God's will as it is communicated through the dream. Joseph perceives the dream coming from an authority higher than the law or religious custom. More generally, in New Testament times, divine revelation is presumed to occur in visions and dreams, and such inner experience is treated as a normal way of God's revelation.

For Joseph, because the dream came from God, it was its own justification. As far as we can tell, Joseph was not judged by anyone for following the invitation of his dream. Nor did anyone seem to challenge him or criticize him for acting upon his dream. As the Latin jurist and a father of the Christian Church, Tertullian (A.D. 160–230), was to comment, "Nearly everyone on earth knows that God reveals himself to people most often in dreams."[3]

Understanding Symbolic Material in Dreams

We are not encouraging people to observe their dreams and carry them out literally and blindly, especially when they seem to be suggesting behavior which is immoral, embarrassing, anti-social, or against the laws and regulations of the Church or government. Nor are we implying that this is what Joseph did. What the dream seems to be asking of Joseph is to look for and follow the highest value in the situation. He is to protect his wife and future mother of the child, Jesus. Also, when his dream is viewed as a symbolic experience, it suggests that the over-riding factor was the creation of new birth by God's intervention in human life, which is exactly what happened through Jesus' life and teachings.

The infancy narratives contain other examples of dreams and visionary experience which are treated as coming from God and inviting a response. In response, the dreamers often take action. Thus, Mary acts on the angelic visitor's message by taking a journey to her cousin Elizabeth (Lk 1:36–40). Joseph acts on the warnings given in his dreams and moves his family away from possible harm (Mt 2:13, 19, 22), the shepherds act on the angelic message that a Savior has been born and go in search of a baby in a manger (Lk 2:9, 15), and the wise men receive and respond to a warning in a dream not to tell Herod where Jesus may be found (Mt 2:12).

An important point to be made in each of these cases is that the Gospel narrator is often telling us only the essential elements of the dream for evangelistic purposes. The Gospel writers are neither historians nor dreamwork researchers. Perhaps the dreams and visions as originally experienced were indeed as clear and explicit as they are reported in the Gosepl texts. More likely, however, the narrator is merely reporting *the meaning of the dream as its symbolic material came to be understood by the dreamer upon reflection.* Certainly Joseph seems to be a very proficient dream observer, since it seems to be the way God communicated most frequently with him. Perhaps Joseph's dreams were filled with symbolic imagery as most of our dreams are, and Joseph is merely sharing with us the results of his dreamwork through which he learned, for example, to flee to Egypt, return to Israel, and settle in Nazareth again.

The dreamwork techniques suggested in this book will help you work with the symbolic content of your dreams. In fact, we recommend that even when your dreams seem explicitly to be giving you a clear message or directive, you process the dream material through appropriate dreamwork techniques in order to verify the intent and purpose of the message, see if there are other likely levels of meaning of the dream, and rationally work out how you can translate the dream's message into appropriate action that furthers your or someone else's holiness and wholeness.

Religious Symbolic Experience

There is much significant symbolic material in both the Old and New Testaments which we do not have space to cover here. Especially to be noted are the dreams, visions and Holy Spirit experiences by the first Christians—Peter, Paul, and others. Marvelous symbolic material occurs in the Apocalypse of John. We have found in our various seminars on dreams and dreamwork that applying dreamwork techniques to biblical material yields meaningful results. A selected list of important biblical dreams and visions is presented at the end of Chapter 18.

We are interested in having symbolic material come alive meaningfully for people, whether it is experienced through biblical imagery and religious practice or as dreams and visions which come spontaneously to people challenging and gifting their spiritual life. The results are for each person to evaluate in relation to themselves and God. Working with symbolic experience as coming from God has a rich tradition in the Old and New Testaments and is revitalizing a growing number of people's lives today.

The prophets spoke in images, as well as in concepts. Jesus himself did much of his teaching in "story-pictures," or parables. While we have no direct report of Jesus' dreams, we do have an excellent record of his parables. Since these are largely teachings in symbolic form which require working with, just as dreams do, in order to arrive at their meaning for ourselves, it is quite possible that Jesus created his parables out of what God sent him—his dreams, his visions, his prayer and meditation experiences. In other words, as Jesus' divine Source communicated to him in symbols, he in turn often spoke to people in symbols.

There is that controversial passage in which Jesus is asked why he speaks in parables. (See Mt 13:10-17, Mk 4:10-12 or Lk 8:9-10.) His reply was that he used parables so that only those who had ears to hear would understand. And what gives certain people ears to understand the language of symbol? Certainly the willingness to follow the truth which is revealed, but probably also a certain facility and practice in working with symbolic material. In Old Testament times, the episodes of new spiritual revelation and direction often included experiences of God communicated through imagery. In the New Testament, Jesus continues this symbolic tradition. Symbolic experience is also clearly present in the appearances of the Christ to the disciples after the resurrection, and in the experiences of Paul and other new members of the young Church.

Implications for living a contemporary spiritual life include developing an ability to work with symbolic communication, especially in order to understand those communications which come to us in dreams and visions.

Jesus' Symbolic Experience at His Baptism

Although we do not have a record of any of Jesus' night dreams, we do have reports of some of his visionary experience—for example, at his baptism by John in the River Jordan. Since this experience was reported by all the Synoptic writers, it was probably as central and important for Jesus as the ladder dream was for Jacob. It implies a new covenant, in which Jesus experiences himself as chosen by God.[4]

JESUS' BAPTISM (Mk 1:9–11)
During that time, Jesus came from Nazareth in Galilee and was baptized in the Jordan by John. Immediately on coming up out of the water, he saw the sky rent in two and the Spirit descending on him like a dove. Then a voice came from the heavens: "You are my beloved Son. On you my favor rests."

Jesus Responds

From our viewpoint, this passage describes a powerful, personal visionary experience evoked in Jesus by his baptism. Much like Jacob's dream, Jesus' experience begins with symbolic visual material—the sky splitting and the Spirit/dove descending—and closes with a conceptual statement, "You are my beloved Son. On you my favor rests." The experience seems to be a private one; no one else reportedly sees the vision. Also, there is no direct mention of God as its source. Jesus feels called and favored, but by whom? He still has to work with the experience to realize its meaning.

To do this, the Gospel writers tell us, he spends forty days in the wilderness, fasting, praying, reflecting, being tempted. The temptations, or tests, all have the quality of challenging and grounding the effects of his powerful baptismal visionary experience. Satan, Jesus' adversary, suggests to Jesus ways of translating his symbolic experience into specific actions such as changing stones into bread, casting himself from the pinnacle of the temple, and worshiping Satan. Jesus rejects each of these actions as self-inflating; instead, affirming the wisdom of the Old Testament, he keeps his focus on God as his source and direction. He never denies that he is chosen by God or that he has been given power by God, but he does not focus on his own ego or identify it with the power of God.

According to the Gospel narrative, Jesus did not begin his teaching until after his baptism and wilderness experience. It was as if he had to do the prayerfully reflective work on his visionary experience and temptations before he could clearly understand the meaning of his divine call and begin his public life. He translated the symbolic experience of being chosen by God into living God's will in the world, no matter what the consequences.

Jesus' Example

While our religious symbolic experience may not be of the same stature as that which Jesus brought into the world, God does speak directly to us through symbolic experiences. In order to integrate and actualize such experiences into everyday living, we need to practice working with symbolic material.

Jesus' parable of the talents (Mt 25:14–30) makes the point clearly. In it, three servants are given different amounts of money by their master who goes away for several years. The one with the least amount hides his money so he will not lose it. The other two, who have more and therefore have the greater risk, invest and increase the money. When the master returns, only the one servant does not show an increase. What little he has is then taken away, while the other two are entrusted with even more responsibility.

In like manner, if we hide or neglect our inner riches, including our dreams and other symbolic material, we may become impoverished. But if we actively work with them or other such material, our whole being will become more alive, enriched, and God-directed.

Dreamwork Technique 3: Key Questions

One of the most important elements of dreamwork, as we mentioned in Dreamwork Technique 2, is dealing with questions the dream seems to be asking us. But we may also ask questions of the dream. This latter technique, called Key Questions, invites us to begin relating to the dream material at another level.

Here, we are talking about questions that are functional and relational, rather than those calling for an answer that is merely informational or descriptive. For example, an informational question might be, "Where did this dream come from?" or "Why did I have this dream?" More functional and relational questions might include, "How am I going to respond to this dream?" or "What is this dream asking of me?" or "What issues in my life or in myself is this dream raising for me?"

As you create a list of key questions you would like to ask your dream, include ones which involve the action and imagery of the dream. For example, if Jesus' baptismal vision were treated as dream material, he might have asked, "What does it mean to me to see the heavens split open?" or "Why would God use a dove to communicate to me now?" Open-ended questions like these are often more productive in dreamwork than questions with yes-no answers, although both have their place.

Once again, we suggest in general that it is better to invite *responses* to questions rather than answers. Questions which ask for responses and reactions tend to develop relationship and expand consciousness.

To call people to consciousness, Jesus often used questions such as, "Who do people say that I am? . . . Who do you say that I am?" Jesus is here asking his disciples how they are experiencing him in relation to the messianic issue, an issue which Jesus seems to leave open in certain ways. And at one point Jesus asks of his adversaries, "Is it easier to say to this man 'Your sins are forgiven' or 'Take up your bed and walk'?" Jesus evokes relationship and expands consciousness by posing alternatives, rather than giving easy answers.

In asking key questions around a dream, we are opening ourselves up to new possibilities, new ways of acting and looking at life. Questions open our perspective.

Dreamwork Technique 3
Key Questions

Procedure:
1. After reading over your dream, list a series of questions about it which occur to you. Do not attempt to respond to any of the questions until you feel you have made a full list.

2. Include key questions about the dream itself such as: What is the central point of the dream? What is the gift in the dream for me? Why am I acting the way I am in the dream? How does this dream relate to the issues in my life right now?

3. Mark the one or two questions that seem most central to you. What makes them central?

4. Write a response to these main questions. Let your response flow, without censoring what comes forth. The point is to be open to new ways of thinking and acting.

5. As an alternative, you may select one significant key question which you commit yourself to focusing on throughout the day.

6. At the end of the day, review the dream, your questions, and your responses. Evaluate how they may have helped you give meaning and direction to your life.

Notes to Chapter 2
1. For a fuller study, see Morton Kelsey, *God, Dreams and Revelation* (Minneapolis: Augsburg, 1974), Chapter 4, "The Dreams and Visions of the New Testament."
2. For a discussion of dates of composition, see Raymond E. Brown, *The Birth of the Messiah: A Commentary on the Infancy Narratives in Matthew and Luke* (Garden City: Doubleday, 1977).
3. Tertullian, *De Anima,* c. XLIV.
4. See, for instance Elizabeth Boyden Howes, *Jesus' Answer to God* (San Francisco: Psychological Studies Publishing House, 1984).

Chapter 3

Dreamwork in the Early Church: God's Continuing Revelation Through Dreams and Dreamwork

◆

The Dreamwork Tradition Carried On

According to Luke in the Book of Acts, dreams and visions occurred frequently and at important moments in the life of the early Christian community. For example, Peter's dream-vision at Joppa proved instrumental in transforming the new Church's attitude toward Gentiles and the Hebrew dietary laws, and Paul's dream redirected his missionary endeavors from Asia to Europe. Others among the early disciples, such as the deacon Stephen who was martyred, reported dreams and visions. Dreams and visionary material were treated seriously and given much authority in the nascent Church.

After the last of the apostles and the others who had known and seen Jesus had died, the young Church continued to grow and expand. From our twentieth century perspective, we ask: What part did dreams and dreamwork play in the lives of the Christian community during the next few centuries? Did dreams, visions, and other movements of the Spirit continue to influence, guide, and direct the elders of the Church? Did God continue to reveal himself and his will to the believing community as he had done during the first fifty or sixty years since Jesus, or did God cease to make direct contact through dreams and visions? Did the leaders of the young Church carry on the Old and New Testament dreamwork tradition?

These are important questions which must be asked of the early Christian writers. These theologians, bishops, preachers, and teachers were the Church authorities who formulated what Christians believed and how Christians related to God—and to their dreams. These were the people who shaped Christianity as it was passed down to us. Their response will be crucial. Upon it depends whether or not we can affirm the existence of a continuing tradition of dreams and dreamwork in the Christian Church.

If we were to address some of those same questions about dream-work to the Christian Church, from medieval times to the present, we would probably find that, at least officially, in Christian asceticism dreams would not be considered an important and common way of discovering the inner life and relating to God. In theological writings and textbooks, dreams and visions would be topics either omitted as insignificant and irrational or rejected with a cursory warning that the Old Testament forbade dabbling in dreams and visions. Certainly, ministers and priests would not routinely include material from religious dreams (their own or others') in their sermons. Today, few in religious ministry are trained in dreamwork skills.

On the other hand, we know from our workshop and counseling experiences that ministers, priests, sisters, and lay people all have vivid dreams, sometimes with clear religious symbolism. We are reminded of a nun, in her early thirties, who had the following dream.

A Modern Dream About Relating to God

I was climbing a spiral staircase of beautiful stone, which seemed to go up into the heavens. But then I wondered, "If the stone staircase began collapsing, would God save me?" No sooner had I let this thought into my mind than the staircase started breaking up, and I in great terror cried out for God to save me. But God did not save me and I fell with the collapsing spiral staircase. I woke up in a sweat.

Some of us may be familiar with the religious experience of the felt absence of God, the *Deus absconditus.* What is collapsing for this religious woman and how may she best deal with it? If God will not save her, who or what will?

Is this spiritually sensitive woman being presented through her dream with only her own feelings about God? Or is there also an issue here about the way God relates to humans? How does God work in catastrophe? Does God rush in like a loving and strong parent to save the situation? Or must we save ourselves? Or does salvation come through some co-creative work involving God and the human soul? The religious dream presents the issues.

When things are not all right, we may be challenged by a dream to work our way through another abyss on our way to God. For this woman and for many others, her dreams offered her an arena to really meet God at very deep levels. Her dream and dreamwork experience took her beyond simple faith, to testing, and then to an experience of resolution.

In a dream re-entry, she went into a meditative state and experienced the dream again. This time she did not resist but let herself fall with the collapsing staircase, keeping a religious attitude that, whatever happened, it would have purpose and meaning. This time she did not ask God to save her. Eventually, she landed softly and looked up to see a beautiful light. Around her the stairs that had been leading her to heaven were in ruins, but it did not matter. She felt safe and found herself in a new place well worth exploring. A soft glow seemed to be over everything.

She accepted this new meditative dream as God's way of giving her a new sense of direction.

The Direction of Religious Experience

The religious sister tumbling back to earth with the collapsing stairway to heaven is a dream symbol rich with theological issues for the contemporary Church. Symbols and their meaning do not occur only in dreams. Almost all religions contain symbolic practices and present figures rich with symbolism and meaning. The cross, for example, is a symbol of direction: pointing upward toward the heavens, downward toward the ground and into the ground, and horizontally to encompass the everyday world. Some of the earliest Christian crosses were equilateral; all of the four beams were of equal length, and the energy in each direction was balanced and in harmony. In the medieval period, the vertical direction of the cross was emphasized by raising the arms of the cross higher and higher. This was the age of Gothic cathedrals with their tall columns and arches. It was also a time in which the theology of the Church was highly rational, focused on transcendence and perfection; in contrast, the actual behavior of the Church on the horizontal (social) plane was often unconscious and even unjust, as in the crusades and inquisitions. Today, when the cross tends to approximate the shape of the human body, the Church has a much more realistic focus, reflected in its many social programs and concerns.

In the religious sister's dream, we see her wanting to go up toward the transcendent, but the dream movement itself takes her in the other direction, down into the depths, apparently even beneath the surface of everyday living. We are reminded symbolically that the cross has not only a transcendent, upward reach toward heaven, but also a downward movement that carries us below the horizontal plane of good works into the depths of the unconscious, to that which is inner and innate.

When theology and belief are highly rational, the direction of Christian life moves primarily upward toward the heavens and perfection. When the focus is on dreams and soul-work, for those striving to be in personal relation with God, the invitation is downward into the innermost being. The soul is quickened at its center. For those who endure the descent, there may come the paradoxical discovery that the way down is also the way up, that in the descent is also an ascent, and that in the darkness a light shines. For many, including the sister with the dream, this is a new attitude and a new place. As she discovered in her dreamwork, it is a safe place and well worth exploring.

Dreamwork in the First Five Centuries of the Early Church

By taking a summary look at the teaching and practice of the Church Fathers up to the beginnings of the fifth century, we can discern a well-integrated tradition of dreams and dreamwork and recognize its continuity with that of the Old and New Testament.

The conviction that God often speaks through dreams and visions may be found expressed in the writings of Justin Martyr, Irenaeus, Clement of Alexandria, Origen, Tertullian, Athanasius, Augustine, John Chrysostom, Anthony, Basil the Great, Gregory of Nazianzen, Gregory of Nyssa, Ambrose, Jerome, Gregory the Great, John Cassian, and many others.[1]

According to John Chrysostom, dreams are enough for God to send to those who are attuned to God, since they do not need visions or other more startling divine revelations.[2]

Tertullian, in his introduction to the *Martyrdom of Saints Perpetua and Felicitas,* spoke of dreams as one of the *charismata* of God, and believed that dreams and visions were promised to people of his own day just as much as they were to the first apostles. Origen in his book *Against Celsus* saw dreams as part of God's providence "for the benefit of the one who had the dream and for those who hear the account of it from him."[3]

Cyprian, bishop of Carthage in 250 A.D., one of the founders of the Latin Church, asserted that the very councils of the Church were guided by God through dreams and "many and manifest visions."[4] And in Gregory of Nazianzen's Church in Constantinople, according to the Church historian Sozomen, "the power of God was there manifested, and was helpful both in waking visions and in dreams, often for the relief of many diseases and for those afflicted by some sudden crisis in their affairs."[5]

Bishop Cyprian of Carthage wrote so much of his direct encounters with God in dreams and visions that twentieth century editors of his writing felt a need to apologize for them.[6] Gregory Thaumaturgus, originally a student of Roman law, was led to the Christian faith in a beautiful dream that involved John the Evangelist and Mary, the Mother of Jesus.[7] Dionysius, a famous student of Origen, received confirmation in a dream to study both the pagan and heretical Christian writings: the voice in the dream assured him he need fear nothing because his faith was secure. Constantine received an important dream-vision before his battle for Rome, which eventually opened up a new era of Western civilization.[8]

"Dreams, more than any other thing, entice us toward hope," wrote Synesius of Cyrene, a fifth century bishop of Ptolemais. "And when our heart spontaneously presents hope to us, as happens in our sleeping state, then we have in the promise of our dreams a pledge from the divinity."[9]

The Personal Uses of Dreams

Origen and other Christian writers clearly recognized that dream images were not simple physical perceptions, as we perceive trees, animals, people, and other things in ordinary waking life, but symbols and images that revealed the nature of the spiritual world. Synesius clearly pointed out that dream imagery was essentially personal, and that symbolic dream material was best understood by the dreamer in terms of his or her personal life.

The early Christian writers were well aware that we all have dreams which we might not share openly in public—dreams of violence, sexuality, and unusual or embarrassing activities.

Athanasius was careful to remind his readers that in dreams the dream ego may manifest unusual capacities which transcend the usual capacities of the body. Basil the Great, among others, pointed out that dreams, sometimes embarrassingly, often reveal inner workings of personality that the rational mind is not in touch with. John Chrysostom added that we are not morally responsible for the thoughts and actions of the dream ego, since these dream images are symbolic expressions of dream language. Dream images are not a fact of physical, outer reality, but are a way of expressing inner and spiritual dynamics.

According to Synesius, whose treatise *On Dreams* remained perhaps the most psychologically and spiritually sophisticated treatment of dreams and dreamwork until Carl Jung in the twentieth century, the entire universe is a unity, and dreams express the meaning of the universe, including our relationship to it and to each other. Anything we do in life can gradually be integrated and harmonized so that we are not at war with ourselves.

In psychological language, when people completely repress their anger because they believe that anger is wrong, then they are repressing a natural emotion which will surface in violent ways. If we are killing people in dreams, it is likely that this may symbolize unexpressed anger. Anger, like sexuality, can be expressed creatively or uncreatively, or it can be repressed.

If we keep a full uncensored record of our dreams over a period of time, we will see almost everything about ourselves revealed. But is this such a bad thing? While some dream images may seem embarrassing until we accept them, other content will seem wonderful and reflect our greatest capacities. The dream itself may give us the most honest and balanced description of ourselves we can know, and it is in this sense that we can work with it as revealing God's purpose in our lives.

Almost everyone who remembers one's own dreams has experienced a dream from time to time in which there is a dream figure who seems to express a dark or foreboding presence. Often the dreamer or the dream ego itself reacts to this figure with fear of being overwhelmed. And, in a very real sense, there are times in life in which even the strongest of us may be overwhelmed by forces such as anger, fear, and compulsive behavior. Better to be prepared for the adversities in life than to hope that we never have to confront much darkness. The question is how to deal with situations of great conflict so that they can be resolved in a meaningful way.

Tertullian wrote that dreams appear to have four sources. For him, some dreams come from demons, although, as he stated, these dreams "sometimes turn out true and favorable to us." Other dreams come from God, and, according to Tertullian, "almost the greater part of mankind get their knowledge of God from dreams." Other dreams come from the soul, and still others are due to "the ecstatic state and its peculiar conditions." But whatever their sources, dreams are meaningful.[10]

In this book, our general position is that since everything in the universe is God's, all dreams somehow reflect God's purposes and plans for our lives. Even the most demonic or terrifying presences in dreams can be worked with and their energy transformed. Dreams, quite simply, present us with what we really need to deal with to fulfill God's need and purpose for our lives.

We are not as concerned with where dreams come from as we are with what we do with the dreams which do come to us. Our methodology and spiritual perspective of commitment to wholeness and holiness should be able to encompass any kind of dream, and offer ways of working with it toward transformation and meaning.

Dreams and Life After Death

One of the significant doctrinal beliefs in the Christian Church is called the communion of saints. This doctrine teaches that persons in God's grace do not cease to exist after death, but live in a non-physical state joined to each other and to Christ in loving, soul-to-soul communion. Early Christian teachers proposed a variety of relations between the communion of saints and dreams.

For example, for many of the Church elders, the dream state gives us some idea of the life of the soul after death. Ambrose believed that dreams and visions were a means of contacting those who had died.[11] More generally, Justin Martyr believed that humans are capable of contact and spiritual communication with non-physical beings.[12] Augustine received a dream that convinced him of the Christian doctrine of life after death.[13]

In discussing dreams that people have of the dead, Augustine did not believe it was the dead person himself or herself who appeared, but probably it was a message from God delivered by angels, who have direct contact with human consciousness and can present their message to the person's imagination in dreams or visions.[14] The point Augustine makes again and again is that, in light of the communion of saints, such dreams are gifts given to us "by the merciful, providential care of God."[15] To treat such dreams as gifts would be to welcome them, examine them, study them, work with them, pray over them. As we see it, this is the purpose of dreamwork.

It is not unusual for those who have died to appear as characters in our dreams in meaningful ways. In dreams, a relationship with someone can continue after their death.

For example, a young woman in one of our dream seminars had a father who was killed in the war, when she was twelve. When she came to the seminar she was twenty-two. She reported a recent dream in which her father appeared wanting to be warm and friendly toward her. She awoke very moved by the dream but did not know how to work with it further.

It was suggested that she could re-enter her dream meditatively and have a conversation with her father. "You might want to tell him how your life has been going since he was killed, and what you have experienced of life and love during your teenage years."

She took the suggestion and had a profound experience of relating to her father, which left her gently crying at the end. Talking with her clarified the fact that something had really changed and been brought to resolution for her. Emotionally, she realized she still had a relationship with her father and the dreamwork experience had helped it move forward.

Are we to say that this dreamwork was merely her own imaginative experience, or is it possible that she actually did, in some way, connect with the spirit or soul of her father and that he connected with her?

Whether such a dream figure symbolizes what that person means to us in our own soul, or represents a personal presence from the communion of saints, or expresses (as Augustine would have it) a message from God delivered by angels, perhaps cannot be answered definitively. We are more interested in helping people confront their dreams than theorizing about them. We know that when such dreams are worked with, profound and transformative feelings are evoked.

We now explore a famous dream in early Christian literature. From it we will be able to see how early Christians related to their dreams.

Saint Jerome's Dream

Let us look at a major dream of St. Jerome, a contemporary of St. Augustine. Coming from a wealthy Christian family and growing up in the port of Aquileia at the head of the Adriatic Sea, Jerome naturally read the famous masters of Greek and Latin literature. He studied in Rome, traveled widely, and collected a library of pagan classics. These were his treasures. As a man of letters, he found the writing style of the biblical authors rough and crude in comparison to the smooth and sophisticated texts of Cicero and Plautus. As you read this dream let its images and actions move you at the feeling level. You are there in the dream, in Jerome's life.

BACKGROUND OF THE DREAM

Jerome was in Antioch with a group of congenial Christian friends who were interested in becoming monks. During this period, he took ill, and the following dream experience happened.

THE DREAM

Suddenly, I was caught up in the Spirit and dragged before the Judgment Seat. The light was so bright there, and those standing around the Seat were so radiant, that I threw myself to the ground and dared not to look up.

A voice asked me who and what I was.

"I am a Christian," I replied.

"You are lying," said the Judge. "You are a follower of Cicero, not of Christ. For where your treasure is, there also is your heart."

Instantly, I became dumb. He ordered me to be scourged and, along with the strokes of the lash, I was tortured more harshly by the fire of conscience. . . .

I began to cry and wail, "Have mercy on me, O Lord, have mercy on me." My cry could be heard amid the sound of the lash.

At last, the bystanders fell down at the knees of the Judge and asked him to have pity on my youth, and give me a chance to repent. The Judge might still inflict torture on me, they insisted, should I ever again read the works of the pagans. . . .

Accordingly, I swore an oath calling upon God's name: "Lord, if ever again I possess worldly books, or if ever again I read such, I have denied you!"

On taking this oath I was dismissed.

RESPONSE TO THE DREAM

I returned to the upper world, and when I opened my eyes they were drenched with tears. Everyone was surprised. My distress convinced them all. . . . My shoulders were black and blue, and I felt the bruises long after I awoke from my sleep. . . .

I call to witness the Judgment Seat before which I lay and the fearful judgment which was held over me—that this experience was no mere sleep or idle dream, such as those by which we are often mocked. After that, I read the books of God with a greater zeal than I had been giving to the books of men.[16]

Jerome's Dreamwork

We can sense the complete absorption with which Jerome experienced this dream. He not only woke up with the bruise marks from his dream scourging, but he followed his vow made in the dream with action in his life.

Soon after his major dream, Jerome went into the desert as a hermit. There he continued his biblical studies. A few years later, he moved to Constantinople and was tutored by Gregory of Nazianzen. He became a great Bible scholar, was called to Rome in 382 by Pope Damasus I, and was urged to undertake the monumental task of translating the entire Bible into Latin. At the time, Latin was the language of the empire. There were few scholars left like Jerome, well-versed in Greek and Hebrew. Jerome's translation, later referred to as the Latin Vulgate, remained the authoritative rendition of the Bible until our own century.

Jerome listened to his dream, paid attention to it, and valued it. He treated his dream as coming from God. He did not question that God was the source of the dream. Although the dream was not asking Jerome to challenge his Church's law, it was asking him to question the supreme value he and his scholarly group of friends had placed on the pagan classics. Jerome acted on the dream's message by giving up reading the classics and by becoming a biblical scholar. He did not apologize to his startled and incredulous friends for following the dream.

This major dream of Jerome's bears a message to him which is self-evident. Other of Jerome's dreams and visionary experiences are full of symbolic material and cover a wide range of dream categories. Many of them must have required much reflection and dreamwork to understand them, such as dreams of his own death and of "flying over lands, and sailing through the air, and crossing over mountains and seas." Jerome was accustomed to telling his own dreams in his letters and apologetic writing.[17]

Following the biblical tradition, Jerome made little distinction between dreams and visions. "In his discussions of the dream of Joseph about Mary's conception," wrote Morton Kelsey, "one would not know whether the vision had been received awake or asleep."[18] For Jerome, God spoke through visions, whether they occurred during sleep or while awake.

In his *Commentary on Jeremiah*, Jerome agrees with Jeremiah that God can use dreaming as well as prophesying as a vehicle of revelation to a person.[19] Such revelation can be a valuable gift from God if the dreamer's life is turned toward God. But, says Jerome, when dreams are sought after and interpreted for selfish reasons, and without any reverent relationship to God or the community, dreamwork can become an idolatrous pastime. For Jerome, the value of the dream depends on the person who seeks it and who helps understand it. Thus, those who are deeply related to God are likely to receive revelations from God in their dreams and dreamwork.[20]

We would also point out, however, that with many people, including Jerome, a strong dream may come which shocks us out of destructive and unconscious ways. And, of course, working with dreams within a religiously committed atmosphere will lead to more powerful dreams and dreamwork.

The Dream Ego and the Waking Ego

Jerome's dream became well known among his friends. No one ever challenged its authority or validity, or claimed that it was not from God. For example, years later when Jerome and his friend Rufinus had a falling out, they each wrote a treatise criticizing the other's position while defending their own. In his treatise, which was written first, Rufinus claimed that Jerome had reneged on the oath he had sworn in his dream never to study and read the pagan masters again. In this, Rufinus confuses Jerome's waking ego with his dream ego. Jerome took the oath against reading pagan literature in the dream and not in his waking life. Is there a difference? For us there is, but perhaps not for the early Christian. We usually work with dreams as giving us invitations and challenges for living a more integrative and spiritual life. No matter what the dream ego does or chooses, our conscious waking ego still needs to make choices on how it will actualize or not actualize the potentials of the dream.

The drama which occurred in Jerome's dream has some special characteristics which are important to the dreamwork practitioner.

Jerome's dream offers an example of an active and participating dream ego. In the biblical dreams we have studied—Jacob's ladder dream and Joseph's dream to marry Mary—we do not see an active dream ego. Neither Joseph's nor Jacob's dream ego seems to do anything but listen, while Jerome's dream ego is involved in considerable action and interaction. In the dream, Jerome stood in front of the Judgment Seat, he threw himself down on the ground, he responded to the Judge's question, he cried out to the Lord for mercy as he was scourged, and he swore an oath in front of the entire heavenly court. Studying the actions, attitudes and feelings of the dream ego, a very powerful and revealing technique, is the focus of dreamwork in this chapter.

Before we leave Jerome's dream, however, it is important to see how the insight of the dream affected him and how he transformed the energy released in the dream into actions and choices in waking life. Although neither Jacob's nor Joseph's dream ego actively participated in the dream, in the waking state they both made decisions and took action based on the dream. Jacob hallowed the ground where he slept and made a covenant with God, and Joseph took Mary as his wife. Was Jerome as active in fulfilling the invitation of the dream in his waking life? How did he transform into action the energy released in the dream?

Jerome put aside his intense devotion to classical literature, and fulfilled his dream by becoming a Bible scholar and a translator of it into Latin. He did not waste the skills he had learned in studying the classics, nor did he bury his talents for literature and scholarship. The dream opened possibilities for transforming his skills and talents into ways of serving the Kingdom of God more directly and more effectively. And Jerome took advantage of them.

Dreamwork Technique 4: Following the Dream Ego—I

Following the Dream Ego is one of the most central dreamwork techniques to be offered in this book, because it helps us understand how our ego, the conscious choice-making side of our personality, is functioning in life.

To live in holiness and wholeness, it is not enough simply to feel devoted to God or religious values. The real ascetical achievement is to translate this devotion into action—to become *effective* in the world and in our spiritual lives. Our dreams can reflect how effectively or ineffectively we are living the strong convictions and spiritual values we profess. Through dreamwork, we can clarify the areas in ourselves that need changing and utilize the energies released from the dream to help make the necessary changes.

Your dream ego is the character or characters in the dream that feel like you, the character to whom you might refer as "I" or "me" when relating the dream. For example, in dreams you may look as you do right now, or you may appear the way you did as a child, or the way you might look as an older person. In a dream, the dream ego may look like an animal, a bird, a flower, or some other object. When telling the dream you might say, "In the dream I was a bird with long wings" or "I was a daisy standing in a field of daisies." Often, too, your dream ego may be dressed in ways you don't normally dress. For example, a woman in her forties recalled a dream in which her dream ego was forty years old but it was dressed in baby clothes, another in which her dream ego was dressed as a Roman Catholic priest, another in which her dream ego looked like her, except that it had bright red hair just like a neighbor's whom she disliked. Jerome reported a dream in which his dream ego was dressed in the Roman toga of a professor of Roman literature. Your dream ego has probably appeared in many different ways in different dreams.

Closely studying the behavior, attitudes, choices and reactions of your dream ego can prove very helpful in facilitating personal and spiritual growth.

Dreamwork Technique 4
Following the Dream Ego—I

Procedure:
1. After writing down your dream and doing some basic dream-work, such as TTAQ and Key Questions, reread your dream noticing the various actions and attitudes taken by your dream ego. Then, on a fresh piece of paper, draw three vertical lines creating three columns.

2. In the first column, titled Actions, *list in sequence the things that your dream ego did*—for example, how it acted, what it said, what it chose, how it responded to the situation. You may have only a few actions to list, or many.

3. In the second column, titled Attitudes and Feelings, next to each action listed in the first column *describe the attitudes and feelings the dream ego had toward that action or situation.* Note any pattern or consistency in your response.

4. The third column may be titled Alternatives. Once you have completed the first two columns, reflectively ask yourself at each step: "Are the behavior patterns and attitudes of my dream ego similar to those of my waking ego?" Then you may ask yourself,

"Am I pleased with the way my dream ego acts and reacts, or would I like to change my behavior and reactions?" If you would like to change, make a note in the third column, next to each action and attitude, describing what your dream ego *could have done* in the dream and how you might prefer it had acted and responded. In each case, generate as many alternatives as you can.

5. Then reflect on your comparisons and contrasts, and ask yourself what you have learned from the experience about your growth process.

Some Variations in Using This Technique

If the dream ego's behavior and attitudes in the dream are *not* typical of your current waking ego's patterns, for example, if your dream ego seems much more self-confident and assertive than you are normally in waking life, you may ask: "Is my dream ego calling me to grow toward greater wholeness and giving me an example to follow?"

Or if, for example, your dream ego seems to be taking a submissive and self-defeating attitude, not typical of your current behavior, you may ask: "Is my dream ego reminding me of how I used to be, and reassuring me that I have come a long way in personal growth?"

To get the most from Following the Dream Ego, it is important to carry out the third, reflective step: comparing what the dream ego is doing to what it might be doing. In this step you are being given new awarenesses and discovering new alternatives for growth toward holiness and wholeness.

What God asks of us is to develop a creatively strong ego, or choice-maker, in order better to follow God's call and serve our highest purpose. As we progress in working with dreams, we see ourselves becoming more assertive and intentional, even in our night dreams. We had the privilege of studying dream ego behavior in a series of dreams of a religious sister.

In earlier dreams, she found her dream ego passively seated at the rear of the church listening to a priest deliver a sermon from the pulpit. In a much later dream, her dream ego was in the pulpit giving the sermon of the day. For her, this shift represented her willingness to take a stronger leadership role in her community and more initiative in her personal spiritual life.

We can learn how well we are dealing with life from accurately observing our dream ego's actions in several dreams over a period of time.

Notes to Chapter 3
Dreamwork in the Early Church

1. For an in-depth survey of the Church Fathers and dreams see Morton Kelsey, *God, Dreams and Revelation* (Minneapolis: Augsburg, 1974), pp. 102–161. For those wishing to study some of the nascent research relating dreamwork and women in early Christian times, see Rosemary Rader, "*The Martyrdom of Perpetua:* A Protest Account of Third-Century Christianity," in Patricia Wilson-Kastner, *et al., A Lost Tradition: Women Writers of the Early Church* (Washington, D. C.: University Press of America, 1981), pp. 1–32.

2. John Chrysostom, *Homilies on Matthew,* IV, No. 18, v. 5.

3. Origen, *Against Celsus,* VI, 21–23.

4. *Epistles,* 53, 5. In his epistles, Cyprian was outspoken in his emphasis on direct encounters with God in dreams.

5. Sozomen, *Ecclesiastical History,* VII, 5.

6. See *The Ante-Nicene Fathers* (Grand Rapids, Michigan: Eerdmans), Vol. 5, p. 266.

7. Gregory of Nyssa, *The Life of Saint Gregory Thaumaturgus* in Migne's *Patrologiae Graecae,* 46, Cols. 911–13.

8. The dreams of Dionysius of Alexandria, Constantine, and many other famous people were reported in Eusebius' *Church History,* written about 315 A. D.

9. Augustine Fitzgerald, *The Essays and Hymns of Synesius of Cyrene* (London: Oxford, 1930), p. 345.

10. Tertullian's metaphysics and theology of dreams is developed explicitly in his introduction to the treatise *The Passion of the Holy Martyrs Perpetua and Felicitas,* where he discusses four of Perpetua's important dreams. See Kelsey's summary of Tertullian's approach to dreams in *God, Dreams and Revelation,* pp. 113–117.

11. See Kelsey, *op. cit.,* p. 147.

12. Justin Martyr, *The First Apology,* cc. 14, 18.

13. Augustine, *Letter CLIX,* to Evodius, 2ff.

14. Augustine, *On Care To Be Had for the Dead,* 12, and *The City of God,* XI, 2.

15. Augustine, *Letter CLIX,* to Evodius, 2.

16. St. Jerome, *Letter XXII,* to Eustochium, 30.

17. See Rufinus, *Apology* I, 11.

18. Kelsey, *op. cit.,* p. 153.

19. See Jerome, *Commentary on Jeremiah,* c. 23, vv. 25ff.

20. *Ibid,* c. 4, v. 23.

Chapter 4

The Disrepute of Dreamwork in the Church: Dreams and Magic

◆

Dreamwork in Disfavor

In the early centuries of the Church, Christians generally welcomed dreams with openness, viewing them as a setting for encounter with God and one's deepest self. A drastic shift in attitude happened between the fourth and fifth centuries. Teachers and theologians turned against the practice of observing dreams. So strong was their disfavor that negative attitudes toward dreams and dreamwork persisted into our own century.

In this chapter we address the questions: What became of the Christian tradition of dreams and dreamwork after the first five centuries of the Church? Why did we hear so little from Christian writers about dreams and dreamwork until the latter half of the twentieth century?

What happened to dreams in the Church as a means of discovering God's will in the lives of the people?

Paradoxically, Jerome proved to be one of the major turning points, Thomas Aquinas another.

Jerome: The Great Mistranslation

In the previous chapter we saw how profoundly moved Jerome had been by his own dreams, yet it is, among other things, because of him that dreams and dreamwork in the Church were held in disfavor for the next fifteen centuries. As far as we can tell, in preparing a Latin translation of the Bible based on Greek and Hebrew manuscripts, Jerome deliberately mistranslated a Hebrew word a number of times in order to include prohibitions against dreamwork in the sacred text. We are indebted to Morton Kelsey for bringing this mistranslation to light.[1]

The Hebrew word in question is *anan,* which means witchcraft or soothsaying; it is usually associated with soothsayers, witches, and those who practiced augury. *Anan* was considered a pagan superstitious activity, so one who practiced it would be classed among sorcerers, serpent charmers, magicians, wizards, soothsayers, necromancers, and witches.

The word *anan* and various forms of it occur ten times in the Old Testament. In preparing the Latin translation of the Old Testament, however, Jerome gave *anan* two very different meanings. Seven times Jerome translated it correctly as "witchcraft" or one of its cognates.[2] But the other three times, where the Hebrew and Greek texts are condemning withcraft (*anan*), Jerome translated it as "observing dreams."[3] Here is the way Kelsey puts it:

> In translating Leviticus 19:26 and Deuteronomy 18:10 ... Jerome turned the law: "You shall not practice augury or witchcraft (i.e., soothsaying)" into the prohibition: "You shall not practice augury nor observe dreams." Thus, by the authority of the Vulgate, dreams were classed with soothsaying, the practice of listening to them with other superstitious ideas.[4]

We cannot absolve Jerome of the mistranslation by claiming that he did not know the meaning of *anan,* since seven out of ten times he translated it correctly. Jerome's mistranslation directly linked dreamwork with witchcraft in the sacred biblical text.

Many of the Church leaders and teachers born in the sixth century and afterward knew only Jerome's Latin Vulgate, and used his new translation of Deuteronomy 18:10 and Leviticus 19:26 as a prohibition to keep people from turning to their dreams for insight, consolation, and hope. The Christian tradition of relating to God through dreams and visions had come to an end. In one deliberate stroke of the translator's pen, Jerome had tipped the scales and changed the delicate balance of history.

Almost all translations of the Bible in use until the mid-twentieth century were made from Jerome's Vulgate and perpetuated the false condemnation of dreamwork.

We shall never know why Jerome took such a devastating position against dreams.[5] It is difficult to understand how a man who so fervently used his dreams for relating to God in his younger years seemed to turn against them later on. Perhaps the mistranslation was a deliberate decision made by the religious authorities of Jerome's day.

Gregory the Great: The Split Develops

The reversal in attitude toward dreams occurred throughout the Latin-speaking Church soon after Jerome's time. Gregory the Great, for example, the last great Doctor of the early Church, who was born in 540 A.D. and was called "teacher of the Middle Ages," manifested both positive and negative attitudes toward dreams and dreamwork. On the one hand, in the first book of his *Dialogues,* Gregory carried on the early Church's affirmative tradition toward dreams and visions, explaining how "God strengthens timid souls with timely revelations in order to keep them from all fear at the time of death."[6] On the other hand, in a later volume of the same work, he strongly cautioned against putting one's faith in dreams, saying that only the saints "can distinguish true revelations from the voices and images of illusions."[7] It was better, advised Gregory, to find God through faith rather than in dreams and visions. Faith was the path he personally preferred to follow. In the end, Gregory and Jerome both seemed to choose faith and doctrine, a more rational approach to God, over ongoing direct experience of God's revelation through dreams and dreamwork.

Dreamwork Among the People

Jerome's mistranslation was not the only source of the problem. The fifth and sixth centuries were a cataclysmic period for the Church, politically and culturally. During the two previous centuries, Christianity had been identified with the Holy Roman Empire. Christians, now out of the catacombs and free from persecution, were safe and secure anywhere in the West. Christian thought dominated the culture just as Christian rulers held sway in political and economic arenas. The Church had forgotten the persecution of its earlier centuries and Christians were, we might say, happily bourgeoise.

A cursory look at the popular manuals of dream interpretation in those days would reveal a preoccupation, not with the God life, but with the good life. People were interested in their dreams insofar as they predicted wealth, good health, good fortune, a lucky turn of events, a successful marriage, a profitable business deal, a new way to make money, a warning to protect one's home or valuables, and so on. Whereas dreamwork in the early Church had focused on God's plan for the Church and how to keep the believing community nourished, nurtured, and spiritually focused, dreamwork among Christians of the fifth century had degenerated into the typical middle class concerns of a very secure and self-centered people. No longer seeking in dreams to find God's will or to heed God's call to holiness and wholeness, people saw dreams as a form of divination—a way, by predicting the future, to increase their power, pleasure, health, and wealth.

Perhaps, as far as ordinary Christians were concerned, Jerome was appropriately condemning the dreamwork of his day as a superstitious practice.

Dreamwork as a discipline of spiritual growth was long forgotten except, as Gregory the Great noted, among the very holy men and women in the Church. For the most part, dreamwork in popular use had become a tool of magic and superstition. As such, it could not receive the support of the Church and its leaders.

Moreover, between the time of Jerome and Gregory, Rome had fallen to the barbarians. The cultural practices of the invaders seemed reminiscent of wizards and witches. Superstition became rampant; so did belief in the all-pervasive presence of the demonic. Dreamwork became the domain of mediums and witches, and flourished among the credulous minds of a superstitious populace.

While the Church's writings during the next five centuries did not deny the possibility of God's spirit being poured out in visions and dreams, neither did leaders encourage the idea. Nevertheless, here and there in each century there were examples of dreams and dreamwork in the lives of the saints reminiscent of the earlier Doctors of the Church.

The association of dreamwork and superstition from the fifth century onward was characteristic only of the Western Church. Christians in the Greek-speaking cultures maintained the original dream tradition passed down from Basil the Great, Gregory of Nazianzen, Gregory of Nyssa, and John Chrysostom.[8]

Greek Influence in the Christian Church

Somewhere around the eleventh century, the Greek language was discovered again in Europe. Perhaps it was brought in by the Moors or Turks; perhaps it was brought back by some of the crusaders. In any case, ancient Greek thought came to life again in the new universities in France and Italy.

This was the second time Greek thought had significantly influenced the Church. In the early centuries, Plato had been the principal Greek influence on the Doctors of the Church. Since he presupposed a spiritual reality behind that of the physical, he was open to the position that dreams have meaning and a divine source. Plato's thought supported the early Christian enthusiasm for dreams and dreamwork.

The eleventh century, however, marked the dawn of modern science. Because Aristotle's works were more compatible with the spirit of research and logic than Plato's, Aristotle's philosophy and language became the basis of modern scientific exploration and even of theological thought.

Aristotle held a firm premise about thinking and knowing, asserting that the only two ways humans can know or experience reality are by *sense experience* and *rational thought.* The human is a *rational animal,* he said, and we are most human when we are acting rationally and logically. Since, for Aristotle, a human can be in direct contact only with sense experience or logical thought, there is no room in his system for viewing dreams as an experience of the non-physical world. Aristotle believed in the divine, but humans, he said, though they may reason and discourse about the gods, can never directly be in touch with them. Thus, for Aristotle, dreams are not to be treated as gifts from the divine, but simply as natural phenomena.

Enter Thomas Aquinas

Thomas Aquinas, a brilliant scholar, who was as deeply impressed as anyone with the power of Aristotle's thought system, set himself what must have seemed like an impossible challenge: to rewrite all of Christian theology, not only in Aristotelian language and categories, but also using Aristotle's premises—that the only ways a human being can know anything are through sense experience and rational thought.

In integrating Christian theology and Aristotelian thought, Aquinas felt he would be thoroughly modernizing Christianity, bringing it out of the dark ages and in line with modern science. In this way, he felt,

Christianity would become a very contemporary religion. This is the incredible feat Aquinas accomplished in writing the *Summa Theologica,* which became the authoritative text in Catholic theological studies until after Vatican Council II in the mid-1960's.

However, from the perspective of dreams and dreamwork, Aquinas' plan to restate all of Christian thought in Aristotelian language posed a dilemma for him. With the rediscovery of the Greek language came also the rediscovery of the Greek-writing doctors of the early Church, who deeply valued dreams and dreamwork. Thomas read their works too, and knew their teachings. He also knew that Aristotle said dreams had no divine significance. What would Aquinas do? Would he affirm the consistent teachings of the Church Doctors about the value of dreams as messages from God, or would he side with Aristotle and keep the presentation of his *Summa Theologica* consistently Aristotelian?

It seemed that he solved his dilemma by avoiding it as far as possible. He certainly does not support the dreamwork tradition of the early Church. In all his thousands of pages of the *Summa,* he found room for only Aristotle's position—that dreams had merely natural causes and thus were of little value.[9] So for Aquinas on the question of dreams and dreamwork, Aristotle's position won and the Judaeo-Christian biblical approach lost.

The influence of Aquinas' work continued to grow in the Church until, for all practical purposes, there was room for no other view. The prevalence of his philosophy and theology for the past seven centuries is one more reason why we have lost touch with our Christian dream tradition.

The Dreams and Visions of Aquinas

Ironically, while writing the *Summa,* Thomas Aquinas reportedly had two very non-Aristotelian experiences—a dream and a revelatory vision—both of which he treated very seriously and acted upon. The first was an instructive dream.

It was reported that for many days Aquinas, probably the greatest mind in the Western world in the thirteenth century, had been struggling to complete a certain theological passage in the *Summa.* He had begun dictating the troublesome passage to his scribes a number of times, but his repeated attempts proved unsuccessful. One morning he came to the scriptorium and began dictating the difficult passage as comfortably and easily as if he had been reading it from another manuscript. When the surprised scribe asked him about the ease and fluency with which he was now dictating, Aquinas announced that in a dream the night before he had entered into a dialogue with the apostles Peter and Paul, and they had instructed him how to deal with the theological issue in question.

The second experience happened near the end of his life when the *Summa* was nearing completion. One morning Aquinas appeared in the scriptorium and announced to the waiting scribes that he would no longer work on the *Summa*. When they urged him to continue, reminding him that the huge manuscript was nearing completion, he dismissed them with these words:

> I can do no more. Such things have been revealed to me that all I have written seems like straw, and I now await the end of my life.[10]

What happened? Did, as some thought, Aquinas have a mental breakdown? It is not likely, for he was too developed and strong a person for us to believe he suddenly collapsed near the end of his work. It is much more likely that he was given a visionary experience—some direct experience of the divine—that was greater than all his rational thought could produce. What could make his work seem like straw if not the transrational and direct revelation of God through a vision or a dream?

While in his great theological works he did not support dreams and dreamwork for the people or for the Church, his life itself reflected an openness to the messages of dreams and visions. While his writing proposed a rational approach to God based on doctrine and logic, some of his important decisions acknowledged the power of the God-given dream and vision which had nourished many practicing Christians throughout the ages. In the end, despite what his books said, he personally chose to follow the dream and the vision. However, it was his books that people read.

It would take centuries to recognize and redirect the course set by Jerome, Aquinas, and others, centuries before dreams would once again be viewed by Christians in general as a path of fulfillment and a way of relating to God.

Dreamwork Technique 5: Dialogue With a Dream Figure

Aquinas dialogued with the apostles Peter and Paul during his night dream. It is also possible to dialogue with dream characters, meditatively, after the dream. Dialoguing with figures or symbols from our dreams is a very powerful and basic dreamwork technique with a wide variety of uses.

Although dreams are reservoirs of psychological and spiritual energies, we usually need help in releasing those energies and relating to them. We need to establish relation to the energies in a dream in order for them to work for us toward healing and wholeness. Almost all dreamwork techniques suggested in this book invite us to relate to the dream and its energies. Some techniques, more rational and structured than others, utilize the brain's logical and linear functions. Other techniques focus on the mind's affective and creative side. Dialoguing combines both sides of the mind's functioning.

Because Dialoguing has the capacity to carry us meditatively back into the dream state, it is especially powerful in releasing spiritual energy and insight. In Dialoguing we have some control over what happens and some responsibility for making the process work to help our needs. On the other hand, Dialoguing is an exercise in surrender, in letting go of control.

For example, when Old Testament prophets entered into dialogue with God during visionary experiences, they had some control over the situation—for instance, they could ask God questions. But they were also open to letting into their awareness truths about themselves or the Hebrew people that they might rather not hear.

If we are open to hearing some truth in a dream dialogue, we may realize our need to change certain attitudes and behavior. But the dream's invitation to change also carries with it the energy to make the change. Dialoguing with dream figures puts us in touch with both the invitation and the energy to change and grow. Dialoguing is the beginning of transformation, for it helps turn the imagery and energy released by the dream into awareness and concepts, so that the energy can be named, evaluated, integrated, and brought into the choices and actions of everyday life.

Dialoguing in dreamwork is quite simple. We choose a figure or symbol from our dream which seems important—it may be fascinating, attractive, scary, or repulsive, as long as it seems important—and begin a dialogue with it. To get started, we ask the dream figure a question and let the dream figure's response come. Usually, this reponse leads us to respond in turn, or perhaps to ask another question. In this way a dialogue may continue.

We usually suggest that people do the Dialoguing technique with pen and paper, writing down the opening question to the dream figure, then writing down what the dream figure seems to reply. The recorded dialogue may be kept in a journal alongside the original dream which inspired it.

One woman began a series of dialogues with a male dream figure.

At first, I simply asked questions to which the dream figure gave responses. I dialogued with the same figure during two more sessions, each time asking questions and listening for replies. By the fourth dialogue, I began making comments and sharing insights about myself rather than simply asking questions, and the dream figure replied with confirming and supportive statements. As in human relationships, the shared dialogues began to change, to balance and expand.

Some Initial Questions

The first time people try this technique, they have questions. One common question is: How do I get a dialogue started?

We suggest you begin by having ready at least three or four questions you would like to ask the dream figure. Some typical opening questions might be:

• Why did you appear in my dream?
• What do you have to teach me?
• Why did you act in a certain way in my dream?
• What gifts do you have for me?
• I am feeling angry (attracted, frightened, loving, etc.) toward you. Please tell me why.

Notice that we are not suggesting source questions such as: Who are you? Are you a part of me? Are you someone outside me? Do you come from God? Are you a messenger? Are you a projection of my mind? These are questions of theory. As such, they may distract from the main task of entering into relationship with the dream figure.

Another problem people have who are doing Dialoguing for the first time is that they are afraid nothing will happen. Our suggestion is: Trust the process. If your first question evokes no response from the dream figure, ask another question, or tell the dream figure of your uncomfortableness and ask what you should do about it. You might ask: "Why don't you answer me? How can I establish a relationship with you? What are you like?"

A third problem people often bring up is feeling silly having a dialogue with a dream figure. Usually, the reason is that they are uncomfortable functioning in a non-rational realm. They might feel just as uncomfortable if the dreamwork task was to draw a picture, mold a piece of clay, write a poem, or improvise a dance. As you practice dreamwork, you grow comfortable working in non-rational realms. You soon realize these realms have their own reality, which is fundamentally a spiritual reality. In time, you find it natural to work with spiritual energy.

People also ask us how they will be able to know what to write down as responses from the dream figure. As you let yourself relax and return to the dream scene, picturing the dream figure, seeing its features, hearing its voice, you will be able to "hear" the dream figure's responses to your questions. If you are reluctant to write what you think you sense the dream figure is saying because you feel the words are simply you concocting a response, we recommend that you write down whatever seems to come. After a few exchanges between you and the dream figure, you will begin to sense the difference between what is coming from your ego, your conscious side, and what is coming through from the dream figure, your unconscious side.

Some Concerns

Some people are afraid that Dialoguing with a Dream Figure is the same as "automatic writing" practiced by some psychics and mediums. We want to assure people that the two techniques are not the same. There are important differences.

In automatic writing, the person's ego gives up its own identity and control, and becomes merely an instrument or channel. The writing thus produced is entirely from the "other." It is the other who speaks continually. Even one's handwriting may appear unfamiliar in automatic writing.

In contrast, in the dialogue technique your ego does not go unconscious or give up control. Rather, it remains conscious and stays *in relationship* to the dream figure. The dream figure does not overpower the ego, but stays in relation to it and affirms the ego's presence, its questions and responses. There is a genuine two-way exchange.

Once when we were explaining the dialogue technique to a group, one woman told how as a child she used to dialogue with her guardian angel, especially at times when she was lonely or hurting. At these times she felt her angel responding and comforting her. Many people in the audience were obviously familiar with such dialoguing experience, for they were nodding their heads in agreement. In dreamwork we are called to be open like children, to allow two-way conversations between us and dream figures to happen in our imaginations.

Some people object to the technique, saying, "It all happens in my imagination," as if that were reason to deny the meaningfulness of the dialogue. At times like this, it is good to call to mind Joan of Arc's reply to the judge at her heresy trial. Joan was not a visionary, but an auditory mystic. She didn't see things, but she did hear voices and claimed they came from God. When the judge interrupted her and corrected, "They come from your imagination," Joan's reply was, "Of course they come by way of my imagination! How else could the voice of God come to us?"

What else but our bodies, feelings, and imagination could God use to communicate directly to us? So, of course, a dialogue with our dream figure will all happen in our imagination. Where else could it possibly happen and still be a direct communication?

Moreover, if a number of people each began a dialogue with a New Testament figure such as Joseph or Mary, the figures would appear differently in each one's imagination and bring different responses to each one's questions. With every person, the dream figure would establish a unique relationship.

Dialoguing doesn't necessarily mean agreeing with everything the dream figure says. We listen, but don't necessarily accept everything that is given. We can challenge or question the dream figures, as Peter did in his dream at Joppa (Acts 10:9–16), or we can refuse to do what they suggest, as Jesus did to his tempter (Lk:1–13). We have this freedom because we are *in relationship* to the figure, not controlled by it.

We find that even if the dream figure seems to be a terrifying force, it is better to establish relationship with it in a dialogue, hearing what it has to say, rather than simply repressing it. This is what Jesus did when he was tempted by Satan in the wilderness. In dialoguing with his adversary, he clarified much about himself and his destiny.

Dark forces, scary situations, and adversaries naturally come up in dreams. There is no need to evoke them, or avoid them. Certainly in their lives the saints had to deal with dreams and visions of strange and scary forces. The dialogue technique is a well-grounded and contained way of keeping such figures and forces in relationship.

In such dialogues, people may want to surround themselves and the adversary figure with the healing forces of the Holy Spirit so that the fruit of such dialogues will be to bring about greater wholeness and holiness. From this perspective, when it arises naturally, even a dialogue with a frightening figure is viewed as a gift from God.

Since the dream figure is given to us as an energy source, we recommend that you ask the figure for a gift, even—and especially—when the figure is frightening or an adversary. You might say, "What gift do you have for me?" or "Please give me a gift for my life."

Asking for a gift is a common practice in the Senoi dreamwork tradition, and it is also a part of the biblical tradition. For example, when

Jacob had the vision of an angel and wrestled with the angel all night long, Jacob held the angel and would not let him go until he gave Jacob a blessing. This is the dialogue they had, in which Jacob was given a new name as a gift:

Angel: Let me go, for it is daybreak.
Jacob: I will not let you go until you bless me.
Angel: What is your name?
Jacob: Jacob.
Angel: You shall no longer be spoken of as Jacob, but as Israel, because you have contended with divine and human beings and have prevailed.
Jacob: Please tell me your name.
Angel: Why should you want to know my name? (Angel blesses Jacob and departs.)

Gen 32:27–29

The blessing comes as a result of Jacob establishing relationship with the angel. With the gift of the new name Israel, the relationship transcends that of two individuals and becomes the people of Israel in covenant with God. A profound dialogue can often change the nature of our relationship to our own spiritual resources.

Personifying a Dream Symbol for Dialogue

Dreamwork, seen as a dynamic process of holiness and wholeness, deals with psychological and spiritual energies. In order to deal with such energies, it is helpful to personify them. Dreams tend to present energies to us in symbolic form. A burning torch in a dream, for example, may symbolize a guiding force lighting our way and offering us the energy to continue following our call from God.

In dreamwork, we also recommend that you personify energies, and therefore would invite you to dialogue with the burning torch, asking it, for example, "Where are you leading me?" "How can I better cooperate with you?" "What is the energy that keeps your flame burning?" And so on.

To be of service to your personality and life choices, any personification needs to become functional, that is, its energy needs to be put to work consciously and creatively. The Dialoguing process can facilitate this kind of energy transformation, especially when your questions to the dream figure seek responses which have to do with your daily life and choices. For example, ask a dream figure: How can I express your energies in my ordinary life? How can you help me take care of my body? How can you help me nurture myself, my family, my community? What do you bring to me that I can use in deepening my faith, my hope, my love?

We encourage people serious about dreamwork to dialogue often with important dream figures or symbols, and to return from time to time in dialogue to re-establish relationship with dream figures met and dialogued with before. And, as with a friend, you always have a choice whether to continue or stop a dialogue, or to take it up again later.

Dreamwork Technique 5
Dialoguing with a Dream Figure

Procedure:

Before beginning a dialogue, do some basic dreamwork and write down several key questions you have about the dream.

1. Choose some character, figure or image from your dream for dialogue. Select one that seems prominent or important to you, either one you want to approach or one you would rather avoid.

2. Make sure it is a time and a place where you will not be interrupted. Let yourself relax, place yourself in a meditative attitude, and in your own way welcome God's presence and guidance as you begin your dreamwork dialogue.

3. Using your imagination, recreate the dream scene where your chosen figure appeared. Let the dream figure come alive again for you. If the figure is a symbol such as a torch, a key, a house, a cloud, a car, a painting, a mountain, or a breeze, personify or name the figure in such a way that you can enter into dialogue with it.

4. Begin with a few opening questions to get the relationship started, write down your first question and in your imagination picture yourself asking it to your dream figure.

5. Then write whatever response seems to come to you as the dream figure's reply. Let your pen move spontaneously as you write, not caring about grammar, spelling or punctuation.

6. Continue the dialogue until you feel something has been changed or resolved, an insight has been gained, or until you want or need to stop. The dialogue itself is a gift.

7. When the dialogue seems to be coming to a natural closing, we recommend you ask one last question—"Do you have anything else to tell me or give me?"—just in case something important has been forgotten.

8. After the dialogue, reflect on what happened, perhaps taking a few minutes to reread the dialogue and find a Title, Theme, Affect and Question for it. Find some way to clarify the energy and insight that may have been communicated to you, and propose ways you might use this gift in your daily life.

Notes to Chapter 4
The Disrepute of Dreamwork in the Church
1. Morton Kelsey, *God, Dreams and Revelation,* p. 159.
2. The passages where Jerome correctly translates *anan* and its cognates are: Dt 18:14, 2 Kgs 21:6, Is 2:6 and 57:3, Jer 27:9, Mi 5:11, and Jgs 9:37.
3. The passages where Jerome mistranslates are: Dt 18:10, Lev 19:26 and 2 Chr 33:6.
4. Kelsey, *op. cit.,* p. 155.
5. Kelsey, *op. cit.,* pp. 154–155, makes some tentative suggestions to explain Jerome's radical shift in attitude toward dreamwork.
6. Gregory, *Dialogues,* I, 4.
7. *Ibid.,* IV, 50.
8. See, for example, G.P. Fedotov, *A Treasury of Russian Spirituality* (New York: Sheed and Ward, 1948) and *Writings from the Philokalia on Prayer of the Heart* (London: Faber and Faber, 1954).
9. See Victor White, O.P., *God and The Unconscious* (Cleveland: World Publishing, 1961) and Kelsey, *Dreams,* pp. 173–178.
10. Thomas Aquinas, *Great Books of the Western World,* Vol. 19 (Chicago: Encyclopaedia Britannica, 1952), p. vi.

Chapter 5

The Rediscovery of Dreamwork Among Contemporary Christians: Dreams and Symbolic Language

◆

The Contribution of Freud

In the twentieth century, independent of the Church, a strong interest in dreams and dreamwork entered our consciousness in three ways:
first, in psychoanalysis beginning with Sigmund Freud; second, in the
investigations in dream laboratories; third, in the general interest in
altered states of consciousness.

Freud's analytic techniques were, to a great extent, based on the interpretations he made from his patients' dreams. Although according to Henri Ellenberger, historian of the unconscious, "investigators of dreams from 1860 to 1899 had already discovered almost all the notions that were to be synthesized by Freud and Jung,"[1] Freud's particular synthesis and terminology made the difference, and helped create the Freudian revolution which made the modern world conscious of the profound and unseen depths of the human unconscious. The conscious ego was no longer seen as absolute. It became clear that whatever was thought or expressed by the rational mind was tied to layers of reality beneath the conscious surface. For Freud, dreams were the "royal road" to the unconscious depths of the human personality. Psychologists before Freud were familiar with the unconscious; they were also familiar with the investigation of dreams. Freud's great insight was to combine the two avenues of research and apply them to the healing of personality wounds.

Freud had finished the manuscript for his book, *The Interpretation of Dreams,* a year or so before 1900. With a sense of the revolutionary impact his book could have, he purposely held publication back, to have the book appear in the first year of the new century. Among his fellow psychologists and psychiatrists, Freud's epoch-launching book received mostly contempt. The book's first edition of six hundred copies took more than eight years to sell. But the revolution did take place, and the importance of dreams as a vehicle of self-understanding could never again be denied. Thirty-one years later, Freud reaffirmed the crucial importance of his dream research in the Foreword to the third edition of *The Interpretation of Dreams.*

> This book ... contains, even according to my present judgment, the most valuable of all the discoveries it has been my good fortune to make. Insight such as this falls to one's lot but once in a lifetime.[2]

In contrast to the medical writers of Freud's day, who for the most part dismissed the dream as a rather purposeless process of random sensory and somatic stimuli, Freud observed ordinary people, unaffected by this scientific judgment, continuing to believe that their dreams have a meaning for their lives, and that this meaning could be discovered by a process of interpretation. In a short treatise *On Dreams,* published shortly after *The Interpretation of Dreams,* Freud acknowledged his debt to the ordinary folk:

> One day I discovered to my great astonishment that the view of dreams which came nearest to the truth was not the medical one but the popular one, half-involved though it still was in superstition.[3]

It is not our purpose here to present Freud's methods of dream interpretation, nor to criticize them. Our wish is to acknowledge this courageous man and scientist for having done more than anyone else in almost fifteen hundred years to make the world aware of the potential for meaning, healing, and growth that await each of us in our dreams. He established in contemporary consciousness the link between dreams and meaning.

Scientific Research on Dreaming

Scientific investigations concerning sleep and dreams during the past fifty years have provided us with much knowledge about the physiological basis of dreams. In 1953, an article in *Science,* reporting the laboratory findings of Nathaniel Kleitman using the encephelograph to monitor dreaming, gave a new impetus to dream research.[4] Sleep and dream laboratories began to spring up, and within twenty years more than twenty-five of them were operating in the United States.[5]

Although the results of this research do not pertain directly to the content of this book, it may be of assurance to readers to know, for example, that all people dream, whether or not they remember their dreams. Dreams seem to enjoy an autonomy of their own, operating outside conscious ego control and independently of external conditions, and the contents of dreams—the images, symbols, and events—are personal and unique reflections of each dreamer.[6]

Dreams and Consciousness

The third stream of contemporary exploration that takes an interest in dreams are those who study alternative states of consciousness. This stream covers a broad spectrum of people—from those, on the one hand, who are researching right-hemisphere brain functioning and studying the formation and functions of images, symbols, and myths, to people on the other hand who are exploring "occult" and "psychic" phenomena. From dozens of different perspectives, these people look upon the dream and its contents as an informative and significant aspect of human life. From some of these groups have sprung an interest in the dream in world cultures and religions.[7] Vine Deloria, for example, has explored the part dreams have played in the Native American Indian cultures,[8] and Kilton Stewart has researched the Senoi people who live in the highlands of

Malaysia, and whose culture was, according to him, based on the daily use of dreamwork in families and tribes.[9]

Rediscovery of the Christian Dreamwork Tradition

The question at issue in this chapter is how and when did Christians rediscover their ancient tradition of dreamwork.

The rediscovery did not come through biblical studies and biblical hermeneutics. In fact, a recent doctoral thesis has shown that in 1980 biblical scholars were just beginning to deal with dream phenomena.[10] So far their conclusions are highly tentative. "Most of them base their judgment of the dream phenomena through contact (not with the dreamwork tradition of the Church Fathers but) with Freud's concepts and interpretation."[11]

Jung's Contribution to Valuing Dreams

Carl Jung was the first to put us back in touch with the style of dreamwork practiced in the first centuries of the Church.[12] First, he treated dreams as very meaningful and practical, helping persons to see what was going on in parts of their personalities of which they were unaware and unconscious.[13] Second, he linked dream imagery to psychological and spiritual energy (not merely to sexual libido as Freud had done) and associated dream imagery to religious texts, myths, and folk tales as a way of releasing their energy.[14] Third, for Jung the dream was an example of an experience expressed in non-rational, imaginal language. Thus, while Freud may be said to have believed that the unconscious used rational thinking but covertly expressed itself in the dream, Jung believed that the unconscious did not communicate rationally, but rather used languages made up of constellations of symbols and metaphors. Thus, for Jung, the dream, which came through the unconscious, was not trying to deceive or distort; it was simply using non-rational, imaginal modes of communication.[15]

Jung developed dreamwork methods and principles which have enriched the traditional approach to Christian dreamwork. He reaffirmed the attitude of the early Church teachers that the imagery of a person's dreams are based on that person's life and history, and that the dreamer is the one best qualified to affirm the meaning of his or her own dream.[16]

One of the hallmarks of Jungian dreamwork is that any outside interpreter must remain open in the face of the dream material and let the
dreamer himself or herself be the one who decides on the correctness of a
dream's meaning. Our book reaffirms this principle. Furthermore, we
agree with Jung's insistence that the dreamer's life and milieu, work and
relationships, past history and memories, conscious associations and psychological state must all be taken into account for dreamwork to be valid
and reliable.[17] Under these conditions, who could be better qualified to
acknowledge the true meanings of a dream through personal dreamwork
than the dreamer himself or herself?

Jung also pointed out that dreams are not simply personal. He
suggested the helpfulness of relating to the images and symbols in a
dream as if they were other people. The unconscious has a life of its own,
he said. It is not merely the receptacle of psychologically repressed
material, but is a living, creative, germinal layer in each of us. For this
reason, many dream characters may be viewed as parts of the dreamer
and many of the dominant qualities of the dreamer may be personified as
dream characters.[18]

Jung encouraged a longitudinal study of dreams. When dreams are
looked at over a period of time they reveal a developmental quality, he
said, showing one's progress toward wholeness.[19]

Jung's primary dreamwork method was *association*—that is, like
Freud, he developed a symbol-linking system, but unlike Freud, who
linked dream symbols to sexual dynamics, Jung linked dream symbols to
more general myths and religious texts.[20]

Although we suggest the symbol-linking method as a dreamwork
technique (see Dreamwork Technique 10: Symbol Association), we do
not recommend it as an initial technique since, as Jung's critics have
noted, symbol association very quickly leaves the scene of the original
dream and focuses on the myth or archetypal symbol with which it is
associated. At the beginning of dreamwork, we prefer to focus upon the
dream material itself, and to utilize techniques which keep us directly
related to our dream, or to other dream material of our own, rather than
to some story or symbol that reminds us of our dream. Used appropriately, however, symbol association can be a powerful dreamwork technique.

Some followers of Jung have, in effect, made the unconscious their
new bible. Some, such as Clyde Reid, believe that spiritual vitality has
gone out of the Church. Instead of looking to the Church for holiness and
wholeness, according to Reid, people are finding God in nature, in
relationships with persons, and through the private messages received in
dreams, meditation, inspirations, convictions, and numinous experiences.[21]

In our book we do not propose dreams and dreamwork as an alternative to faith or membership in a believing community, but as one way among many of maintaining and nurturing one's relation to God, to self, and to the community. Dreams often put us in touch with current dynamics in our relationships; our healing and growth in interpersonal relationships naturally affects the life of the community in which we live.

Modern Christian Explorers of Dreams

There are two persons most directly responsible for the rediscovery of the Christian dreamwork tradition. We have mentioned their names before. They are John Sanford and Morton Kelsey. Both of them, Anglican priests and counselors, were led to research the roots of dreamwork in the Church through their studies of Jungian psychology. Kelsey wrote:

> My search for some of this material started from an important footnote in Jung's *Psychology and Religion: West and East*, in which he quoted two writers who had summarized the thinking of the Middle Ages on dreams. One was a Jesuit priest, Benedict Pererius, and the other, Gaspar Peucer, was the son-in-law of the Protestant reformer Melancthon.[22]

For Kelsey, the encounter with dreams and dreamwork effected a personal conversion.

> As I began to take an interest in my dreams, I became aware for the first time in my life that God wanted to speak to me. It was during a difficult time that a friend advised me to pay attention to my dreams. I soon noticed that there was a wisdom greater than mine that spoke to me in my dreams and came to my aid.[23]

As a result of his experiences, Kelsey began to study dreams and dreamwork throughout the history of Christianity. The results of his research were published in 1968 in a scholarly book, *Dreams: The Dark Speech of the Spirit*, the only recent study of the dream in Christian culture.[24] He showed that throughout Christian history the dream had been "a channel often used by God to talk to his people."[25] For the historical parts of our book we have utilized Kelsey's research extensively.

John A. Sanford, formerly a pastor of an Episcopal church in San Diego, is now a counselor in private practice. He was trained at the Jung Institute in Zurich and authored what was perhaps the first contemporary book presenting a Christian approach to dreams and dreamwork, *Dreams: God's Forgotten Language*.[26] Sanford's purpose in writing was to restore the dream to the place it held in the Old and New Testaments as a major medium—along with visions—of God's communication to humans. Throughout his book, Sanford consistently treats dreams as revelations from God. "The divine authorship of the dream is found from first to last in the Bible."[27] He feels, as we do, that the dream needs to be rediscovered for the Church's use today so that we may hear God speaking to us just as directly as he spoke to the people in biblical times.

Holiness and Wholeness

With the advent of modern psychology, two important shifts of focus in dreamwork happened. First of all, with the awareness of psychological development mirrored in dreams, there was a strong interest in understanding dreams in the light of personality. This new interest allowed dreamwork to be viewed as a way of getting in touch with the deepest parts of the person—conscious and unconscious—in order to develop wholeness, or "individuation" as Jung named the process. Priests and religious leaders who were trained in modern psychology began seeing a close relationship between spiritual holiness and psychological wholeness, so that the two processes in the individual coalesced into one.[28] For Victor White, a Dominican priest, the *psyche* which Jung explored in therapy and dreams was nothing other than the *soul* which Church teachers had explored for centuries in their disciplines of spiritual growth.[29] The new integrative approach to dreams, which we follow in our book, uses dreamwork to foster spiritual as well as psychological growth. In fact, the position we take is that the full practice of a spiritual life involves psychological development. For example, personality problems can block spiritual development, and certain personality problems do not seem to become resolved without a spiritual perspective.

The second shift in focus in modern dreamwork again broadened the usefulness of dream methodology. Most of the ancients, and indeed many of the writers down to present times, were particularly interested in prophetic and telepathic dreams—thus the tendency throughout much of the history of Christianity to link dreamwork with the magic and divination of fortune tellers.[30] In their fascination with the possibility of foretelling or predicting future events, people often lost sight of dreams as an arena where a basic relationship to God and the world of spirit might be developed. Hence, dreams that did not seem to be predictive or telepathic were often disregarded as uninteresting. With modern psychology's interest in dreams came the belief that every dream has meaning. And from a spiritual perspective came the awareness that dreams can be helpful to the person desiring to grow psychologically and spiritually. In our book, we are primarily interested in the dreamwork which daily challenges us to come to consciousness about who we are and how we are uniquely called by God along a path toward holiness and wholeness.

Toward a Fuller Methodology for Dreamwork

We have seen how the psychological traditions of Freud and Jung, combined with recent dream research documenting the necessity of dreaming in order to preserve mental health and well-being, have impressed on the public a newly-awakened interest in dreams. And within the Christian tradition, Morton Kelsey, John Sanford, and Victor White have all spoken for the value of dreamwork as important to the spiritual life. These authors, as well as others, have shown that following one's dreams as revelatory of God's will was central to ancient Judaism and early Christianity.

What seems wanting in the contemporary Christian approach to dreams is a fully-developed methodology for helping today's Christians understand their dreams. If we recognize that God wants to touch our lives and that God is already doing it in our dreams, how do we systematically pay attention to the inner images and voices emerging from the depths of our soul? How do we work at an everyday level with the symbols that surface in our dreams as healing and revelatory forces in our lives?

The dreamwork methodology presented in this book was developed and synthesized from many sources. Besides using attitudes and practices gained from study of dreams and dreamwork in the Old and New Testaments and the writings of the early Christian teachers and theologians, we have used the insights of Jungian psychology, certain key concepts attributed to the Senoi people of Malaysia, techniques researched and developed at the Jungian-Senoi Institute in Berkeley, California, under the direction of Strephon Kaplan Williams and published in his book, *Jungian–Senoi Dreamwork Manual* (1980)[31] and other refinements and techniques developed by Louis M. Savary and Patricia H. Berne at Inner Development Associates in Washington, D. C.

In the following pages, we have tried to clarify and systematize a series of dreamwork techniques for dealing with important symbols that occur in dreams.

Dreamwork with Symbols

In dreamwork, a symbol refers to any dream image which evokes an emotional response, either during the dream or after it. For example, in your dream you may have seen a vase on a table. If the vase was just one of many things on a cluttered table, none of which evoked a response in you, then symbol-dreamwork with the vase may not prove very helpful. If, however, the vase caught your attention because, say, of its beauty, or because it was chipped, or because you remember your grandmother had one just like it in her house, then you are dealing with a symbol, and dreamwork with it will probably prove fruitful. It is the energy inherent in a symbol that causes it to catch our attention and evoke an emotional response.

A dream symbol may be a visual image, but it may also be a sound (my mother's voice, the chanting of monks, a hurricane's winds) or a smell (the odor of incense, the scent of roses, the aroma of coffee), or, less frequently, a touch or a taste. A variety of sensory items may provide symbolic energy and deserve symbolic processing in dreamwork. Activities and experiences such as flying in a plane, being attacked, finding a lost coin, or falling over a cliff may also be treated as symbols. In short, almost any word, image or action in a dream may be viewed symbolically.

Symbolic Language and Literalness

One thing we strongly emphasize is *not* simply to take the words, images or actions in a dream literally. For example, if in a dream your dream ego is changing jobs or leaving a marriage, don't assume the dream means that you must change (or are destined to change) your career or your marriage partner. Instead, we would ask you to do dreamwork with the symbol of "your job" or "your marriage." You cannot *assume* to know what the dream means without doing some discerning dreamwork. Dreams don't usually give literal commands to act; rather, dreams ask questions, reveal issues, suggest alternatives, open up new possibilities, invite responses.

We may be tempted to assume, from some biblical texts, that people of the Old and New Testaments did things because they were literally commanded so by their dreams; however, such an assumption may be unwarranted. For example, it may seem that Joseph's dream told him to marry Mary; upon closer reading, however, we see that the angel did not tell Joseph to marry Mary, but rather *not to be afraid* to marry Mary. Instead of commanding, the dream was, among other things, confronting

Joseph with his attitudes and feelings toward Mary. The information Joseph was given about the baby in Mary's womb opened up new possibilities and alternative plans for them. For Joseph to respond adequately to his dream, he would have to do more than simply take Mary into his home and marry her; he would have to deal with his feelings, his attitudes, and his values—toward his own self-image, toward Mary, toward the other villagers in Nazareth, and to the Mosiac law.

Furthermore, we recommend that when you choose to deal with a symbolic image or event in a dream, don't try to define it or translate it. Instead, *relate* to it. It is important to remember that symbols, which form the usual language of the unconscious and of the spiritual dimension, function at a level more primary than words, or even concepts. Symbols are not as easily manipulated by the rational mind as words or concepts are, since they are more complex and multi-dimensional. Nevertheless, once we have had the symbolic dream experience, we need conceptual thought—words and sentences—to make it conscious, to give it perspective, to release the energy it contains, to bring it into daily life.

The five dreamwork techniques suggested in the following pages are designed to release a symbol's energy and help us bring it into consciousness in a way that makes it useful in our daily life and decisions. These techniques are called Symbol Immersion, Carrying the Symbol Forward, Carrying the Symbol Back in Time, Symbol Amplification and Symbol Association. Each technique has a clear function and will prove useful and helpful with certain kinds of dreams.

Dreamwork Technique 6: Symbol Immersion

If a dream symbol, such as a vase, can be said to have a life of its own, then it has a past, a present, and a future. For example, the vase in our dream may have had a *past* when it belonged to our grandmother; at *present*, let us say, in the dream it stands on a table among many other items in an estate sale; and if the dream ego does nothing, the vase may find its *future* with a potential buyer looking at it admiringly in the dream.

The technique called Carrying the Symbol Forward deals with the symbol's future, Carrying the Symbol Back in Time deals with its past, and Symbol Immersion deals with the symbol in its present form in the dream. In each technique, we begin with the symbol as it appears and acts in the dream, letting the dream come alive again in our imagination. If we were to do symbolic dreamwork on the vase dream, we would begin in imagination by picturing the vase on the table and getting a sense of our feelings about it and our relation to it.

In Symbol Immersion, we focus on the symbol and experience its unique qualities *just as it is,* without letting the symbol change its appearance or activity. We want to see it, hear it, feel it, smell it, know it as it is in all its detail, so that if we were ever to meet it again, we would recognize it instantly.

In Symbol Immersion, while the symbol stays in the same place, we can, using our imagination, change our viewing place—now coming closer, now distancing, now picking up the vase, feeling its weight, touching its texture, peering into it, looking for identifying marks on its bottom, etc.—in order to learn everything we can about the symbol in its present state. Perhaps in the original dream we thought we saw a mark on the vase, or a crack; in Symbol Immersion we look closely to verify our suspicions, to see if what we thought we saw in the dream was really there. Immersion often allows us to discover details about a symbol we never noticed in the original dream.

In the spiritual life, one of the issues we often work at is our relationship to people and things. We do not want to go on viewing people simply from our subjective biases—who we imagine certain people are or who we expect them to be; we want to develop the ability to experience them as they really are. Immersion helps us relate to things deeply, yet objectively. Objectivity need not be cold and merely rational; it can involve seeing things in their totality and in their relation to us. The spiritual discipline of Symbol Immersion, whether in dreamwork or meditation, helps us see our place in the scheme of things and helps us relate deeply to important symbols—personal, cultural, natural, religious. We often suggest Symbol Immersion outside of dreams as a spiritual practice. For example, spend some time in a church when hardly anyone is present. Choose a symbol—one you may have seen there for many years, but never related to as deeply as you could have—and do Symbol Immersion.

When choosing dream symbols to work with in Immersion, go to the symbol with the strongest energy. What most attracts you? What most repels you? What is most vivid? What evokes a strong reaction? Or choose dream symbols that are considered important in general—for example, Christian symbols such as the cross, rainbow, church, fish, lamb, rock, bread, wine, candlelight, key, Bible, and so on. Other dream symbols to choose for immersion are symbols of healing and wholeness. Since much of our lives is conflictual and we are pulled in many directions, it is often helpful to focus on healing symbols.

Dreamwork Technique 6
Symbol Immersion

Procedure:

1. In rereading your dream report, select an image or symbol from the dream which attracts you, which seems vivid, and of which you would like to be more aware.

2. In your imagination, let your dream come alive again and focus on your chosen symbol. Keep the symbol in the state it was in the original dream; do not let the symbol transform itself or move into the past or the future. (You can let it do that later.)

3. Relate to your symbol in any way that makes it more vivid and important to you. For example, in imagination change your position in order to perceive the symbol in greater detail, so you may always remember it.

4. If you are with a dreamwork partner or in a dream group, let them ask questions that will make the symbol clearer to you. Relating factual detail to the others allows them in their own imagination to see the symbol in all its detail as clearly as you do. The objective here is to perceive the symbol as clearly as possible *and to relate to it.*

5. After doing the Symbol Immersion technique, you will want to ask yourself *how you are now relating* to the symbol. It is from this relationship that the symbol's energy flows to you; it may bring you peace, healing, wholeness, wisdom, insight, new possibilities, all of which may be carried into your daily waking life.

Dreamwork Technique 7: Carrying the Symbol Forward

When you choose to re-enter the dream to work with a major symbol, we suggest you do Symbol Immersion first. This initial procedure grounds you by helping you experience the symbol just as it is. Once a symbol has become vivid and deeply familiar to you, you are ready to go forward or backward in time with it.

Often, merely by re-entering the dream and focusing on the symbol, we discover that it naturally wants to change or move. We often don't have to choose consciously to make the symbol change, but merely by looking at it the symbol begins to evolve or to initiate action before our very eyes. For example, in the dream, if the person admiring the vase were to buy it and take it away, we in doing Carrying the Symbol Forward would follow the vase as it left the house with the buyer and see where it led us, all the while staying in touch with our feelings toward the vase.

If the dream symbol we choose to follow is a person, it may perform some action for us or in relation to us that will have significance for us. Or it may bring into the experience other symbols that have new spiritual energies or insights for us, something perhaps that we need.

Carrying the symbol forward or backward in time is often a way to keep its energy from being overwhelming. These techniques offer us the opportunity to work toward healing from a new direction or perspective. (When the very action of the dream is carried forward in time, the procedure is called Carrying the Dream Forward; it is presented as Dreamwork Technique 28.)

Dreamwork Technique 7
Carrying the Symbol Forward

This technique works most effectively on symbols with which you have first done Symbol Immersion.

Procedure:

1. In imagination, re-enter the dream and focus on the symbol. The symbol may spontaneously change or act in such a way that it proceeds forward in time. If the symbol doesn't do this automatically, you may invite it to do so by asking it questions such as: Where are you going to from here? What are you going to do next? What will become of you? How can I begin relating to you to bring about healing or a resolution of a problem in my life?

2. Once the symbol begins to move forward in time, simply follow its change or movement. Notice how the symbol relates to you and how you relate to the symbol. Mark any emotional changes in your relation or response to it.

3. When the procedure comes to a natural stopping place, you might offer gratitude to the symbol. Then reflect on the process, asking yourself questions such as: What have I learned about the symbol?

What have I learned about myself in relation to that symbol? What energies, feelings or insights have been released in me? How can I stay in touch with those energies? How can I utilize them in my daily life for healing and wholeness?

Dreamwork Technique 8
Carrying the Symbol Back in Time

This technique is best when it follows Symbol Immersion on the chosen symbol.

Procedure:

1. Meditatively, re-enter the dream and focus on the symbol. The symbol may spontaneously change or act in such a way that moves backward in time—like a motion picture running in reverse. If the symbol doesn't do this spontaneously, you may invite it to do so by asking questions such as: How did you get to be here? Where did you come from? Where were you before this? How could I have related to you before this time? What do I need to know about your past history so that you could be a force for healing and wholeness in my life?

2. Simply follow the movement and changes in the symbol as it regresses in time. Notice how the symbol relates to you as it changes, and how you relate to the symbol.

3. When the procedure comes to a natural stopping place, offer gratitude to the symbol, and reflect on the process as with the previous technique.

It is sometimes profitable to use all three techniques—immersion, going forward, and going back in time—on the same dream symbol. Such a combination of techniques can put you in touch with the life history of that symbol in relation to you.

Dreamwork Technique 9:
Symbol Amplification

People often confuse Symbol Amplification with Symbol Immersion and Symbol Association, but there are clear differences.

Symbol Immersion is basically an imaginative and often emotionally laden technique which requires that the dreamer go back into the dream state (or appropriate altered state of consciousness through meditation) and relate to the symbol. In contrast, Symbol Amplification is a rather logical, left-brain activity and takes place in rational consciousness outside the dream state.

Association is, for the most part, a subjective, symbol-linking procedure in which a dream symbol reminds us of another symbol (a word, object, or experience from our own life, from literature, or from known-to-us history), which may in turn remind us of a third symbol, and so on. In contrast, Amplification stays focused on the dream symbol itself, reflecting on its inherent qualities. Amplification evokes symbol-inherency rather than symbol-linking.

We believe Symbol Amplification should usually precede Symbol Association because it is important to view the symbol in its inherent qualities and functions before we color its meaning and character by subjective association.

Amplification involves the conscious enumeration of a symbol's generally recognized characteristics, both sensory and functional. For example, we ask: How does this symbol function in outer life? If we ask this question of a vase, we can begin to enumerate its normal and generally recognized functions such as holding flowers or decorating a table. Moreover, some people collect vases as antiques or works of art; others use them for storage or for hiding things; they are also a common gift.

Amplification also studies the characteristics and functions of *this particular symbol,* asking what is unique about this vase that makes it different from other vases, visually and functionally.

Symbol Amplification as a dreamwork technique helps us understand and know a symbol through objective eyes. It shows that even in dreamwork we can approach symbols helpfully and productively in other than subjective ways. In amplification we often begin to hear metaphors that relate to our present life.

Dreamwork Technique 9
Symbol Amplification

Procedure:
1. Choose a dream symbol you wish to explore, and, in a rational frame of mind, consciously enumerate its common characteristics and

its usual functions by responding to the following questions: What are some ways this symbol functions in outer life? What are the unique qualities and functions of the particular expression of this symbol in my dream (e.g., this particular vase)?

2. Reflect on how you relate to the qualities and functions of the symbol in the dream, and how you relate to them in waking life.

3. After listing characteristics of the symbol in itself and as it functions in the dream, generalize or group these characteristics under a common theme, to help you arrive at what would be for you the essential function or chief characteristic of the symbol. This process will suggest what the symbol most likely means for you. For someone else, amplifying the same symbol may produce a different chief characteristic. This is true especially when working with major symbols. For example, to different people a cross appearing in their dreams might point to such different meanings as a crossroads in life, the value of suffering transformed, a redeeming factor at work in a troubled relationship, attunement with Christ's passion, or something else. It is important that you choose which characteristic of the symbol seems most central for you at this particular time, and work with it to discover meaning in your life.

Dreamwork Technique 10: Symbol Association

Association is symbol-linking. It answers the question: "What does this remind you of?" or "What comes to mind when you think of this symbol?" While Symbol Amplification strives to be objective, Symbol Association evokes a strictly personal, and often biased, response.

Meaning and healing often occur when there is a blend of our personal experience with a more universal experience. A spiritual perspective toward life accepts things such as vases as worthy of being recognized objectively for what they are and do; to know reality in this way is to experience God's creation as it was meant to be experienced. At the same time, a spiritual viewpoint recognizes that it is necessary to be aware of our associations to a symbol *as associations.*

While associations can lead us to healing and new insight, they can also remain unconscious and bias us away from experiencing things as they really are. As a dreamwork technique, Symbol Association helps make conscious our own personal coloring of dream symbols, while amplification maintains an objective viewpoint. Together they help us honor symbols in their being and value, and offer us a holistic perspective. The view they offer together is more total and whole than either taken alone.

Dreamwork Technique 10
Symbol Association

Procedure:

1. Choose a dream symbol that evokes a strong emotional response in you. If possible, spend a short time using Symbol Amplification on it to ground and balance the associations you make.

2. Ask yourself the questions: What does the symbol remind me of? What does it make me think of? What story, person, memory, place, situation does it call to mind? What emotions does it trigger, and when and where do I remember feeling those same feelings or feelings like them?

3. Continue associating—linking symbols and memories—until some awareness clicks in your mind (or body). Even though the final awareness may seem to have nothing directly to do with the original dream symbol, you have reached this awareness by a series of symbol-links that began with your dream symbol. Although you seem to have left the original dream symbol far behind, you are still related to it; that relationship can be traced, if need be.

4. Combine the characteristics you have discovered through amplification and association into a single whole. In doing this, it may help to complete the following statement: *When I think of, or feel my way into, this symbol it ultimately represents to me . . .* What you are searching for is the essence or chief characteristic of this symbol for you, the characteristic that seems to bring the other characteristics together.

5. Next, turn the essential meaning of your symbol into a statement or principle about living life. Here, you are taking a characteristic and turning it into an action statement so that you may more fully bring the symbol's energy into your daily life. For example, if the

vase as my symbol has for me the chief characteristic of *containment*, then I might transform this into an action statement such as "My life energy needs containing so that I can feel more grounded in what I am doing with my life right now." Many other such statements are also possible, since in this step you are making the essential life of the symbol relevant to your own life.

Notes to Chapter 5
The Rediscovery of Dreamwork
Among Contemporary Christians

1. Henri Ellenberger, *The Discovery of the Unconscious* (New York: Basic Books, 1970), p. 311. See also pp. 303–311.

2. Sigmund Freud, *The Interpretation of Dreams* in *Basic Writings of Sigmund Freud* (New York: Basic Books, 1955), p. 181.

3. Sigmund Freud, *On Dreams* (New York: Norton, 1952), p. 15.

4. See E. Hartmann, *The Biology of Dreaming* (Springfield, Ill.: Thomas, 1967), p. 5.

5. See Patricia Garfield, *Creative Dreaming* (New York: Simon and Schuster, 1974), p. 11.

6. Readers wishing to explore the scientific aspects of sleep and dreaming may be interested in the following: Shirley Motter Linde and Louis M. Savary, *The Joy of Sleep* (New York: Harper & Row, 1980); U.S. Public Health Service, *Current Research on Sleep and Dreams* (Washington, D.C.: Government Printing Office, 1966), publication no. 1389.

7. For a general treatment of dreams in their social and cultural impact see G.E. von Grunebaum and Roger Callois, *The Dream and Human Societies* (Berkeley: University of California Press, 1966).

8. Vine Deloria, *God Is Red* (New York: Grosset and Dunlap, 1973), p. 203.

9. See Kilton Stewart, *Creative Psychology and Dream Education* (New York: Stewart Foundation for Creative Psychology).

10. Daniel H. Newhall, *Dreams and the Bible* (San Anselmo: San Francisco Theological Seminary, 1980), an unpublished doctoral dissertation, p. 6.

11. *Ibid.*

12. See C.G. Jung, *Psychology and Religion* in *The Collected Works of C.G. Jung* (New York: Pantheon, 1958), 11:57.

13. See C.G. Jung, *The Analysis of Dreams* in *Collected Works*, Vol. 4.

14. See C.G. Jung, *The Practical Uses of Dream Analysis* in *Collected Works*, Vol. 16 and C.G. Jung, *On Psychic Energy* in *Collected Works*, 8:3 ff.

15. See *The Practical Use of Dream-Analysis*, p. 149. See also C.G. Jung, *Man and His Symbols* (New York: Dell, 1968), p. 80.

16. C.G. Jung, *The Theory of Psychoanalysis* in *Collected Works*, 4:147.

17. *Ibid.*, p. 200.

18. C.G. Jung, *The Meaning of Psychology for Modern Man* in *Collected Works*, 10:151.

19. C.G. Jung, *On the Nature of Dreams* in *Collected Works*, 8:289.

20. *The Meaning of Psychology for Modern Man*, p. 152.

21. Clyde Reid, *The Return to Faith* (New York: Harper & Row, 1974), pp. 22–26.

22. Morton Kelsey, *God, Dreams and Revelation* (Minneapolis: Augsburg Press, 1974), p. 167.

23. Morton Kelsey, *Dreams: A Way To Listen to God* (New York: Paulist Press, 1978), p. 9.

24. Morton Kelsey, *Dreams: The Dark Speech of the Spirit* (New York: Doubleday, 1968). This book was later reprinted by another publisher as *God, Dreams, and Revelation.* See note 22.

25. *Dreams: A Way To Listen to God,* p. 9.

26. John A. Sanford, *Dreams: God's Forgotten Language* (New York: Lippincott, 1968).

27. *Ibid.*, p. 102.

28. See Josef Goldbrunner, *Holiness and Wholeness.*

29. Victor White, O.P., *Soul and Psyche: An Enquiry into the Relationship of Psychotherapy and Religion* (London: Collins and Harvill, 1960), pp. 11–31.

30. See Pedro Meseguer, S.J., *The Secret of Dreams* (Westminster, MD.: Newman Press, 1960), p. 35.

31. Strephon K. Williams, *Jungian–Senoi Dreamwork Manual* (Berkeley: Journey Press, 1980). This book is the first published comprehensive manual for working with dreams that we know of, and is a major innovative approach to Jungian psychology.

Chapter 6

Dreamwork and Prayer: Waking Dreams and Dreamwork

◆

Getting in Touch with Self and God

In the past five chapters we have traced the Judaeo-Christian history of dreams and dreamwork, seeing how the tradition developed, degenerated, was lost and was found again finally in the twentieth century, enormously enriched by medical research and the experience of thousands of therapists and their clients. We have seen that although one strand of theological tradition claims that dreams are probably meaningless and misleading, a stronger strand affirms that in dreams God communicates with us. And although one segment of psychological tradition pays little attention to the content of dreams, a far larger segment affirms that dreams when worked with can reveal our conscious and unconscious depths. Opting for the psychological and spiritual tradition that affirms dreams as meaningful, we begin to realize that dreams when worked with appropriately can help us get in touch with our deepest self as well as God.

Some questions we are then faced with are: How can we introduce dreams and dreamwork into our spiritual practices? How do they fit into what we are already doing? Where is a good place to begin doing dreamwork?

Applying Dreamwork Techniques to Meditation Material

If you plan to do dreamwork by yourself, one of the best ways to begin learning dreamwork techniques, oddly enough, is not to practice on your night dreams, but to use dreamwork techniques on material from your meditations and contemplations, especially if that material contains images, feelings, and other forms of inner sensory response.

For example, consider the kind of contemplation proposed by Ignatius Loyola in his *Spiritual Exercises.*[1] In contemplating a scene from Christ's life or one of his parables, we are asked to bring the scene or story alive in our imaginations—by seeing the persons, how they are dressed, what actions they take; by listening to their words; by touching things in the scene with the fingers of our imagination; by getting in touch with our own feelings as well as those of the persons in the story; by entering into dialogue with them. In this Ignatian approach, the biblical scene or story is dramatized in imagination. Thus, ideally, we as meditators enter into the story, interacting with the story's characters.

Such contemplative material is like dream material in a number of ways: it comes to us in the context of God's presence; it is treated as a gift of God; it involves imaginal experience and affective experience; it often happens in a deeper than normal state of consciousness; ideally, it also gets us involved in the experience.

Contemplative material differs from dream material in a number of ways, too. Contemplative material usually possesses a more ordered character, is generally dramatically composed, reveals clear connections, and is easier to remember; in contrast, night dream material is sometimes fragmentary, confused in memory, and logically discontinuous (though not symbolically so). For these reasons contemplative material may be easier to use than night dreams for practicing dreamwork techniques.

Ignatius recommended that the meditator spend a period of time (say, fifteen minutes) after every contemplative period in order to reflect on the prayer, draw wisdom from it, and put the wisdom to use in daily life.[2] We have taught dreamwork techniques to many Christians as a way of reflecting on their prayer experiences. Many of the techniques presented in this book may be used to enrich a review of a contemplative experience, including the ten presented so far: Dream Report, TTAQ, Key Questions, Following the Dream (Prayer) Ego, Dialoguing, and five techniques for symbol processing. Again and again, people report deeper understanding and insight from their prayer *once they begin applying (dreamwork) techniques to the meditative material.*

Particularly satisfying contemplative experiences, as Ignatius recognized, call for repetition and deepening. In such cases, we recommend doing Dialoguing or symbol work with these experiences as the main work of some future prayer period. Thus, a woman who in prayer had let the parable of the prodigal son come alive in her imagination found herself quite taken by the pouch of money the father handed to the prodigal. She utilized a later prayer period to focus on the pouch, first doing Symbol Immersion with it, then Carrying the Symbol Back in Time and Forward in Time. During the process, she became conscious of many hidden attitudes she had toward money and toward her own father and, indeed, toward God.

In using the dreamwork techniques with the more structured imaginal material of prayer, we grow familiar with their potential. We learn the art of choosing which technique to use and when. Undoubtedly, the more we practice the techniques, the better they will serve us in helping us gain energy and insight from our night dreams.

The Waking Dream Technique

From workshops on dreamwork, we have discovered the Waking Dream to be a valuable technique.[3] In a Waking Dream, as we use the term, persons apply the method of Ignatian contemplation to a dream, vision, or scene reported in the Bible. In a meditative mood, usually intensified by listening to appropriate musical selections, participants relive, in imagination, such dreams as Jacob's ladder-to-heaven dream or Joseph's dream to marry Mary.

In helping participants begin a Waking Dream on Jacob's dream, for example, we might ask them to imagine Jacob selecting a stone for his pillow and then lying down on the sanctuary's floor. "You may want to join Jacob," we might suggest, "finding your own stone and taking a place near Jacob." Usually we have already read the biblical passage to them, so they are familiar with the story. "See the ladder in your imagination," we might suggest. "What is it made of? See the angels ascending and descending. Notice how they move. Look at their faces. Are they bringing or taking anything? Let the story unfold before your eyes. There are no right or wrong things to do. There is only an ancient dream from God being given to you anew today." We ask participants to stay in touch with their feelings and their dream ego's responses.

As the music plays, the Jacob dream (now modified because they have become observers and participants in it) unfolds uniquely in each one's imagination.

When the music is over, we ask them to find a stopping place for their Waking Dream, acknowledge to God the gift of the dream, and begin journaling the dream. When they seem to have finished writing, we ask them to do Title, Theme, Affect, and Question (Dreamwork Technique 2) based on their Waking Dream. Then we usually invite them to talk and share in the group.

A Waking Dream on Jacob's Ladder Dream

For Ann this day, her Waking Dream on Jacob's ladder dream was "a sensate experience." She was aware of the stars and the cool night before Jacob's dream happened. During the dream, "I identified with Jacob," she said. "God surrounded me and enveloped me. It was a healing experience." Ann's TTAQ were:

T: Jacob's Junction
T: Forgiveness and promise
A: Peace, calm, serenity
Q: Have you made the right career decision?

For Nancy, the experience seemed as real as being awake. The ladder for her was wooden. It glowed with radiance, while there was darkness all around. She felt the awe of approaching mystery, and as the waking dream ended she expected to get a last look at the ladder, but instead found herself letting sand (mentioned by God in the prophecy) sift through her fingers. Nancy's TTAQ were:

T: The Presence of Yahweh
T: God always with us
A: Weariness, wonder, warmth, belongingness, awe
Q: How will God work through you?

Gary climbed to the top of the ladder, felt a sense of peace there, attracted by a place that seemed soft, lush, beautiful. After the view from the top, he came back and lay down on the hard ground—and it felt soft. Gary's TTAQ were:

T: See What Lies Ahead of You
T: The revelation of God's love for me
A: Relaxation in a sense of peace
Q: Sometimes you still don't trust me?

Waking Dreams do not always stay with the biblical story, and that is all right, for as a source of communication from God, dreams spontaneously become unique to our life. What is revealed in dreams and dreamwork seems to be tailored to our individual needs.

For example, in Pamela's waking dream, "Jacob's golden ladder transformed into a stepladder in front of a Christmas tree. My children were going up and down the ladder decorating the tree. After they went to sleep, my husband and I put presents (presence) under the tree. As the waking dream continued, Santa came and took the presents away to give them to others more needy. He left behind what seemed like an empty sack. When the children opened the sack, butterflies with angel faces and wings flew out and perched on the Christmas tree." Pam's TTAQ were:

T: The Ladder and the Christmas Tree
T: What Santa (God) does with our gifts and decorations
A: Frustration, and then wonder
Q: What are your real gifts, and what are you doing with them?

Dialoguing After Joseph's Dream To Marry Mary

In a similar way, other dreamwork techniques mentioned might be applied to material from a waking dream. For example, after a waking dream based on Joseph's dream to marry Mary, participants were asked to select a character from the dream or events surrounding it and dialogue with that dream character (Dreamwork Technique 5).

One woman dialogued with Joseph himself. She asked the dream figure of Joseph how he felt about his dream. Was he relieved, confused, frightened? Would he tell his own parents? How would he explain his actions to his friends?

Others chose to dialogue with the angel, with Mary, with Joseph's mother, and with Joseph's father.

Again and again, participants, a bit apprehensive about doing the dialoguing technique for the first time, said, "It flowed smoothly, which surprised me" or "It was easier than I thought it would be."

Participants also remarked how the dialogue brought them into relationship with the dream characters. "Joseph is a real person to me now; he never had been before" or "I think Joseph could understand how I feel about a very difficult decision I've had to make about a relationship."

Jung and Active Imagination

The contemplative process we use in the Waking Dream technique is related to a process Jung called "active imagination."[4] In a letter to a Mr. O., Jung directly suggested that he use active imagination on his dream material:

> The point is that you start with any image, for instance, just with that yellow spot in your dream. Contemplate it and carefully observe how the picture begins to unfold or change. Don't try to make it into something, just do nothing but observe what its spontaneous changes are. . . . Note all these changes and eventually step into the picture yourself, and if it is a speaking figure at all then say what you have to say to that figure and listen to what he or she has to say.[5]

Jung came to believe that active imagination, which involved turning willfully to the unconscious while awake, was a basic condition for the integration of the personality.[6]

Relating to Joseph's Energies

We asked workshop participants what questions the Waking Dream on Joseph had asked of them (the Q part of TTAQ). For some, the issue of trust and the energy of trust came to the fore. One felt asked by the dream, "Could you make a decision like Joseph's based on trust in God?" Another, "Do you trust God when God seems to guide you toward the almost impossible?" For others, the energies of love and gratitude came to the surface. Questions the Joseph dream asked of them included: "Do you really realize the gift of life I have given you?" and "How much do you love me?" One young woman needed to move a situation in her life from a response of great pain to one of acceptance. "Why does this situation hurt you so much still?" the dream asked her. "When will you be able to say, 'Into your hands'?"

Through relating to the Joseph figure in a Waking Dream, a very intellectual minister was able to let go of an exclusively rational perspective on the Bible and express his feeling side in a safe manner. After the waking dream, the minister came to the classroom half an hour before the next session and, sitting alone in the room, wrote a simple and moving lyric for a love song which he in his waking dream saw and heard Joseph singing to Mary. He asked the group if he could read it aloud for everyone to hear. The entire group was moved by the powerful emotions his words evoked. We asked him if he often wrote poetry or lyrics. He said, "Never," and insisted the words he had read to us were Joseph's, not his.

The Joseph figure acted as a containing, supportive, symbolic structure for the minister to release his own religious feelings without experiencing this affective energy (locked up in him for so long) as chaotic or overwhelming. He offers an example of how working with waking dreams that contain important spiritual and religious symbols is often good preparation for working directly with more individualized and original material that occurs in our night dreams. This same minister a few days later, in response to a night dream, was able to write another deeply emotional poem and own it as his own, probably thanks to the preparatory step of writing "Joseph's" song.

Using religious symbols and images as material for waking dreams allows us to experience words and phrases of our religious language in holistic ways, since the process uses both our thinking capacities as well as our emotional capacities at the same time.

Dreamwork Techniques Applied to Parables

Dreamwork techniques enjoy wide applicability. They may be used with any parable of Jesus in order to re-experience the biblical story and thus enliven our spiritual life. For example, we might begin by using the technique of Dialoguing with the prodigal son, asking him, "What message do you have for me in terms of my life right now?" or "How am I like you?" or some other significant questions. He may reply by pointing out areas of inadequacy or mistaken values in our life or ask us what would it mean for us to "return to my Father."

The purpose here is to experience the energy that awaits us in the story *through its re-enactment,* rather than to try to understand or reinterpret the story through an interpretation system, such as Jung's or Freud's, or even those of traditional beliefs. Because our method deals with energies and how to release them, the dreamwork techniques are effective not only with dreams but with any symbolic experiences such as biblical stories, events in the life of Jesus, or parables Jesus told. In telling parables, Jesus was trying to communicate in symbolic language the presence of the Kingdom of God, that is, God's direct intervention in the lives of humans like us. When we re-experience stories and scenes like the prodigal returning to his father, by applying dreamwork techniques such as Dialoguing, Waking Dream, and Symbol Immersion, we recontact the Source-energies embodied in these texts for ourselves and our communities, and we can systematically learn to use these energies to enliven and fulfill our lives. In applying dreamwork techniques to these texts, we find a source of meaning more sustaining and far greater than our personal selves. These texts also invite us to take advantage of healing sources other than those of our own making, specifically the direct experience through prayer and dreamwork of God working in our lives and in our communities.

As biblical scholar Walter Wink suggested in his book, *The Bible and Human Transformation,*[7] many people find certain biblical exegesis deadening rather than enlivening. An exclusively scholarly and complex interpretation of biblical texts may be fruitful for a theologian, but it may not provide enough for the person seeking direct and personal experience of the richness of the Christian tradition.

Dreamwork and Dealing with Illness

A hospital chaplain we know has changed his approach to patients from talking at them to inviting them to work experientially with religious texts as well as their dreams. Rather than telling them his own ideas about, say, the parable of the prodigal son, he encourages them to re-experience it. To accomplish this, he may teach them how to do the techniques of Waking Dream, Dialoguing, etc., and may assign them the task of using one or other of these techniques on the parable.

From his new perspective, the chaplain feels he is allowing the Holy Spirit to touch his patients' lives and to direct their spiritual process. They, in turn, report a deepening of their religious perspective in dealing with the trauma and challenge created by their illness. In sharing with him the results of their "dreamwork," they learn to speak comfortably and directly about their needs and fears as well as the psychological and spiritual issues involved. "In the long run," he said, "I spend a lot less time talking small talk with my patients and a lot more time dealing with their true needs and helping them get a perspective on their illness."

Dreamwork Technique 11
The Waking Dream

Procedure:
1. Choose a biblical dream, a parable, or story from the life of a holy

person that seems to relate to some energy you need or issue you're working on. Read the text of the story. This makes sure that you correctly understand the facts and structure of the story or dream.

2. Set aside at least fifteen minutes of time when you can relax completely and not be disturbed.

3. Let yourself grow quiet and become aware of God's presence, opening your consciousness to the spiritual energies and gifts contained for you in the story or dream.

4. Recreate in your imagination the starting point of the story in as much sensory detail and movement as you can. For example, if you are doing a Waking Dream on Joseph's dream, you might ask your imagination to provide the following details: What does Joseph's face look like? What kinds of emotions does it reveal? What color are his eyes? His hair? His clothes? How is he lying as he sleeps? On his back? His side? And so on. (Your imagination should feel free to respond in any way it wishes, since the biblical text does not specify any of these details.) Imaginative sensory involvement helps to open the channels to your deepest self, so that the energy of the story may flow into you.

5. Once started, let your imagination spontaneously carry on the story. Trust it to carry you wherever you need to go, even if it takes you "away" from the text. You may find yourself involved as a participant in the action of the story and/or having a conversation with one of the characters.

6. You may play suitable music during this period to facilitate the movement of your imaginal, prayerful drama.

7. During the waking dream, your body may respond to the experience; so may your feelings, as well as your mind. The thoughts, feelings, and images that occur are worth noting.

8. When you come to a suitable stopping place, close the experience, express thanks to God, and gently bring yourself back to normal consciousness.

9. Afterward, write down the details of the experience, put a date on the paper, and do the TTAQ technique. If your Waking Dream seems to call for more dreamwork, you might try Dialoguing, Key Questions, and/or some techniques that explore symbols, as well as dreamwork techniques to be presented in the following chapters.

1. *The Spiritual Exercises of St. Ignatius,* trans. Anthony Mottola, Ph.D. (Garden City: Doubleday Image Books, 1964). See, for example, Ignatius' directions for the contemplations on the incarnation (p. 69), the nativity (p. 70), and the application of the five senses (p. 72).
2. *Ibid.,* Additions #5, p. 61.
3. The classic reference to the waking dream, in the sense that we are using it here, is Mary M. Watkins' *Waking Dreams* (New York: Harper Colophon, 1977). Strephon Kaplan Williams in *Jungian-Senoi Dreamwork Manual* (Berkeley: Journey Press, 1980), pp. 165–66, uses the term "waking dream," but in an entirely different meaning from the way it is used in Watkins' book and in the present book. His use of the term "waking dream" describes situations such as actions or other interventions of fate in which the person's own unconscious dream pattern seems to leak out into waking life. According to Williams, the waking dream is a life event in which a particularly strong synchronicity, or meaningful coincidence, occurs. To work with such events as with a dream can yield deep meaning.
4. See Aniela Jaffe (ed.), C.G. Jung: *Memories, Dreams, and Reflections* (New York: Random House, 1961), esp. "Confrontations with the Unconscious." Also Watkins' *Waking Dreams,* pp. 42–50.
5. Gerhard Adler and Aniela Jaffe, eds., *Selected Letters of C.G. Jung* (Princeton: Princeton Univ. Press, 1973), pp. 459–60.
6. C.G. Jung, *Archetypes and the Collective Unconscious* (Princeton: Bollingen Collected Works, 9, 1959), p. 180.
7. Walter Wink, *The Bible in Human Transformation: Toward a New Paradigm for Biblical Study* (Philadelphia: Fortress Press, 1973).

A Summary and Invitation

Throughout Part I our theme has been relating to God through dreams and dreamwork. We saw that, unlike recent practice in the Church, Old Testament and early Church communities related extensively to their dreams as messages from God.

We saw also that when the ancients opened themselves to God speaking through dreams, God related to them and revealed wisdom to help them and their communities live a new and deeper spiritual life.

We, too, as contemporary religious people can establish a direct connection to God through our dreams and spiritual dreamwork. Major religious and personal issues of our lives appear in our dreams and can become more clearly understood when worked with using dreamwork methods.

You have only to choose to make a commitment to exploring the dreamwork techniques at your own pace and perhaps with a small group of like-minded people. Experiment with the process. In it you may find answers to your own questions and searchings.

Part II

Relating to Yourself Through Dreams and Dreamwork

◆

Chapter 7

Dreamwork as Personal Journey: Welcoming the Dream's Perspective

◆

Questions About the Life Journey

Part I of this book deals with our relationship to God through dreams and dreamwork. Part II focuses on aspects of our relationship to ourselves discovered in dreams and dreamwork. We begin by exploring our life journey from the perspective of dreams and dreamwork.

Do you view your own life as a journey? How would you characterize your regular daily journey? Using a typical day as a symbol or metaphor of your life journey, you might ask, for example, "In the morning what is my pattern of waking up and getting started? How do I move from unconsciousness to consciousness? Do I live my day fully? What is the most exciting part of my daily journey? Who are the people who journey with me—at home, at work, at school, at church? Do I live my day consciously? Do I fill my day with choices, affirming myself and others?"

Can you make a list of your conscious choices? Remembering is one of the essential ways of becoming conscious and whole. If you were asked at the end of a day to record what you said and did, would you remember much of your day?

As you journey through life, what is the major value you go about making real in the world? Where did you get that value? From your parents? From someone else? Do you feel you are living out the value that is actually most important to you?

What are your typical attitudes in facing a day in your life? For example, would you say: "I'm happy," "I'm depressed," "I feel inadequate," "I feel pressured," "I'm always helping others and leave no time for myself," "Money and work are what life is all about," "I can't believe I'm lovable," "I have to be strong for my family's sake," "I don't have enough confidence," or something else?

When we are stuck in unproductive and unwanted attitudes, dreamwork can offer a way of bringing to light our habitual attitudes and offering suggestions for changing them. Following the Dream Ego (Dreamwork Technique 4) is especially helpful in this regard.

Two Primary Energies in Life

Two basic innate kinds of energy seem to operate during our lives. One may be called the energy of the *journey;*[1] it is an energy that keeps us moving forward on our path with little radical change. Those who value life when it is a steady movement toward the future, comprised of a series of predictable choices and decisions, are most in tune with journey-energy. Such people are usually surprised and upset by the presence of the second kind of life-energy called *death-rebirth.*[2] This is the energy that carries us into and through crisis, illness, loss, separation, major life changes, and radical transitions. Persons who have a crisis-personality— who seem at their peak when under pressure—usually operate well with death-rebirth energy.

Traditionally, faith in God provides a resource in times of crisis. We can also look to our dreams for support, strength, and suggestions for coping with crises. In general, we need to learn to be at home with both journey energy and death-rebirth energy in order to balance our lives. Dreams and dreamwork help us keep these energies balanced.

It is not enough simply to know about these two energies; we need consciously to choose to be journeyers and to face the crises and transitions of life, welcoming both kinds of energies as we relate to God's gifts and graces along the path.

Relating on the Journey

If our life may be described as God playing a song through us and we are the instruments, then the individual events of our lives are the notes of our melody. Musically, each note is an important step in the journey of the song from beginning to end. Dreamwork can help us be in resonance with the song being played through us. For we are not completely passive instruments in God's hands, but can be free and conscious persons. And we are called to relate to the song of our lives with what might be called "dynamic passivity," freely and consciously aligning our will with that of God. Dreams suggest how to relate to our journey in this way. Relating is a key word for a journeyer.

On our journey, many things fall into our path. When something beautiful happens to us or we receive a blessing from God, we can relate to it without identifying with it. We simply recognize it as a gift given to us. As long as we relate to things without trying to possess them or claim them as part of our identity, we can keep moving forward on our journey. Some people, however, do identify with blessings, gifts, and talents, such as a beautiful singing voice or a skill in mothering. For example, a young woman, because of a dream she had shortly after the death of her child, realized she had placed her entire identity into mothering. She had not related to her gift of mothering, but had seen herself as synonymous with mother. Through dreamwork, she made a choice to return to her parents' farm for a year to learn to relate again to the ways of nature including the energy of death-rebirth.

People tend to be possessive not only of talents and blessings, but also of more conflictual experiences and chaotic events. For example, persons can attempt to possess or identify with sickness, depression, failure, anger at a friend's betrayal, etc. In each case, whether in times of good fortune or bad, the holistic task is to relate without being possessive. Dreams often point out when we are being possessive of something, but usually it is a waking-life crisis that makes us fully conscious of how tenaciously we are identifying with something or possessively holding on to it.

Death-Rebirth Energy

How do we relate to the accidents and tragedies which seem to break the natural flow of our journey? If we lose our job, or get sick, or have a dear friend terminate our relationship, how are we as journeyers to cope? How can these events be viewed as sources of energy, as opportunities, as gifts?

These events relate to the death-rebirth energy, which is the bringer of crisis. Out of the crisis comes consciousness of a need to change, or a call to a more humane and integrated way of living, or a push to go out and create new opportunities, or a drive to refocus our attention on the greater, larger task to be done.

Sometimes we do not look far enough ahead to see that today is only one event in a larger journey ordained by God and in God's hands.

Our Task

As journeyers, our task is to look at each crisis, recognizing the force of adversity in it, but remaining open to its divine origin and its place in the divine scheme. Our task is to remember that our whole life is the journey, to trust in our own journey, and to live in anticipation (rather than fear) of what lies ahead. Although we cannot avoid the adversity in our path, we can choose our attitude toward it and the levels of consciousness from which we respond to it.

The task of the journeyer is to live consciously, filling the soul with value, meaning, and sources of healing. To wish for rebirth is to wish on some level for death; to wish for joining is to wish for some separation. To choose to journey up the mountain is to choose to leave certain things behind.

Taking Responsibility

The movement toward holistic health involves the development of our ability to take responsibility for our own health, rather than projecting that responsibility onto some authority. Learning dreamwork and working at our own holiness and wholeness is a big step in taking responsibility for ourselves. Of course, there may be times when we need the help of psychological and spiritual professionals, just as we sometimes need the help of physicians. Nevertheless, the overall care of integrating our bodies, minds, and souls belongs to us.

Traditionally, in the area of dreams and dreamwork, and certainly in the case of psychoanalysis and certain other forms of therapy, the emphasis was on consulting a dreamwork professional or dream interpreter. It was believed that dream language was so complex and confusing that only an expert could ever decipher what a dream was trying to say.

Gradually, writers on dreams in our era of self-help and self-responsibility began to encourage dreamers to work with their own dreams. However, aside from recommending that people write down their dreams, make associations to them, or learn Jungian psychology (a sophisticated psychological and spiritual system), there was little methodology to be found for those following a spiritual path and interested in doing their own dreamwork. Certainly there was nothing comprehensive in the religious literature that took into account the wide range of dream content and function.

A not unusual example was to have a person come to us who said that during a retreat their director had told them to watch their dreams and record them, but had not said anything more methodologically about how to deal with dream material or find insight in it. Evidently certain spiritual directors had read somewhere or been told that a person's dreams were important, and passed this wisdom on to their retreatants without teaching them any dreamwork techniques to help them bring the grace and energy of the dream into everyday life. It is also not unusual for us in workshops to find people who have been faithfully keeping a written record of their dreams for months and even years (often at a spiritual director's suggestion), but who have done nothing more than journal their dreams simply because they had no idea what else to do with them.

A spiritual director's advice to keep track of our dreams is an excellent idea. After all, where else could we get more unique spiritual direction for our life nearly as well as we could from our own inner wisdom and our personal point of contact with God? Dreams and dreamwork are, of course, not meant to be a sole and exclusive source of spiritual direction, but to complement our own faith, our participation in the life of the believing community, and our own conscious effort at holiness and wholeness, with and without the guidance of a spiritual director.

While we present a method for doing dreamwork that does not demand the help of a professional, we suggest a clear place for the professional in enhancing dreamwork done by individuals. (See Chapters 14 and 15.)

Where To Begin

A very simple question about dreamwork that needs to be answered at the outset is: Which of my dreams do I work on? Obviously, there would not be enough time (or need) to do serious dreamwork on all the dreams one has on every single night throughout the year. Dreamwork of such magnitude would literally consume most of your waking hours.

Our approach is to work first of all (1) with special dreams and (2) dreams that occur around special occasions. Special dreams are those that feel important, those that affect us strongly, those we can't seem to forget, those which contain images or symbols that stand out in our minds, those which repeat and recur, those that cause us to wake with anxiety, and those that occur during periods of stress, anxiety and ambivalence. Another kind of special dream is one that is requested. (See Dreamwork Technique 17: Seeking a Dream.)

Special occasions to observe dreams are at *transitional points* (moving from one home to another, graduation, taking a new job, retirement, marriage, the birth of a child, illness, surgery, divorce, getting a promotion, starting therapy, initiating a new relationship, etc.) and times of *religious celebration* or *spiritual events* (Christmas, Easter, Pentecost, other great holidays and special feast days, birthdays, anniversaries, times of retreat). To honor the major transitional times in our lives in their fullness leads to a richness in spiritual growth. Our dreams at these times may release journey energies as well as energies of death-rebirth.

A Symbolic Approach to Daily Life

To think of ourselves as journeyers is to add the dimension of symbolic activity to the literalness and details of daily life. Dreamwork shows us how to deal with events symbolically. For example, adversity usually contains within it, symbolically, the level of sacrifice. Sacrifice is a journeyer's spiritual act, utilizing death-rebirth energy in the relationship to God. It consists in our consciously choosing, in the face of the new, to let go of that to which we are most attached.

On New Year's Eve a spiritual man, of both Christian and Jewish background, had this dream about sacrifice.

> A number of us were to be executed. In front of me in the line was an older woman, a wise old woman. She stepped forward when her turn came to be executed. I awoke before my turn.

"For a long time I couldn't understand this dream," he said. "How come the old woman could step forward to be executed and I couldn't?"

After doing dreamwork, he realized, "I was being asked to sacrifice what I most held on to, my life—not literally to give up my life but, at a more ultimate level of belief, to give control of what was happening to me over to God."

Every one of us has a certain number of dreams in which our dream ego is being asked to do things it does not want to do or is put in situations in which it does not want to be. This may mean in part that we are being asked to be open to change and to develop a new relationship to God and to our own soul. Something is required of us, and how do we respond? Such awarenesses often come with keeping a dream journal.

Dreamwork Technique 12: Keeping a Dream Journal

It is one thing to record dreams on isolated pieces of paper or even on a tablet, but another thing to keep a Dream Journal. A Dream Journal is a record of dreams and dreamwork kept over a period of time. It has the feeling of a diary because it is that place where we can write most intimately—as if to a close friend—about what's going on in our life and how life events seem to relate to our dreams.

When people keep a dream journal, who is listening to what they write? To whom are you writing when you record your dreams? We suggest you build a relationship with your journal as you would with a spiritual friend. One woman who left off keeping her dream journal told us, "I miss the interaction after having kept up the writing for a long time. I miss it the way I miss a friend—the closeness of a good friend I've failed to visit."

A dream journal can be a written record of a life journey—the physical, emotional, psychological, and spiritual parts of it. In keeping dreams and dreamwork recorded in a journey journal, we add a concrete record of how we value our relationship to our dreams. It becomes a barometer of our journey and our growing relationship to ourselves and to God.

A dream journal is meant to be completely private, and not to be read by others without permission. For this reason, it is wise to let others, even spouses, know that this journal is an intimate part of ourselves and its private nature deserves to be respected. You need to be able to say to yourself, "I feel free to write anything I want in my journal, knowing that my privacy will not be violated."

In keeping a dream journal, some people record only their dreams and dreamwork. Others choose also to include life experiences, fantasies, inspirational sayings, pictures, creative writing, poetry, important personal or world events—anything that seems to have relevance to the journey.

Simply to write down the events that happen to us is to keep a *diary*. In contrast, writing down dreams and dreamwork and reflecting on them in the light of significant events usually produces new consequences. We discover as we keep a dream journal that we begin writing things that are beyond our known perspective. As we enter into relation with our dream journal—which may be, at once, a relationship to our soul, to our Higher Self, and to God—we are likely to be receiving insight, wisdom, guidance. A dream journal is not merely a record of what's going on; it is a record of a journey in relationship.

When you write about an outer event, you may wish to apply the techniques of dreamwork to the characters or symbols of the outer event—for example, asking Key Questions, doing Dialoguing, Amplifying Symbols, making drawings, and so on. In this way you are seeking to understand and give meaning to your life as a journey.

After keeping a dream journal for a period of time, patterns and themes may begin emerging. The style of these patterns and their web of possible meaning forms the context of the journey. It is said that each person has a myth or story to live out, a particular unique destiny to fulfill, a destination toward which to journey. In dreams and dreamwork, many symbols and events arise to reflect the pattern of our journey and our response to it. When, for example, horses, cars, trains, planes, boats, buses, trucks, and other symbols of travel and journeying appear in our dreams, it is interesting to look for dreamwork techniques that might reflect the pattern of our journey. If we dream of climbing mountains, exploring caves, looking at new houses, following a path, going through some initiation rite, we can follow the dream ego and notice how it responds to the journey symbols, asking ourselves questions such as: Do you feel lost? Are you active and eager? Do you make choices? What do you take with you?

One elderly woman dreamed of preparing for a train trip and discovering she needed to take only two suitcases with her instead of four. Through dreamwork, she understood her dream to be suggesting that now, during her retirement, she needed to cut back on her activities and obligations in order to have more reflective and personal time with herself and a few close friends.

Benefits in Keeping a Dream Journal

There are a number of benefits that come from keeping a dream journal over a period of time. First, as we review our dreams and dreamwork, we begin to notice a *pattern in our attitudes toward life* as a journey, and we see where we are being asked to question our values.

Second, we see, in perspective, *potentials for a unique and meaningful destiny.* Dreams are a manifestation from our inner depths of our own meaning. Watching their pattern over a period of time may reveal the trajectory of our journey and emphasize what we are really meant to do in life.

Third, to help us in the process, the dream journal highlights *major transition points* in our lives and helps us understand adversities in the light of our larger destiny. In the journal we notice how a number of dreams reflect *issues important for us to deal with* in making the transitions of our journey.

Fourth, dreams offer us *key symbols* that we can relate to on our journey, so that we may know where to look for the major energies that are available to us. One of the most productive tasks to do with a dream journal is to go through its pages marking or underlining images, issues, characters, and themes that repeat or that recur in various forms or guises.

Fifth, in working with a dream journal we gain *a larger perspective on life,* more than any single dream might give us. Looking over a broad scope of dreams and dreamwork in our journal, we become aware of the immense power and scope of the world to which dreams are a gateway for us personally and as members of a believing community. We begin to see the call to holiness and wholeness as an exciting goal toward which our journey is leading us. We strive to bring into balance and harmony more and more aspects of our life and personality that are slowly being revealed, including what we naturally do well, what we don't do well, what we like and what we don't like.

A journey implies both a goal and a process. People often confuse the two. The goal of life is to become holy and whole, but we are not usually made whole or holy instantaneously. God is also involved in the process of our becoming whole and spiritual. For our part, the task is to become conscious of new aspects of ourselves and to integrate these new aspects into our developed personality. For example, just because we have made a commitment to God and to doing God's will, it does not mean we have thereby created a living, vital relationship to God. To accomplish this, there is still much work to be done, a process to be lived out.

Our life is a gift from God. Our task is to honor that gift by managing our life and its optimal development. Our journey is also a part of that gift. In keeping a dream journal, we honor that gift by keeping a record of our inner life, as well as our everyday life and choices.

Dreamwork Technique 12
Keeping a Dream Journal

Procedure:

1. To begin a dream journal, use a notebook, loose-leaf binder, or some other way of keeping all your dreams and dreamwork material in order and in one place. Identify the journal as your private domain.

2. Put a date on every entry you make in your dream journal.

3. Keep an orderly record of your dreams in the journal. Some journalers write their dreams only on one side of each page, saving the facing page for dreamwork.

4. Keep a record of your dreamwork before, after, or alongside the words of your dream. For example, put Title, Theme, Affect and Question at the head of your dream; note results of Key Questions, Symbol Amplifications, Symbol Associations, etc. on the facing page alongside the dream; include dialogues and other symbolic processes after the dream.

5. Make note of any outer life events or choices that might have had a bearing on your dream. These include issues in your life that are prominent or sensitive, decisions you are struggling with, or events happening which concern you and over which you have little or no control. The presumption is that dreams are usually speaking to your current needs, problems, issues, making you more and more conscious of the present stage in your journey.

6. In the back of your dream journal you might like to begin an index of recurring symbols, issues, and themes. After a time, you can use these special pages to review the development of your major themes and issues and reflect on their meaning for you.

7. Also after a time, you can do a more complex version of Following the Dream Ego, comparing a series of dreams, to notice

any changes or continuing patterns in the actions, attitudes, and choices of your dream ego. Do the dream ego's patterns reflect those of your waking life? Are you happy with those patterns? Would you like to begin changing any of them?

8. Keep a record of your dreamwork tasks, those assignments for outer life which you give yourself in order to actualize your dreams and dreamwork in your daily activity and choices. Make note also of the insights you gained from carrying out those tasks.

9. Journal important life events or situations, positive and negative, which evoke energy and strong response in you. Treat them as you would a dream and apply dreamwork.

10. At the end of each year review your journal work and summarize the most important events, choices, personality changes, dreams, dreamwork, and dialogues. Share your spiritual growth process with friends and like-minded people.

Notes to Chapter 7
Dreamwork as Personal Journey

1. For a discussion of the energies of the journey and death-rebirth, see Strephon Kaplan Williams, *Jungian-Senoi Dreamwork Manual,* pp. 276, 298–300.
2. *Ibid.,* p. 275.

Chapter 8

Dreamwork and Spirituality: The Dream as Question and Quest

◆

Spirituality Defined

Spirituality is one's way of responding to God's call, a style of living that is open to the energies of God's spirit. More generally, it is one's way of being and acting in the world in light of ultimate values. While spirituality may involve prayer, it is more than a way of praying; it is a way of living. It is lifestyle based on the availability and invitation of the often forgotten spiritual dimension of life. While prayer's primary intention is a deeper relationship with God, spirituality involves the broader consideration of one's own needs and choices in the light of more ultimate values.

For persons using dreamwork, their spirituality involves ways of channeling energy released from the inner world into the everyday world. For them, it is a way of living that keeps them conscious of the journey, its goal and its process; it is a way of living that strives to be more and more conscious of one's personal self and the larger process.

Consciousness Defined

Consciousness may be defined as *awareness followed by appropriate action.* Consciousness combines being and doing. Simply being aware of something, whether grasped through the outer senses, the mind's reasoning, or inner realization, does not qualify as consciousness. To be aware is to recognize and see things as they are; this is a state of being, one that happens, for example, in meditation or while reading or conversing. The more centered one is, the more clearly and penetratingly one is aware.

Awareness is a powerful state of being, but it is not of itself consciousness. To be fully conscious, one needs also to act. One needs to take the energy released by the awareness and actualize it in some appropriate manner in the world. Doing is the state of action that complements the state of being achieved in awareness; taken together, they produce consciousness. To be conscious is to be affected by our perceptions and awareness in such a way that we are led to action. Consciousness is the energy of awareness transformed into appropriate concrete behavior in our own life and in the world.

Dreamwork and Consciousness

Dreams are a call to consciousness—to awareness and action. Certain dreamwork techniques lead to awareness and insight—the release of energy. Such awareness techniques include, for example, TTAQ, Key Questions, Dialoguing, and techniques that explore symbols. Other dreamwork techniques, such as Personality Tasks and Outer Life Tasks, focus on the actualization of the energy released in a dream. People who do not use some of the former techniques may not be able to reach an awareness of a dream's meaning. People who do not use some actualization techniques may not successfully actualize the energy released in a dream.

What Is a Question?

To live as consciously as possible is a major objective of the spiritual life. Thus, any genuine spirituality will involve a way of being and acting in the world that promotes ever fuller consciousness.

Two major avenues to fuller consciousness are the question and the quest.

The ability to ask a question or respond to one may well be one of the great evolutionary milestones in the history of humanity. It marks a beginning of spirituality and of humankind's relation to God and God's creation. In the primal story of consciousness, the Garden of Eden story, there are significant questions asked of Adam and Eve by both God and the serpent. We can assume the questions in that story are posed in order to evoke and bring about awareness and responses in Adam and Eve. Jesus frequently used questions to help bring his disciples and his audiences to new levels of consciousness and commitment.[1]

Learning the nature of questions and question-asking in spiritual practices and in spiritual traditions may be of central importance to the whole process of living more consciously in relation to our destiny and to God. Certainly it is often true that it is more important in a relationship to ask the right question than to have the right answer. Questions tend to open up possibilities, while answers tend to close them down. Perhaps, ultimately, there are no absolute answers to questions, only responses and choices. Making choices in response to such questions and issues is the daily bread of our journeys.

We particularly emphasize the question as a consciousness-raising tool because dreams, perhaps more than any other kind of spiritual communication or knowledge, do not allow themselves to be taken as quick-and-ready answers. This is not to say that dreams are vague images and without meaning. Rather, when the dream is viewed as a question, or when the dream is approached with deeply felt questions, it reveals much to us that we can use in everyday life.

Insight almost always comes from a dream, but it is usually grasped only after asking questions and struggling with the energies the dream evokes in us. And since dreams usually reveal deeper possibilities than our present waking consciousness can grasp or allow, we need to approach the dream with openness and curiosity. The dream also asks us: "Will you consider using the new knowledge I bring you in meaningful and appropriate ways in your life?"

The Quest

If questions usually bring about the awareness aspect of consciousness, a quest usually evokes action. The word "quest" is usually associated with medieval knights and their famous deeds. The great spiritual quest of the Middle Ages was for the Holy Grail, symbolized by the cup used by Jesus at the Last Supper. In the medieval epics, the questing knights had visions of the Grail but never seemed really to find and possess it. What was important was that they spent their lives seeking it.

A quest is, by definition, something worth a lifetime of seeking. A quest is a journey seeking the ultimate value of life.

In different periods of history, the symbolic object of the quest changes. No one literally searches for the Holy Grail today, but the attitude of questing still remains. If we are to remain motivated on our spiritual journey, we need to focus upon a goal more ultimate than our own self. The quest is something beyond what we can attain simply by our everyday effort, yet it is something which calls forth that everyday effort to an ever more committed degree.

Symbols of the quest in our age include wholeness, peace, true friendship, social justice, and planetary consciousness. Our contemporary quests tend to be interior, relational, and communal.

Even though a goal may be ultimately an "unreachable star," we need to feel a sense of relation to it. Just as the medieval knight experienced the Grail in a vision or a dream, so we can use our dreams as a way of relating to our quest. Perhaps in our dreams our quest appears as a path up a mountain, a treasure hidden in a field, a beautiful castle, a prize at the end of a race (as it was for Paul the apostle), or some other symbol. When such a quest symbol occurs, we suggest meditating on it.

One woman dreamed of a beautiful oriental rug which seemed to have special meaning for her, even though she did not understand precisely what that meaning might be. She assigned herself the task of meditating on her rug-image every morning for two weeks. As she meditated she felt in very vivid ways the harmony of its texture and colors. For her, it became a symbol of the wholeness for which she was striving. And her meditations enriched the awareness and quality of how she lived her day.

This same woman, later diagnosed as possibly having breast cancer, dreamed of standing in a hospital hallway in front of a closed door to the cancer ward. She meditated on this closed door for days. At first, she was conscious only of her fear of what might await her behind it. Days later, during her meditation, she experienced the door opening, and found the room full of light and growing things. In that meditative process her attitude toward the possibility of cancer changed from fear to inner peace and openness. The transformation was a spiritual one, for she chose to handle her life-and-death fears within a spiritual context, opening herself to whatever God might present to her on her journey. The quality and direction of her quest became clearer.

Success in the quest is not measured by reaching the goal but by reaching out for it, not in attainment but in the quality of our lives as seekers. Yet paradoxically we may at times reach achievement-points on the journey, which evoke a profound sense of resolution and transformation.

At times, major stages along a personal journey, such as being chosen for a big job, getting married, buying a home, having a child, recovering from a serious illness, and so on may seem like the achievement of our goal, but they cannot be our ultimate quest. They are experiences to be integrated into our selves as we continue the journey. Dreams continue to remind us of our quest, usually through the reappearance of key symbols. In dreams we find encouragement and support on our way, and confirmation of choices we make which are in line with our quest.

The Nature of Tasks

A task is at once a work of consciousness and a step on the journey toward our quest. A task combines both awareness and action, and thus contributes to consciousness. And since every task requires an objective and a plan of action, it also participates in the journey and the quest. Tasks are what ground the spiritual life and test its growth.

A task may be defined as *a specific project, including a commitment to carry it out in a specified amount of time.* For example, the woman who dreamed of an oriental rug committed herself to the task of meditating on it every day for two weeks. The commitment is made by the conscious side of the personality, that is, by the ego, the choice-maker. The ego is the part of us that governs and arranges our waking life.

From every dream emerges a large number of possible tasks, projects for both inner and outer reality. It is usually by means of tasks that we actualize dreams and translate their energies into personality growth and into service in the community.

We may respond to a dream with three levels of task: (1) *dreamwork tasks,* (2) *personality tasks,* and (3) *outer life tasks.*

Working with a Dream

Dreamwork tasks include those dreamwork techniques that make the dream more vivid, real, graspable, and understandable. Such techniques include writing down the dream, asking key questions, naming its title, theme, affect, and question, dialoguing with dream figures, doing symbolic process, and so on. At this level, the objective of the task is to turn the energy released in the dream into concepts in such a way that the ego can begin to understand the dream and plan actively to use its gift of energy.

At this level, too, we acknowledge the Source that gives the energy and the dream—as well as the energy and insight that comes during the subsequent dreamwork. A frequent spontaneous response to the awareness of the gift of energy is worship, often expressed in meditation and prayer. Worship following dreams and dreamwork usually involves acknowledging God as Source, or, in the prophet Daniel's expression, God as the revealer of mysteries.

Dreamwork Technique 13
Choosing Dreamwork Tasks

Procedure:
   If you have only about fifteen minutes for dreamwork,
1) Write out the dream.
2) Do the TTAQ technique.
3) Express gratitude to God for the dream and dreamwork.
Or alternatively
1) Write out the dream.
2) Try Dialoguing or Symbol Immersion.
3) Acknowledge what comes for you.
If you have thirty minutes or more,
1) Write out the dream.
2) Do the TTAQ technique.
3) Respond to Key Questions or choose another dreamwork method.
Then either:
4) Dialogue with a symbol or character from the dream that has energy for you, or
Do Symbol Immersion on a key symbol.

5) Acknowledge God's gifts in the dream and dreamwork.

Once you have learned many dreamwork techniques and know when and how to apply them, it will be up to you—just as an artist who has learned to use the tools of his or her craft—to choose your own dreamwork tasks, your own sensed artistry and creative self-expression.

Some observations:
1. Don't try to do every dreamwork technique on every dream. Choose those that seem appropriate and helpful.
2. For a major dream, we recommend using a number of techniques to mine the riches of energy and insight to be found in it.
3. You need not do all dreamwork immediately after waking. It is enough at that time to write down the dream and, if possible, do the TTAQ technique.
4. Often dreamwork on a single dream, spread out over days, weeks, and even months, can prove very productive in fostering personal growth.

Dreamwork Technique 14
Honoring Dreamwork

Procedure:
1. In a few sentences, write down how you feel so far about working with the dream. How does this feeling differ from the way you felt when you woke up from the dream?

2. Make note of what you have learned so far from your dreamwork on this dream.

3. Express what was happening to you as you were doing the dreamwork. What value did it seem to have for you?

Realizing the Power of Dreamwork

Responses to these questions help make us conscious of the relationships to our inner self and to God that are building through dreamwork. It keeps us aware that behind the dream is a Thou, and that even *in the dreamwork* there is a Thou. The power of dreamwork reflected upon may be sensed from some comments people have made to the technique just described.

> "I begin to see why I had this dream now."
> "I never realized how important this issue was for me."
> "I think I have a handle on something significant."
> "I'm beginning to articulate something that's only been a vague feeling till now."
> "The dream has given me a different perspective on a problem I've been struggling with."
> "The dream gave me a way to talk about this issue to a friend who wants my help."

Changing Personality Patterns

Personality tasks are tasks designed to change personality patterns—behaviors, emotional responses, attitudes, and other psychological mechanisms. At this level, the objective of a task is to turn the energy released in the dream into personal change.

One woman, consciously aware that her habitual defensiveness was a response to the fact that her mother died when she was a child, had a dream in which she was given a new, nurturing mother which she need never fear losing. Her personality task was to begin actualizing the nurturing, protective energy released in the dream so she felt free to change her personality by behaving in less defensive ways.

It is essential to our spiritual growth to manifest in our everyday lives the potentials coming to us from God as Source. We are given free will and choice in order that we may choose to make specific in our personalities what God needs and wants of us.

Selecting the appropriate task to work on is important. Some chosen tasks are unrealistic in their expectations and unrealizable within the time specified. Tasks should reflect the energy released in the dream and channel that energy in such a way as to keep it flowing.

It is important to utilize the energy released as soon as possible, to affirm it, and to treat it as a gift. Otherwise, it tends to sink back into the unconscious from which it came.

In dreamwork, a personality task is often difficult to concretize and specify. Our tendency is to enjoy the upsurge of energy released by the dream and to let it recede without ever channeling it into our own personality. Dreamwork is designed to facilitate opportunities for the ego to make choices in order to utilize the energy released in a dream. In doing tasks, we are building a healthy ego, not letting it dissolve in the feeling of energy or get detoured in the dead-end of criticism and judgmentalism, but challenging it to work to manifest the potentials of that energy concretely in personality and in outer life.

Dreamwork Technique 15
Choosing Personality Tasks

Procedure:

Dreams frequently reflect some issue or theme related to our own personality, calling us to greater wholeness and holiness. When dreams and dreamwork release energy that may be channeled to personality development, it is wise to select personality tasks to implement. Some of the following questions may be helpful:

1. In what ways does the dream bring up a personality issue that I need to deal with—some attitude, value, behavior, habit, preference, opinion, or bias that may need to be reviewed and changed?

2. What kinds of emotions and energies are being released in me as a result of the dream and dreamwork? In what direction do they seem to be leading me? In what area of my personality would I like to make some choices for change?

3. Choose some finite, reasonable, and measurable personality task that can channel the energy released. Choose a personality task that you can begin as soon as possible.

4. Start the process with small steps. Build on your successes. As the energy begins to flow into your waking life, you can continue creating further personality tasks in order to keep the energy flowing.

Tasks That Affect the Community

Outer life tasks involve choices, based on dreamwork, to act or continue to act in ways that constructively affect the community or some part of it. The energy in a dream is given as a gift to be released into the world. The application of dream energy to outer life is part of the full sequence of dreamwork. If the dream provides an insight that affects our relationships or the life of our family, friends, and community, dreamwork asks about our commitment to live this insight: What will I do to embody this insight in my outer life? How will I channel the energy of the insight into some task so it will be spiritually alive in me and in the world?

Dreamwork Technique 16
Choosing Outer Life Tasks

Procedure:

1. It is often possible to ask: How is this dream a gift to the community? How can the dream energy released through me be directed into the larger world, beyond my own personality?

2. It is helpful to clarify and specify the energies being released in the dream, and then to ask: How do these energies connect me to the community? In what way are they energies or insights that can be used in serving others—specifically, my family, my friends, my schoolmates, my workmates, my religious community, the larger world?

3. Choose specific actions that can be performed. Give yourself a deadline for beginning. If your outer life task seems unusual or in any way questionable, ask a dreamwork partner, or someone who knows you well, if he or she thinks it's a good idea for you to do this. Treat the response as important input for your decision. The decision, however, remains yours. The dream energy was a gift given to you. How you use it is ultimately your responsibility.

Note to Chapter 8
Dreamwork and Spirituality

1. See Miriam Louise Gramlich, "The Questions of Jesus: Calls to Commitment," *Review for Religious* 42:2 (March/April 1983), pp. 233–239, where she comments on more than sixty-five questions of Jesus. "These questions represent only a fraction of those Jesus asks in the gospels," she notes. "It would be impossible to include them all in a single article" (p. 239).

Chapter 9

Dreamwork and Destiny: The Soul in Dreamwork

◆

What Is Destiny?

Our destiny involves our purpose in life; it is that to which God ultimately calls us. Destiny evokes questions such as: "Why was I born at this particular time, with these particular talents and liabilities, within this family and set of relationships, in this country?" "What is the purpose of my life within God's larger plan?" "What am I personally called to be and do in the world?"

If our *quest* is that which we seek from God and from life, our *destiny* is what God and life itself seek from us. And while our *journey* is expressed in our own personal experience, our *destiny* may lie primarily in the mind and heart of God.

Dreams and dreamwork keep guiding us to fulfill our destiny, or life purpose, even though we may not always understand it. For example, we will never know many of the places where we have made an impact and touched others' lives, where something we have said or done has rippled out and made a difference in the world. We may not have very much control over our destiny, yet we seem to be unerringly guided to fulfill it. In doing dreamwork, we can receive a sense of being called and guided toward our destiny, and in this way we have an opportunity consciously to say yes to our destiny and to surrender to it. This is an important point in spiritual growth.

A young priest at a workshop was assigned a young woman as a partner for certain activities. They worked together very well and felt an immediate bond with each other. Trying to understand why this woman had impressed him so strongly, the young priest sought wisdom in a dream. "What part does she play in my destiny? Why is she in my life?" he asked the dream. He woke up with only two words in his mind: "For direction." One dreamwork task for him was to list in his journal the kinds of life-directions she might evoke for him, and then to choose and reflect upon those which might most offer him a sense of direction in his life.

Destiny as Paradox

Destiny involves us in paradox: we seek fully to know our destiny, yet accept the fact that we will never fully know it. While we are called to try to understand our ultimate purpose and to live as consciously aware of it as possible, we are also called to give up having to know exactly the ultimate meaning of our own life's experiences. *Our destiny is where God's mystery and our mystery intersect.*

If we give up seeking to know our destiny and choose instead to go passive and unconscious, then we cannot consciously cooperate and co-create our life with God. And while we can't demand to know fully God's heart and mind for us, we can choose to be conscious of God's relationship to us and to live in accordance with what we hear as God's call for us at any given moment.

Dreams and dreamwork allow us to increase our consciousness of God's call and relationship to us. Jacob's dream at Bethel and Joseph's dream in Nazareth were both destiny dreams inviting these persons to live consciously in accordance with God's call.

Dreams and Destiny—An Example

Dreamwork may bring dream images and destiny issues into consciousness in such a way that we may spend years working them out.

Nevertheless, dreamwork does give us a handle on them for working them out. A young woman therapist described to us the following destiny dream and some of her dreamwork with it.

> Six months after my father-in-law died, in a dream I was given a death's head on a stick (very much like the kind we used to carry around as kids on Halloween). I was instructed to put it in my home and give it a place of honor there. Though I didn't find the head attractive, I did as I was instructed. I placed the head in a little shrine in my home. I was then given another head on a stick. This time it was not a skull, but the head of a lovely woman with her hair pulled back in a knot. I was told in the dream that since I had given the death head a place of honor in my home, I was given this beautiful head to look at and put in its place.
>
> When I awoke, I began describing the woman's head to my husband. "The figure is like a cameo with her hair in a Psyche knot," I said to him. And as I said the words, I realized it was indeed Psyche's head I had been given. After doing some basic dreamwork, I realized the dream was telling me that if I could accept death and honor it in my life, I could look upon and own my psyche and live with it comfortably. I would get to see and know my own soul.

This young therapist said about herself, "It had been important to me to know why I felt called to be doing all this psychological training. I learned it was helping me make a place in my life for my own soul. I would have the gift of my own psyche as a result of the process. It was important for me to deal with the process of loss, sickness, grief, aging and death in order to live."

Part of her destiny was to reclaim her own life and also to help others through processes dealing with fear of death, sickness, loss, aging, and separation. "After I realized that the dream was letting me know that this was part of my destiny, I was able to go through my own grieving and loss process more consciously and willingly," she said. "Otherwise I probably would have resisted and resented the process."

Before her dream, she had been so (unconsciously) preoccupied with the fear of death, sickness, injury, or loss that she would not let her children ride bicycles on the street, and worried excessively about their health and safety. She had a personality pattern, created by this fear, that needed changing in order for her to meet her destiny and allow her soul to develop.

As persons standing alone in life, we are ultimately insecure. As individuals choosing to live within God's purposes for our lives we can feel grounded and find strength to deal with whatever confronts us.

What Is Soul?

We define the soul as that dimension of us most directly connected to God. Our soul carries the destiny (*telos*) energy. That may explain how some people under special circumstances have known the future.

Moved by the grace of God, our soul guides us to sense our destiny by using dreams. Dreams have been described as the voice of the soul at work. Through dreamwork we attempt to relate to our soul and learn its guidance. Dreamwork is the area of activity where our ego and soul relate and cooperate. While our ego does not know our destiny, it has the responsibility of relating to our soul in order to discover our destiny as it is being revealed to us.

Soul is an essential dimension of the person. In the Christian tradition, the soul is viewed as a unique, individuated principle of existence. It is the personal expression of life, vitality, and energy in an individual. The soul accounts for the possibility of transcendence. It is the medium of relating between our self and God. It is sometimes referred to as a spark of God, or the place in us where the God-spark originates and lives. The soul is at home in the entire person, conscious and unconscious.

The human soul is not identical to the unconscious. Although there are functions of the soul which are not conscious, for example, its vital or life-giving operations, and its interaction with unconscious archetypal energies, there are several faculties of the soul which are normally conscious, for example, the intellect, will, imagination, and memory. As a spiritual reality, then, the soul operates on both the conscious and the unconscious levels.

God and the Unconscious

God is not identical to the collective unconscious, as is sometimes inferred. In the Christian tradition, God is seen as having both conscious and unconscious aspects. We understand God to express the conscious functions of intellect and will and personal relationship, as well as unconscious functions implied in terminology such as the ground of being or, more popularly, the Force. The collective unconscious with which we humans are in touch and from which we receive new energy seems to partake in some way of the infinite nature of God. Just how this is true we do not know. Much about God and the unconscious world remains mystery to us. And it is somewhere in this mystery—so fascinating to us—that dreams happen.

Fate as Reality

There is one other element that needs to be taken into account here, and that is what is variously called the Reality Factor, the Inevitable, Fate, or simply "the given." It is what both God and we must deal with. On the obvious level, it includes sickness and death, new births and events coming into our lives, accidents and delays, miscommunication and misunderstanding, being late and missing a connection, being given a magnificent opportunity, non-changeable facts ("My mother is dead; I cannot bring her back to life") and irreversible decisions ("I chose this job and refused that one").

Thomas Merton described fate in his book *Contemplation in a World of Action:*

> That I should have been born in 1915, that I should be the contemporary of Auschwitz, Hiroshima, Viet Nam and the Watts riots, are things about which I was not first consulted. Yet they are also events in which, whether I like it or not, I am deeply and personally involved.[1]

Choice and Fate

While we may often have preferences and clearly know what we would or would not like, there are times when, because of inevitables and unavoidables, we cannot choose what will happen—to us or to those we love. Since we often don't acknowledge the inevitable and unavoidable as part of the total reality, we are tempted to despair when a child is born with muscular dystrophy, or a promising young person dies, or we arrive too late to catch the last plane home. Much pain comes into the world through resistance to what is unavoidable in life.[2]

The inevitable is what is given to us. Yet by our choice we can turn the inevitable into our destiny—into a way of fulfilling what God wants of us.

It seems to happen in this way: when because of something inevitable I cannot choose to make happen what I would like to happen, there is an alternative to despair or just giving up. I can *choose* to surrender to the inevitable. In this way, instead of denying its reality, I integrate it into my journey. I recognize its finality, its adversity; I feel my responses of anger, fear, frustration, disappointment, excitement, etc.; I pick up the pieces that remain, or let them go, and carry on. By my choice I have made it a part of my destiny. I look for the larger meaning in what happens to me.

A Sense of Journey

If *destiny* is what God wants of us, and *quest* is what we want of God, then *the inevitable* (fate) is what both God and we must deal with. Our *journey,* then, may be viewed as the manifestation of the intersection of these three great forces—destiny, the quest, and the inevitable.

Our essential destiny is a spiritual factor, an energy source, a guiding force transcending ourselves and beyond our choosing, which influences our thoughts and actions and calls us to our greatest wholeness and holiness.

This destiny, of necessity, is influenced by what is inevitable and unavoidable, and it evolves in response to these elements in our life, just as Merton's destiny evolved as he journeyed affected by the given facts of Hiroshima, Auschwitz, Vietnam and Watts, and eventually his own accidental death by electrocution in Thailand.

A sense of journey means living life consciously and in tune with our evolving destiny, which we choose to allow to permeate our life.

The Commitment

Making a commitment to one's destiny and journey produces at least six consequences for spiritual growth.

First, I find that I choose *not* to have my ego (with its images, attitudes, wishes and wants) always come first.

Yet, second, I continually strengthen my ego as choice-maker so that it can help to manifest a purpose greater than its own.

Third, I seek to improve my relation to the Source of my destiny, my call.

Fourth, I am willing to have visions, to be surprised, to be called out of a pattern.

Fifth, I am willing to deal with the adversity of the inevitable and to choose to move forward, through development and diminishment, to my destiny.

Sixth, I choose to accept as fully as possible the fruits of my commitment as expressed in increased vitality and meaning and representing God's purpose on earth.

In this chapter we present four dreamwork techniques that relate to destiny—the end (*telos*) toward which God is calling the individual.

Dreamwork Technique 17:
Seeking a Dream (Incubation)

Destiny dreams are those which help us find our true relation to God and to the human community evolving on its way to completion. There are highly symbolic times in life when our purpose in the community and our relation to God are celebrated and called forth. These include personal moments that have a social and familial dimension such as birthdays, anniversaries, and times of major choices and changes. Such symbolic times also include religious holidays such as Christmas, Easter, Pentecost, or the feast days of saints and holy people to whom we are specially attracted.

One way of enriching the celebration of special events is to treat our dreams at these times as having to do with our destiny and purpose in life.

Near the beginning of his reign, King Solomon, who loved God, went to a famous sanctuary at Gibeon to offer sacrifice, and most likely to have a destiny dream (1 Kgs 3:4–15). On one level (offering sacrifice), he was clearly seeking God's blessing on his reign, but on another level (observing a dream), he was seeking to know his destiny and the destiny of his people, now that he was their ruler.

The dream turned out to be a dialogue between God and Solomon's dream ego. In the dream God put the choice to the dream ego, asking Solomon to say what gift he would like to have. Solomon asked for "a heart to understand how to discern between good and evil, for who could govern this people of yours that is so great?" (1 Kgs 3:9). Unselfishly, Solomon asked for something that would benefit his people. Most people given their wish would probably selfishly choose a long life, riches, or victory over their enemies. But since Solomon asked for a discerning heart, God gave him what he asked for *plus* a long life, riches, and a victorious reign.

Many people experience depression around holiday times. Psychologically, such depression may be related to childhood disappointments, current strained family relationships, or some other emotional dynamic. It is also possible that such depression may have soul-dimensions. The symbolic energies released at these special spiritual times and seasons may be focusing us on our life's purposes and possibilities, and making us aware of missed opportunities. One way of dealing with depression around holiday times is to work with our dreams.

Since these symbolic times usually evoke special energy, the spiritual resources of dreamwork may be used to help deal with it. Dreamwork may help relieve the depression and allow a deep energy for celebration to surface.

Dreamwork Technique 17
Seeking a Dream (Incubation)

Procedure:
A dream may be sought or incubated at any time. Destiny dreams may most naturally be asked for during times or events which are symbolically charged for you or the community.

1. When seeking a destiny dream, it helps to prepare yourself for it, generally, by prayer and some form of fasting or sacrifice and, more specifically, by having a pen and pad near your bed and by requesting a special dream from God, the revealer of mysteries, just before you fall asleep.

2. You may "plant a dream seed," or use some other symbol as you lie in bed at night by imagining a seed being placed in you and beginning to sprout. Some people prefer to plant a dream seed in their heart, others in their head. Picture the dream seed planted wherever you choose, and as you grow more sleepy continue to repeat your request to God for a special dream (or whatever symbol you choose).

3. As soon as you awaken, write out the dream and do dreamwork on it, with the expectation that it will have something to reveal about your destiny and purpose in life.

Dreamwork Technique 18: Rewriting an Unresolved Dream

When you have a dream which, upon awakening, seems unresolved, you may use a rewriting technique to help give it a healing resolution. Psychologically, rewriting helps orient the soul in special circumstances— for example, when our personality may be locked into a destructive pattern or wounded by a painful memory. Usually, such patterns or memories are buried deep in our unconscious, but when they are brought to the surface by a dream, it is an indication that we are ready to deal with some part of them, and that we are called to heal the wound they caused so we can better fulfill our destiny. The dream may be asking us consciously to begin dealing with this issue in order that we can open ourselves up to new levels of personal and social wholeness.

Rewriting is not usually the first technique you use with an unresolved dream. Do basic dreamwork first, to discover the emotions and issues that are being called to your attention. Clarify the wounds the dream points to and the level of healing being called for. Otherwise, you may not consciously get in touch with the pattern or memory to be worked with. Experience the disturbing energy for a while before you move into healing.

The principle behind the rewriting technique is this: if it weren't for this psychological or spiritual wound, you probably would have experienced the material of this dream as a creative and whole person. To facilitate the healing of this wound, therefore, it is helpful for you to be able to re-experience the dream in a positive, healing way, to re-experience it as a person whom God loves and wants to be happy and whole.

An unresolved dream often reveals a part of the personality that needs to be healed, redeemed, and re-educated. The ego's task, then, is to find ways consciously to facilitate such healing and relearning. This it does by rewriting the dream material in ways that bring about a healing resolution.

Dreamwork Technique 18
Rewriting an Unresolved Dream

Procedure:

After doing basic dreamwork with an unresolved dream and experiencing its destructive or painful energies for a time, it is possible to evoke a healing element by rewriting the dream with a healing resolution. Here are two different ways to do it.

1. Imaginatively reinsert yourself in the dream at a place *before the destructive patterns or painful feelings would have taken over,* and then with pen and paper write out a new scenario for the rest of the dream, changing whatever needs to be changed in order to bring about a satisfying ending. You may also spell out in the text how the revised behavior and feelings might continue to be a part of your waking personality as well as of your dream ego.

2. An alternative approach is to rewrite the dream as a life story, myth, or folk tale, including in it a healthful resolution. Thus, the rewritten dream might begin, "Once upon a time there was a woman who . . ." The objective here is to write a story that deals with the

issue that appeared in the night dream, but resolves it in a way that its patterns appear in a positive light and the memories provide opportunities for future healthful growth.

3. Following either approach, allow time to reread and reflect on the rewritten dream. Invite yourself to welcome the healthful patterns and feelings that it contains, in contrast to those of the original night dream, and possibly share your work with others.

Fulfilling the Unresolved Dream's Purpose

It is sometimes argued that in rewriting a dream we are rejecting the original dream, the gift from God. In reality, however, we remain connected to and related to the original dream in its theme and purpose. Thematically, the original dream brings to our attention a destructive personality pattern, an unlived potential, or a painful memory and reminds us in the very drama of the dream that these issues remain unresolved in our life. The original dream's purpose is to make us aware of these issues so that we begin to deal with them successfully and healthfully. The original dream also informs us that we are ready to face these issues and that we possess the inner energy to begin dealing with them. In doing the rewriting technique, we acknowledge the information revealed by the original dream, we remain focused on the same issues, we are ready and energized to face these issues, and we proceed to use the dream material in ways that are likely to lead to a healing resolution of the issues, thus fulfilling the unresolved dream's purpose.

Dreamwork Technique 19: Researching a Dream Theme

A destiny theme can often be detected more clearly when one's dreams are studied thematically over a long period. If you have been keeping a dream journal, you may have been making note all along of the major themes and chief symbols active in your life. These themes and symbols tend to reflect dominant patterns of behavior and attitudes in your waking life. They may have to do with your parents or family, your work or school, your spiritual life or emotions, your relationships, or something else.

This researching technique asks you to focus on an important issue in your life, to list chronologically the dream material found in your dream journal related to that issue, and to reflect on its progress.

In light of your soul's destiny or call, you may bring this major issue into a spiritual perspective, perhaps in a meditative setting, to help facilitate its transformation and resolution. In this dreamwork technique, the idea is to work at the issue in a sacred and healing context.

For example, a young woman who clearly felt called to public life was ripped apart by anxiety every time she had to speak before a group. Over a period, she noticed that the anxiety-in-front-of-crowds theme appeared a number of times in dreams that were often unresolved. Crowds of people were the trigger that released her anxiety, even in dreams. This she learned from researching her dreams. The technique further advised her to bring her anxiety into a setting that connotes sacredness for her, so she introduced her anxiety-provoking crowd symbol into her meditation. Actually, during her prayer she would recall a sacred place that appeared regularly in her dreams and visualize a crowd before her in that sacred place. She combined two strong dream symbols into one meditation: the anxiety-provoking crowd and the healing, sacred place. These meditations (for she repeated this procedure a number of times) confirmed her awareness that her destiny involved speaking in front of crowds, and allowed her to view the crowds not as people coming to criticize and reject her, but as people who were coming to learn from what she had to say. Through this dreamwork she was able to step out of her own personal bias and see the situation from a healthy perspective.

Dreamwork Technique 19
Researching a Dream Theme

Procedure:
1. When dealing with an ongoing issue that needs resolution, review its expression in your dreams over a period of time—weeks, months, years. On a piece of paper, make a chronological list of dream material pertinent to the issue, and observe the progress of your dream ego in dealing with that issue.

2. If the issue needs to be brought into a spiritual perspective to foster its transformation and healthy resolution, bring the issue or its major symbol into a sacred, healing context. For most, this is best done in a prayerful setting.

3. Specifically, choose a sacred, healing place that may have occurred in your past dreams and symbolically introduce the issue needing transformation into that place. The sacred place may be a cave, a meadow, a mountain, an altar, a church, etc. If you cannot identify such a sacred symbol from your dream material, perhaps you can choose one from your waking experience.

4. Continue quietly bringing the two symbols together in meditation, over a period of time, until a new attitude, response, or way of behaving begins to surface.

5. As you explore and test these new ways of responding to your troublesome issue, watch your future dreams for signs of confirmation of your new attitudes and responses.

Dreamwork Technique 20: Resolving a Remembered Dream

Dreams remembered from childhood often stay with us because they have something to tell us about our destiny. When such dreams are also unresolved dreams, it is even more important to return to them and work with them. Often their resolution reveals a basic pattern in our life, usually a stuck place. Resolving such dreams can also help put us more clearly in touch with our own destiny. We know a man who today works with people who are dying of terminal illness. His earliest remembered dream is of himself as a child standing before an open grave, looking with concern, not terror, at a corpse in the grave. After consciously re-experiencing his childhood dream in a waking state and doing basic dreamwork techniques on it, he began to see it as a dream that did indeed foretell (and now confirm) his choice to dedicate his life to caring for the terminally ill.

Dreams remembered from childhood are to be treated as important gifts. If they seem to require more dreamwork than other dreams, they deserve it.

Dreamwork Technique 20
Resolving a Remembered Dream

Procedure:

1. In working with a dream remembered from youth or childhood, especially one that seems unresolved, re-experience the dream in a relaxed, meditative state with eyes closed. This time let yourself, as dream ego, take a more active role in the dream. There is no need consciously to change or control the imagery; rather let the imagery change as the dream ego interacts with it.

2. Then, write out your experience as you would an ordinary night dream, and use whatever other dreamwork techniques seem helpful.

3. If the dream is still unresolved, use the Rewriting a Dream Technique to bring some resolution.

4. Use various objectifying techniques such as Key Questions, Symbol Immersion, and Symbol Amplification to ground your search for a destiny pattern.[3]

Notes to Chapter 9
Dreamwork and Destiny
1. Thomas Merton, *Contemplation in a World of Action* (New York: Doubleday, 1973), Image Ed., p. 161.
2. There is a fine line between what is given to us (as inevitable and unavoidable) and what we choose for ourselves albeit unwittingly or unconsciously. For example, poor health may be a genetic inheritance (inevitable) or it may come from our choosing not to live in healthy ways.
3. See also Strephon Kaplan Williams' *Jungian–Senoi Dreamwork Manual* for a thorough and advanced description of how these methods for bringing resolution to dreams and life events work.

Chapter 10

Dreamwork and Personality: The Ego-Self Relationship in Dreamwork

◆

Personality Development

To begin dreamwork seriously is to begin personality change and development. A commitment to dreamwork implies a commitment to personal growth. Through dreamwork, parts of our personality of which we may be unaware are often revealed; unhealthy and unconscious personality patterns can be recognized and changed. Through dreamwork, it is possible to change these patterns below the level of insight and concept, at their source level in the personality. For example, a young woman who had a difficult time relating to men had a recurring rape dream. Through re-experiencing her rape dream in a meditative state with her therapist, she was able symbolically and emotionally to change her pattern of response to men at the source level of her inner world. The fact that she no longer had the rape dream at night, plus her ability to begin successfully relating to men in her waking world, was concrete evidence that a personality change had happened within her, without her having to conceptualize the process. Her dreamwork reflected the fact that shifts had happened directly in her inner world. She went on to a fulfilling marriage with children of her own.

Resolving Situations Through Dreams

Some problems cannot be worked out in outer world relationships, but they can be worked out in the dream world, as in this example.

> I had a dream in which I felt sad that Robert and I weren't able to stay married. In the dream, I cried and told him how sadly I felt. He acknowledged that he had treated me very badly. (In the waking world, Robert would never acknowledge such a thing to me or to anyone; it's not in his character.) By his doing so in the dream world, I was finally able to hear inside myself that I could give up assuming total responsibility for the failure of our marriage.

> My response to him in the dream brought further wisdom to the surface. "We were both very young and immature," my dream ego had said. This gave me an understanding on yet another level that made the divorce seem not so much *our* failure, but stated the fact that we were both part of the human condition. We were both immature. The dream put our relationship in perspective for me for the first time—five years after the separation.

It was very important for this woman to bring to waking awareness the insight that had been revealed in the dream world. Just to have had the dream—without the dreamwork—would probably not have put her in touch with the resolution process happening in the inner world through the healing power of the dream. "Once I acknowledged the dream's meaning," she explained, "I felt an inner shift in my body that underlined my body's affirmation of the rightness of my understanding of the dream."

Much can be learned about the personality through dreamwork. Besides allowing us to deal with issues that cannot be resolved in the outer world, dreamwork allows a way of objectively looking at ourselves so that we can take a conscious role in our development. We need not feel totally dependent on feedback from others or our own personal musings about who we are. Dreams, symbolically but clearly, show us how different aspects of our personality function. They put feelings, conflicts, and unresolved issues into figures and forms that we can grasp. They put us in touch with missing or forgotten factors that help us understand ourselves. One woman who consciously recalled feeling shame at being beaten by her parents throughout childhood discovered through dreamwork that she was also *angry*. This discovery enabled her to release her anger and initiate a healing process.

Relating to God

With dreams and dreamwork as a help to personality development, our conscious rational minds do not have to be the only source responsible for our wholeness. The ego does not have to remain in total control, nor is it expected to be all-powerful. Dreams and dreamwork are most helpful allies, and often make up for what is lacking in our conscious processes.

When we work with dreams, we are in touch with destiny sources. When we do dreamwork with devotion and commitment we feel a response from the divine Source. In relating to God through dreamwork the soul is energized, the power and meaning of life is felt, and integration and healing occur again and again.

In our view of personality development, we use a model of wholeness and integration. Thus, we feel that a spiritual perspective is integral to the development of personality. If we humans are made in the image and likeness of God, we reflect God in whatever we do.

The idea of personality development, what we might today call self-actualization, was not foreign to the thought of the early Church thinkers. Neither, of course, was spiritual development. Following the Greek tradition of education, or *paideia*[1] (the holistic development of the human mind and spirit), theologians such as Origen, Basil the Great, Gregory of Nyssa and Gregory Nazianzen spoke much about the formation of the Christian's personality (*morphosis*)[2] and the transformation of the Christian's spirit (*metamorphosis*).[3] Just as personality development involves a continuous and lifelong effort, so the soul slowly makes its journey toward the high point of its destiny. Thus, the more fully-functioning and vitally alive our personality is, the more we are able to actualize God's will and our destiny in our lives. Irenaeus put it simply: "The glory of God is humanity fully alive."

Personality Dynamics in Dreams

There seem to be three central dynamics of the personality which play a key role in dreams and dreamwork. These are the ego, the Self, and the relationship between them. Let us look at each in turn.

The ego carries out many important functions of the personality. Primarily, it is the choice-maker and the consciousness-carrier. The ego also has developed a set of attitudes and values as the context within which it makes its choices. Dream material often brings into awareness and calls into question the ego's style of choicemaking, its ways of dealing with consciousness, and the appropriateness of its attitudes and values.

The ego also has images with which it tends to identify our personality. For example, when we are parents we may identify our whole personality with being father or mother, and we tend to live as if we were nothing but mother or father. Similarly, we can identify with other images and roles such as teacher, friend, spiritual person, etc. In terms of the personality, one function of the ego is to maintain wholeness by not identifying the total personality with one of its parts to the exclusion of the other parts. As choicemaker, the ego's task is to make choices which help develop a balanced personality. To choose is to apply energy in one direction rather than another. To foster the wholeness process, the ego makes a conscious commitment to serve, not its own wishes, but those of the inner self, the integrative function of the personality.

The Self. At the core of our being is the inner self or integrative, self-transformative, self-regulating center of our personality. It corresponds to the personal aspect of the archetypal energy complex Jung named the Self. For the most part, we are unconscious of the inner self and its integrative, transformative work in our personality. However, its presence and its energies of growth and creativity are often revealed in dreams and meditation. The Self seems to know the inner and outer potentials of our personality, and while it does not make choices (for that is the ego's function), it does reveal possible choices, and integrates (or tries to) what is eventually chosen. In dreams, the inner self also challenges and questions the ego's awareness, attitudes, and choices by presenting alternative healing possibilities to our consciousness. In dreamwork, we come to realize that at times the inner self is asking for cooperation in the self-transformation process from the conscious, ego-directed side of the personality.

The Ego-Self Relationship

There is a clear need to establish an ego-Self relationship in the personality. The ego and the inner self cannot operate successfully for very long when they are out of touch. As long as such a relationship is maintained, the exchange of creative energies between the conscious and unconscious levels of the personality flow smoothly and productively. Without the ego, the inner self cannot fulfill its function of integrating the personality. Therapists realize that one of their first tasks with clients is to see that the client develops enough ego-strength to make choices, to remain conscious of reality, to develop relationships in the outer world, and to relate to the inner world. All these activities are continually required of the ego if a healthy and whole person is to emerge. On the other hand, if the ego remains weak, it is dominated by unconscious energies—for example, it is liable to *identify* itself with persons, images, and roles rather than relate to them. Or, if it relates to others, it relates to *roles* rather than to persons. A weak ego prefers sleeping or being in ecstasy over making strong, committed choices. Dreams and dreamwork invite us to maintain a healthy ego, listen to the inner self, and develop the ego-Self relationship.

As Jung commented on the essential relationship between the conscious and unconscious mind in dreamwork:

> Experience has taught me that a little knowledge of dream psychology produces a tendency to exaggerate the importance of the unconscious, to the detriment of conscious decision. It should not be forgotten that the unconscious functions satisfactorily only when the conscious is fulfilling its role to the limits of its ability. Then dreams may perhaps add what is still lacking or lend a helping hand when our best efforts have failed.[4]

Following the Dream Ego technique, presented in Chapter 3, may be used in connection with dreamwork techniques suggested at the end of this chapter to strengthen the ego and to develop the ego-Self relationship.

The Ego in Relation to the Self and to the Soul

From Chapter 9 we saw that the ego (the conscious part of our personality) is in relationship with the soul; in this chapter we see that the ego is also in relationship to the inner self. How do these relationships differ?

When we talk about the ego in relationship to the self, we are taking the perspective of personality development; here the ego's task is to cooperate with the self's integrative and transformative functions in developing the personality's fulfullment: wholeness.

In contrast, when we talk about the ego in relation to the soul, we are taking the perspective of destiny, of a larger, lifelong purpose and meaning: holiness. It is perhaps the energy released by a sense of destiny in the soul that motivates the self and the ego to work together toward wholeness.

The call is to achieve not only an integrated personality, but also a deeply spiritual and committed life. While the inner self continually invites the ego to relate to the task of personality development, the soul is inviting the ego to relate to God and to the task of developing a loving community on earth.

Developing the Ego

The much maligned ego is a *sine qua non* for helping the soul and the self become realized. Instead of scolding and demeaning the ego and putting it out of sight, as if it were a delinquent child, we can choose to educate and nurture it into a healthy maturity. Rather than emphasize its weaknesses and the problems it causes, perhaps we can treat it as a child that needs to be loved, valued, nurtured, and brought into the family. Perhaps we can begin to see the ego as a gift whose functions are absolutely necessary and irreplaceable if we are to become fully-actualized human beings and fulfill our destiny.

Instead of an ego focused only on its own personal glory and gratification, we can develop an ego that begins to approach life with full energy, in harmony with the soul and the inner self. The ego can be part of the fully functioning, fully alive person, cooperating with the body, with the inner self, and with the soul. Rather than having an ego-less life, we have an ego that can cooperatively participate in life, and is not threatened by living. Such an ego can become strong enough to be in touch with personality weaknesses and wounds without being overwhelmed by them; strong enough to be vulnerable without fearing new challenges and risks; strong enough in its own identity to surrender to its soul's destiny without letting go of its conscious connection to the soul. (An ego is able to surrender to its soul's destiny just as an ego is able to surrender to the body, as in riding a bicycle where the body, *not the ego,* maintains the balance. A healthy, mature ego, which is flexible and resilient, does not surrender itself; it surrenders its control and its resistance, i.e., its purely limited point of view.)

The Dream Ego and the Waking Ego

The dream ego relates (or does not relate) to other characters and symbols in the dream. In dreamwork, we can observe the quality and style of the dream ego's relating. We can see if the dream ego relates positively and assertively, or passively and helplessly, or violently and destructively. We can ask whether the dream ego becomes involved in the drama of the dream, or does it act more like a curious but distant observer? Does it stir up conflict in the dream, work toward cooperation, or feel out of place and lost? Does the dream ego seem to have lots of energy, or do its intentions usually get frustrated and blocked?

Because the dream ego often reflects the waking ego's attitudes and behavior, we can use dreamwork to help understand our waking ego. In dreamwork, we can see how the dream mirrors the ego's condition on three levels: dreams reflect how the ego relates to the inner self (the Self), how it relates to the soul (destiny), and how it relates to its own maturity, i.e., developing its own skills, gifts, choice-making powers, ability to relate to persons in the waking world, and a clear identity and sense of self. To process ego-related material through dreams and dreamwork, we suggest the use of the technique called Following the Dream Ego (Chapter 3) as well as the techniques described at the end of this chapter.

The dream ego mirrors the ego's relation to the inner self and to the other energies of the unconscious. These energies of the unconscious may be reflected symbolically in the various characters, figures, images, symbols, and words in a dream. In dreamwork, we look to see how the dream ego is relating, or not relating, to these elements in the dream. Look for signs of the dream ego being connected to, or related to, or involved cooperatively and productively with such figures. This may be a sign that our ego is connected to our inner self and that the energies of the unconscious are flowing smoothly. Or it may be that we need to develop the ego-Self relationship. When the dream characters and figures are challenging or threatening the dream ego, or trying to evoke response, study the dream ego and its responses. See if it is asking that a stronger connection be made between the dream ego and the inner self.

The Dream Ego and Relation to the Soul

The dream ego may also mirror the ego's relation to the soul and its destiny. Dreams in which attitudes and values are affirmed or questioned, or where one's identity and purpose in life are involved, can be seen as reflecting the ego-soul relationship. In adult life, many people experience a spiritual crisis, sometimes referred to as a mid-life crisis or second birth. Carl Jung is often quoted as saying most of the patients who came to him after the age of thirty-five were involved in such a spiritual crisis. Mid-life crises are clearly recognized in developmental studies of the adult personality, though they are seldom discussed as spiritual crises. The maturity process clearly involves a soul search, since the mid-life crisis is often characterized by a questioning of one's major values and life commitments, and accompanied by feelings of meaninglessness and worthlessness. For example, persons find that merely working to satisfy their personal needs and wants, no matter how successfully, no longer suffices, and they feel a need to deal with larger issues of the community and with the meaning and purpose of their lives. In dreams related to soul-growth, we may see the dream ego choosing certain values and working toward certain goals. This activity is usually accompanied by feelings that are satisfying or unsatisfying. Here, working with the symbols and following the dream ego's attitudes and choices will help bring such issues into clarity. Such dreams also contain surprises.

For example, a forty-year-old woman dreamed that she heard her baby crying in the nursery. Being very attentive to this beautiful child, she ran to the nursery to comfort it, but when she looked into the crib the baby was comfortably sleeping. However, the crying continued. At this moment, the woman discovered a door in the nursery she had never noticed before. When she opened it, she discovered to her surprise another nursery with an identical crib and a child in it. This child was hungry, weak, emaciated. How could she have forgotten she had this other child, she wondered. After dreamwork, she discovered it was an undeveloped spiritual side of her life. It might be noted that since the dream, for the past eight years, she has been working to develop that side of her. Spiritual development is not a short and simple process.

The Ego Reflects Itself

Finally, the dream ego also mirrors the waking ego's own development and maturity. It is in this area that much contemporary psychological dreamwork has been focused. From dreams and dreamwork, the ego learns to identify its self-defeating attitudes and egocentricities. It learns to recognize when it is truly making choices for the good of the total personality, and when it is merely playing out certain socially acceptable roles and behavior. Dreams may mirror stages of ego-development from childhood to fullest maturity, and remind the ego that, as an adult, it can no longer make choices simply for self-enhancement at the expense of the needs of those depending on its cooperation. Through dreamwork, the ego learns that it is being challenged to stay conscious of changes and to accept new challenges rather than to slip back into the unconsciousness of sleep (what Deikmann calls the "trance of ordinary life")[5] or ecstasy (where the ego is passively entertained, drugged, drunk, or merely searching for an escape-high).

In all these kinds of dreams—relating to the ego, soul, or the inner self—the waking ego's task is to make conscious whatever personality dynamics the dream seems to reveal, and then to integrate and transform them by appropriate choices.

When the ego responds to the invitation of such dreams, making them real in some way in the waking world, there will usually follow some confirming dreams showing the dream ego and other figures of the dream operating together in more cooperative and effective ways than before. It is as if the dream not only asks for integration and development, but acknowledges it when it occurs.

Dreamwork Technique 21: Following the Dream Ego—II

Dreams often mirror the condition, needs, and strengths of the personality. Dreamwork allows us clearly to recognize these conditions and to make appropriate choices in response to them. Often this is not a simple matter, and for this reason people may consult professionals for help and confirmation in working toward strengthening the ego and personality. In ordinary growth and personality development, however, most of us are capable of learning many helpful insights from our dreams and of making appropriate choices for personality growth as a result of dreamwork. Usually, we do not lack the energy to change, but rather miss the proper perspective. Dreams and dreamwork can offer such perspective, thus allowing us to utilize fully the inner energy available to us.

There are some dream theorists who say that people must never tamper with their dreams, and that it is enough to gain insight about oneself from the dream. We have found, as an alternative, that people can "tamper" with their dreams and the characters in their dreams to utilize the healing energies reflected in them. Thus, while a record of the original dream is kept, a dream can be worked with, re-entered, rewritten, expanded, and completed in such a way that a new healing relation is established between the waking ego and the dream.

For example, Following the Dream Ego—I technique asks us to make three columns: the first describes the actions and choices of the dream ego at each stage or episode of the dream; the second observes the dream ego's corresponding attitudes, reactions, and feelings at each stage; the third contains alternative ways of acting, choosing, feeling, and reacting—things the dream ego was *not* doing or feeling. As you work with third column material—looking at what the dream ego was not doing but might have been doing—you begin to see new potentials or alternatives. The technique offers a creative way of opening up your perspective and suggesting concrete ways of taking on (or at least trying on) new intentions, attitudes, and choices. The technique for this chapter which we call Following the Dream Ego—II involves rewriting the dream by utilizing material from that third column.

Dreamwork Technique 21
Following the Dream Ego—II

Procedure:
    This technique, designed to open up alternatives for personality development, works well when a general change, e.g., to become more assertive, or more decisive or more in touch with feelings, is desired but still needs to be concretized and applied to specific life situations.

1. First, complete the three columns referred to in Following the Dream Ego—I (Dreamwork Technique 4). Pay special attention to the third column. List there as many alternatives as you can think of.

2. Then, using material from the third column—you will have to pick and select from available alternatives—rewrite the entire dream (or at least major portions of it) giving the dream ego a new set of attitudes and choices. In this way, you recreate the original situations of the dream, stage by stage, but now you present the dream ego with a fresh approach, a new level of involvement.

3. Afterward, compare your waking reactions both to the original dream and to the rewritten version of it.

4. If you like some of the new attitudes and choices in the rewritten version, ask yourself if those new attitudes and choices are typical of your waking attitudes and choices. Usually, they are not, but rather

are more an expression of ways you would like to be. If so, ask yourself where in your daily life you could begin to practice such new attitudes and choices, and start practicing them. (See also the following technique, Working on Personality Issues.)

Strengthening the Waking Ego

Some observations about this technique are in order. Rewriting the dream invites you to re-enter the dream with a more committed and value-centered ego, and usually with a more active, conscious, and involved ego than in the original dream state. We are here talking about the waking ego, for in doing this technique the waking ego is getting practice in choice-making and creating new behavior patterns. In this way, the ego strengthens itself as well as the entire personality. Its reward is the experience of greater effectiveness. It begins to feel itself as a significant part of a greater meaningful totality—the whole person. In listing alternatives and practicing choosing them, even in a dreamwork exercise, the ego realizes that it does have access to the necessary inner energies to choose and behave in more satisfying ways.

Researching the dreams of depressed women, Roslyn Cartwright of the University of Illinois at Evanston[6] found their dreams were also depressing. Dreams seemed to be mirroring personalities. She asked these women to rewrite their dreams with a sense of joy and creativity, and she taught them how to suggest to themselves that they dream optimistic night dreams as well. Results seem to indicate that after a period of time the women's attitudes toward life moved from feeling depressed and ineffective to feeling creative and effective.

In order to insure permanence of new attitudes and feelings, it is most helpful to translate them into personality-oriented tasks. This is the simplest and most direct way of utilizing energy released from the inner world in outer life.

Dreamwork Technique 22: Working on Personality Issues

Suppose in dreams we consistently find we are haggling over the price we pay for dinner, clothes, entertainment, appliances, etc., feeling quite stingy and sometimes not even getting things we really want because of it. One possible personality task might be to go out and spend a generous amount of money on ourselves and then to confront the emotional anxiety it might provoke in us, and see if our attitude could be changed, as a result, toward a greater sense of freedom and healthy self-nurturing.

To take another example, suppose someone's dream ego always says yes to whatever is asked of it, even when it would rather not say yes; one personality task in waking life might be to try saying no to others once or twice when it would be appropriate to do so, or even not so appropriate. Similarly, if the dream ego is always agreeable, even when it feels like disagreeing, perhaps a waking-life task might involve disagreeing a bit with the opinions of others. It may be that the dream is inviting us to develop our capacity to say no and to disagree with others, thus differentiating us from others. The task is to try the suggested behavior in our waking personality and examine our response to the experience. Personality-oriented tasks coming out of dreams are often fun as well as potentially healing.

They are healing because they work toward wholeness. Always to be agreeable and always to say yes is to be one-sided. Dreamwork invites us not to get stuck at one side of a polarity. Personality tasks allow us to test and welcome both sides of a polarity, preparing us to be able to be disagreeable, angry, bitchy, and to say no when appropriate. Anger, disagreeableness, and so on, may not in themselves be desirable but they form a very real part of the personality's repertoire, a part which is often kept hidden beneath the surface. When we are not conscious of these polarities, they surface in unconscious ways. For example, when we have not learned to say no directly, we may manipulate others to say no for us. Being able to say no when appropriate is a sign of an integrating personality.

One woman in a dreamwork group prided herself on being self-sufficient. "I don't need anyone's help," was her comment. "I can do it myself." She had a dream in which she found the dream ego asking help from someone else. In dreamwork, she discovered the dream was not mirroring who she was in outer life, but pointing to a capacity she lacked—the capacity to ask others for help, the capacity to be interdependent. She assigned herself the personality task of asking each of the other members in the dream group to help her with something she needed. From one she asked for a ride to an appointment, from another she asked for help with a term paper, from a third she asked for suggestions in decorating her apartment, from the fourth she asked for help in finding a good garage mechanic.

Dreamwork Technique 22
Working on Personality Issues

Procedure:

1. Choose some personality characteristic that is showing itself, through dreams and dreamwork, to be in need of change.

2. Assign yourself a specific behavior or choice to make in your waking life that responds to the needed change.

3. If your new behavior meets the four general guidelines listed below that govern appropriate personality tasks, then set yourself a deadline for carrying them out.

4. Observe subsequent dreams for confirmation or corrective suggestions.

General Guidelines

If a certain choice or behavior is suggested in a dream, should the dreamer take it literally and act it out in the waking world? For example, if I dream that I am taking a certain course at the university, or that I am getting a divorce, or that I am marrying a certain person, or that I am killing my mother-in-law, shall I obey the dream by enacting in outer life what is being dramatized in the inner world? As a rule, most dreams are not to be interpreted literally. The dream communicates in symbolic language; thus the purpose of doing dreamwork is to clarify the dream's meaning and to arrive at an appropriate way of taking action in response to the dream. Here are some general guidelines for choosing personality tasks in response to a dream.

1. Do some dreamwork before actualizing any of the dream's content literally in the outer world. Dreamwork techniques help focus and clarify many subtle areas of a dream.

2. Subject each important personality task suggestion to the test: Does this action further my growth, bring about relationship with my fellow human beings, and further God's work in the world through me? This question is most important when the course of action suggested by a dream involves significant decisions and important life changes.

3. Evaluate the proposed action in terms of its appropriateness, i.e., is it in conflict with the laws of society, the laws of God, or the laws of re-

ality? For example, if a dream seems to suggest that I donate my complete retirement savings to the Church, test its appropriateness by obtaining the advice of wise counsel.

4. Evaluate the consequences of your proposed action. Ask yourself: "If I say yes to this or no to that because of a dream, what will happen in the future because of my choice?" For example, to leave a marriage or change careers has long-term consequences that must be weighed carefully.

In general, a dream is to be treated more as a question than as an answer. And when it speaks, it usually presents possibilities, perspectives, and alternatives the conscious ego may not have thought of. Dreams as a rule present a *context of choice* rather than the actual choice to take, the context here being a pattern of attitudes and values within which I make my choices. Thus, if I ask my dream the question: "Should I continue this relationship or not?" a subsequent dream is not likely to answer in a simple yes or no fashion, but might instead show me the pattern or context in which my friend and I are relating. In this sense it would not be surprising to have two dreams which are superficially contradictory—one in which I see myself creatively relating to my friend, and a second in which we are in strong, unresolvable conflict. In reality, the dream in both instances is presenting factors involved in the context of the issue or question. Once I am aware of these issues, through dreamwork, I am more able to make healthy, holistic, and meaningful choices.

Notes to Chapter 10
Dreamwork and Personality

1. For a three volume work devoted entirely to an understanding of *paideia* and its development in Western civilization, see Werner Jaeger, *Paideia: The Ideals of Greek Culture* (Oxford: Oxford U. Press, 1939–44), and, more specifically, *Early Christianity and Greek Paideia* (Cambridge: Harvard U. Press, 1961).

2. See Jaeger's comments in *Early Christianity and Greek Paideia,* p. 140, n. 1. For example, Jaeger reports that the passages in Gregory of Nyssa "in which the word *morphosis* and its derivatives occur are too numerous for me to collect them all ..." (p. 140).

3. Here the Church Fathers follow and develop Paul's use of *metamorphosis* as found, for example, in Romans 12:2 or 2 Corinthians 3:18.

4. C.G. Jung, "De la nature des reves," *Revue Ciba,* September 1945, p. 1612.

5. See Arthur Deikmann, *The Observing Self* (Boston: Beacon Press, 1982), pp. 119–131.

6. Reported from personal conversations between Roslyn Cartwright and Strephon Kaplan Williams in 1977.

Chapter 11

Energy and Symbols in Dreamwork: The Language and Function of Dreams

◆

Symbolic Language

It is not accurate to say that the language of outer reality is literal and factual while the language of the dream is symbolic. It is likely that we continually live and communicate on the symbolic level, and we do it naturally and spontaneously, whether in waking life or in the dream world. For example, when we send someone a birthday card, it symbolizes our care and love; when we give someone a gift, a message is communicated on a symbolic level; when we cook someone's favorite food for dinner, it symbolizes more than satisfying one's caloric and protein needs. And when we forget to appear for an appointment, what might we be saying symbolically?

The early writers and homilists of the Church were aware that the passages of the Bible were meant to be heard on more than the literal or historic level. Clearly, for them, the text contained symbolic messages on the eschatological and spiritual levels. Because of their imagery and action Jesus' parables are meant to be taken symbolically. Work is left for us to do in relating to them.

Similarly, although at times dreams seem to contain direct messages meant to be taken literally, as when the angel appeared in a dream to Joseph and told him to take Jesus and his mother and flee to Egypt, the Church teachers who wrote on dreams were very conscious of the symbolic language of dreams and how dreams often communicated multi-leveled wisdom.

Since dream language is symbolic, we deal with dreams on more than one level. Even before we look at the details of a dream, we realize that the dream is a gift. To begin dreamwork is to acknowledge that we have been given a gift of challenge, healing, and revelation from God. As we make conscious in dreamwork the symbolic level of the dream, we are making conscious how God operates in the world in relation to us.

Signs and Symbols

It helps to understand "symbol" in contrast to a "sign." While a sign is an image used to express one specific meaning, a symbol is an image with overtones that can have many levels of meaning. These levels are a function in part of the complexity of the symbol itself, its context, and what it evokes for us psychologically and spiritually. Anything can become a symbol for people. For early Christians, the fish, the butterfly, and the cross came to symbolize various aspects of Christ's life and message.

Symbols also seem to contain energy or numinosity, which evoke a response from us. Symbols seem to have their own aliveness and stimulate us to find out what they mean. Powerful symbols seem to reveal layer after layer of meaning and energy.

In the outer world, symbols are often expressed in products of artistic craftsmanship, such as the Rose Window in the Cathedral at Chartres, Da Vinci's painting "The Last Supper," or the liturgical vestments worn by priests. Ritual is also a symbolic action: from an ordinary handshake of greeting, to the "kiss" of peace offered to fellow Christians, to the elevation of the sacramental host and cup at the eucharistic liturgy.

Symbols and Inner Life

In the inner world, symbolic images and ritual actions are most easily recognized in visions, fantasies, poems, parables, and, of course, dreams. Everyday gestures such as shaking hands may have great symbolic significance when they occur in a dream.

For example, a middle-aged woman explained, "I don't often dream of Church rituals and traditionally holy images, but I dream of packing for a trip, embracing a friend, and boarding a train. For me, such images are very symbolic and religious." She was well aware of the journey symbolism in the New Testament—Jesus' journey to Jerusalem, the Way of the Cross, the parables that involve travelers, etc. She was also aware of the feeling energy released in her when she dreamed of herself on a journey.

The questions she heard her dream asking of her were: "How do you live your journey on an everyday level?" And further: "How about your willingness to go on a journey each day, to be flexible, to take risks, to be open, to face loss, etc.?"

When we asked how she responded to these questions she replied:

> I am in a transition place in my life. I often dream of boarding a bus or a train or walking along a path, at times losing my way, looking for the light. The dreams confirm what I am living out in the outer world. In one dream, someone came on a motorcycle to find me and lead me out of a lost place. After that I became more open to seeking help for some personality problems. On the spiritual level, the dream reminded me that when I am most lost, intervention comes. Right now spiritually my personal resources seem exhausted, and I am open to seeking and receiving help.

Her dream is spiritual in that it presents her problems in a larger context than just her personal life. The dream indicates she is on a journey toward meaning. It gives her the motivation to seek help and spiritual renewal.

Symbols and Energy

People often ask us to give samples of the kinds of energy released by a dream symbol. For example, suppose the symbol in a dream is a woman caring for her child. It is likely that the energy being released is related to nurturing, nourishing, and protecting something in her life that may need her care. Again, if the symbol is strong and hero-like, it is likely that the energy being released is related to courage, risk-taking, accomplishment, healing, and the like.

If a symbol in our dream is an adversary character, it is likely to be releasing in us energies related to challenging, testing, limiting, diminishment, destroying, and the like. Perhaps after doing dreamwork we discover that we are being asked to sacrifice (destroy) some inadequate or unhealthy attitudes in our life. The adversity symbol might be indicating that we have the energy to rid ourselves of that attitude at this time.

There are other symbolized energies such as those for structuring, developing, changing, or holding on to certain aspects of our life.

Behavior in Dreams

In this light, it is important to remember that characters in our dream are better worked with as symbols than as representing activities we do in the waking world.

For example, a woman dreamed she was standing at a bus stop masturbating, when someone came up to her and threatened to tell her friends. Nevertheless, the dream ego continued masturbating and reached orgasm. If we were to look at this dream literally or moralistically, it would be taken as a sexual act being done in public, inappropriately. However, when we ask "What kind of energy is being symbolically expressed by the dream ego?" the dream takes on a very different meaning. Symbolically, masturbation is a form of self-expression in which one manifests and releases one's energy. It may symbolize self-motivation (self-stimulation). In the dream the dream ego is able to release her energy successfully (come to orgasm) in public, despite threats and disapproval. When we learn that the woman who had the dream had recently decided to start a small retail business by herself, a public venture none of her friends had ever dared, we can begin to understand how she could see the masturbating dream as a confirming sign from her inner self that she possesses the energy and the capacity to carry out her new business successfully.

Similarly, symbolic dream language expressions such as murder, execution, rape, incest, abortion, and so on are to be treated as *symbolic expressions of inner energy,* not as a literal statement which would be viewed as immoral or illegal in outer life.

People with very weak egos or under great psychological stress may interpret such dream content literally and may try (or feel obliged) to act it out. Certain people are afraid of their dreams because they fear that the strong symbolic dream action may actually happen in their outer lives. This is why working with dream symbols as inner experience can relieve persons of unnecessary insecurity and anxiety.

Dreams present the dark and light sides of life for us to deal with. The cross is a symbol both of transcendent light and overwhelming darkness. If we had Jesus' attitude, we would not simply resist (or deny) evil; we would deal with it in dreamwork. To go the second mile is to do the inner work.

The Cross as Symbol

Literally, a cross can be viewed as two pieces of wood whose centers are fastened together at right angles. As a symbol, however, it creates a special way of releasing energy, a specific way of manifesting God's purpose on the earth. When represented in the form of a cross, energy is expressed in the form of polarities integrated. The energies that reach vertically from heaven to earth, and the energies that flow horizontally to embrace the human planet, all meet at the center of the cross. Suffering and healing, for example, are held in tension in the Christian cross. In Catholic hospitals, a crucifix may be found in every room, symbolizing Christ's suffering, but also his healing presence. As one hospitalized man explained the symbolic energy the crucifix brought to him:

> Just as Jesus suffered out of love for me and his suffering was not in vain, so my suffering can have purpose too. Living with a physical illness, I am reminded day and night by that crucifix that suffering can have redemptive value. I know that there is death and rebirth, that there is sickness and healing, that all healing is not physical.

The Protestant cross, which does not display the crucified Christ, can also be seen as the intersection of the earthly and spiritual life, at the center of which is mystery.

Religious Symbols in Dreams

While symbols are definitely personal, they are not merely personal. There is not just "me and my cross." Many symbols and their expressions often reflect things happening in the community, the culture, and religion as well. Such symbols have universal aspects as well as personal ones. In dreams, we may experience a universal symbol, such as a cross, crucifix, or a church, in particular forms relevant to our lives and our journeys. Doing dreamwork with such symbols calls for different levels of awareness to be applied. We could explore, say, a dream image of a Church on a personal level, but also on a more universal level. Personally, we might ask: What is happening to my dream ego in relation to that Church image? What is my dream ego's emotional relation to it? What are the qualities of that Church that apply to me?

On a more general plane, since a Church is often symbolic of a religious community or an organized religion, we might ask: What is my relationship to my experience of going to church, or to the religious tradition to which I belong? Since a church or a temple can symbolize a sense of the sacred, a holy place, or God, we can ask, for example: What is my relation to sacred things and holy places? How strong is my relation to God? Such questions help reveal the symbol's meaning for our lives; they call us to choose to realize God's plan in our lives; they release the energy inherent in the symbol and relate it to us.

The symbol is the locus of the energy and the medium by which it becomes usable by us. Once the symbol is given to us in a dream, we can relate to it in dreamwork and translate the energy released into specific actions which enliven our lives and make them meaningful. For example, if a cross symbolizes the unity of the opposites, suffering and healing, how can I unify and transform certain tensions in my life right now so that my suffering becomes redemptive and healing? In order to release the energy of the symbol in our lives, we need to act and react. Well-designed dreamwork questions can enable us to act and react.

Dreams can also help us to use the energy released in a symbol. First, often a dream presents the issues in our life needing clarification, usually at the level of feeling: I am angry at my boss, I'm afraid I have not been a good parent, I'm resistant to change or to taking risks, I feel unacceptable to God, I feel constricted on my creativity, I am frustrated trying to organize my life. Second, often a dream suggests a direction or a way of working at the issue to resolve it. Thus, the dream may inspire us with new potentials, especially new attitudes. Or we may have a dream in which we are acting in decisive, non-fearful ways; or in our dream a helping figure may appear to aid us in dealing with a situation in a spirit of love, courage and caring.

The dreamwork techniques presented in this chapter suggest ways to manifest the energy released from the symbol in our everyday life, or at least to bring the energy to the surface and express it in some artistic or cultural form.

Dreamwork Technique 23:
Artwork with Dream Symbols

The symbolic and cultural arts—painting, sculpture, pottery, poetry, music, drama, dance, movement, mime, etc.—offer specific ways of releasing, focusing, concretizing, and increasing the energy evoked in dream symbols.

Shaping a wisdom figure (or a terrifying figure) from a dream into clay helps the symbolic energy come more fully alive for us, yet at the same time its energy feels more contained and clearer to relate to. The energy feels so because it has been expressed in something very tangible and because we have chosen to work with it and demonstrate our acceptance of it, indeed, our physical involvement with it. With clay or drawings, we have a concretized symbol to hold onto, relate to, live with, and be stimulated by. The clay figure kept on a special shelf, or a drawing on our wall, remains present to us and evocative.

Many people hesitate to display a piece of personal art, for they feel they cannot paint or sculpt well, or that their guests would find it strange to see personal artwork in a home or apartment. In working with art materials, it is important not to feel you have to be a professional artist before you can do dreamwork techniques that involve art materials. We all have an innate ability to express images, even if our expression seems crude, primitive or unusual. It is better to form the symbol inadequately than not at all. These dreamwork techniques are designed to honor the symbol's being and energy, not to produce artifacts worthy of aesthetic admiration.

These products of our imagination are our children, so to speak. We learn to accept them as any parent would accept a child at its natural and appropriate level of development. Artworks, like children, have a personal meaning for us and are best kept where we are involved with them frequently.

Concretely, this might mean setting aside a place and a wall in your bedroom for your personal artwork, or even a closet which you reserve as a sacred area within your home. Some people use a special table or dresser top as their sacred area. It is often important to have a religious symbol which you yourself have created and not just depend on commercially available religious objects of art, no matter how aesthetically beautiful or meaningful they may be.

Dreamwork Technique 23
Artwork with Dream Symbols

Procedure:

1. When a dream contains a symbol (or symbols) which seem to evoke strong response, use some art form—paint, clay, music, wood, poetry, etc.—to express and concretize the symbol. Let the symbol come out the way it wants to, even if it appears differently from the way it appeared in the original dream.

2. Reflect on the insights and feelings that surface as you make your drawing, clay figure, poem, song, etc. Sign and date your work in some personal way.

3. When working together in a family or group, it is often beneficial to share your artwork and your experience of it. After an individual shares, we suggest that other group members not comment on or interpret his or her artwork or dream. Asking a question, however, may help bring out other aspects of the person's experience, and would indeed be helpful. But to tell someone else what you think his or her art or dream means is basically projecting your own attitudes and feelings onto someone else's experiences.

4. Afterward keep your work in a special place where you are likely to be involved with it frequently. It may produce new insights and release renewed expressions of its energy in you.

The Versatility of Artwork

Even symbols that release frightening or negative energy, such as beasts or adversaries (the word "satan" means adversary), are good for putting into artwork, for to put the figure into art is a way of containing the energy. Some people who felt uncomfortable, for example, painting a devil or destructive figure came up with the idea of including in the painting a balancing, containing, or healing symbol. To balance the frightening energy, one person drew a Christ figure next to Satan. Another encircled a frightening figure in a sacred circle of divine light in order to contain it. A third added the cross into her drawing as a healing symbol.

Some people use a number of art forms in releasing dream energies. One person who dreamed of going to her closet in order to dress for a party acted out her dream by going to her closet, choosing clothes, putting them on, and dancing as if she were at a party. Later she did drawings of scenes from the party as she imagined them in her dream. Finally, she composed a song on her guitar—one, she said, she had heard in her dream. As a result, her creative expressive experience helped balance some of the more painful and stressful aspects of her life.

After doing a waking dream on Joseph's dream to marry Mary, one woman did a clay figure of Joseph and the child. She called it a Joseph Madonna. She explained:

> Doing the artwork, took me beyond the dream to new insights. I experienced the joy and love Joseph had for Jesus, a profound, responsible love. My relation to Joseph in the clay was healing for me. I saw how he held his little family together through all their trials. I found a new love and respect for my own husband and my own child. In fact, when I took my sculpture home, I was so happy I wanted to dance. I explained to my three-year-old son about the Joseph Madonna and we both danced around the sculpture.

Dreamwork Technique 24: Metaphoric Processing

We mentioned thinking of our artwork as our children. That's metaphor. Obviously, pieces of art are not little human beings, but it is productive to ask how our artworks are our "children." To respond to this question is to begin metaphoric processing. In dreamwork, metaphoric processing means using the content or structure of a dream as a way to process some life experience. For example, if I dream of a war, I may treat the dream as a metaphor and ask myself: "What wars are actually going on in my life right now and how am I responding to them?" If in a dream I am running away or hiding, I might ask: "Where in my life do I tend to run away from responsibility or hide when a conflict surfaces?"

More generally, we can ask ourselves: How does my dream of last night metaphorically reflect (1) my childhood, (2) my present relationship, (3) my job, (4) my sexuality, (5) my spiritual process, (6) my attitude toward my physical body, (7) my anxiety, and so on.

How do we know what metaphor to choose? Certain dreams seem to present themselves as metaphors for outer life situations. For example, a catastrophe dream or an impending-disaster dream might suggest how we respond to crisis situations. Or if, in a dream, we are preparing for a test, use the dream to reflect outer life testing situations, for example, testing our new assertiveness skills, applying for a raise, participating in a sales competition, etc. Look at what is inherent in the words and issues of a dream, and ask how they might apply metaphorically in waking life.

For example, in a dream of war there may be many metaphoric applications: conflicts, how we prepare for stress, how we protect those dear to us, courage and risk-taking, fear, etc. Each of these levels may be explored with a single dream, as long as the exploration is productive.

Treated metaphorically, a dream can have at least five levels: (1) personal and attitudinal, (2) relational, (3) spiritual, (4) communal or political, and (5) universal. If we learn to view dreams at various levels, we can choose to do dreamwork tasks and/or personality tasks at these various levels. For example, a woman in our class reported and worked with the following dream:

> I am having a war dream. I am putting away a year's supply of food in the basement, and choosing the safest place to protect my children. I am procuring all that may be needed for feeding, protecting, and comforting them in the event of attack. I hoped my husband would be at work if and when an attack should occur, so that I wouldn't have to deal with his feelings and needs, as well as those of my children.

On the *personal and attitudinal level,* the woman found herself dealing with a fearful situation actively and practically. She was able to recognize and honor these qualities in herself.

On the *relational level,* she recognized the broad range of her concern for her children's well-being and proper nurturance during time of stress; she also recognized her need to deal with her relationship to her husband, since she felt it might be too much for her to care for him as well as for the children.

On the *spiritual level,* she recognized that the dream was asking her to deal with the sense of helplessness she might feel trying to avoid something that was out of her control. The dream did indicate that she could be in control of *preparations* for such an event and that she did want to actively prepare herself for the spiritual crises that might come her way.

On the *community level,* the dream showed that she was personally involved with her own children, but that there was little or no sign of community or political involvement. When asked what her dream ego was *not* doing in this regard, she replied: "I'm not actively involved in any anti-nuclear activity. I've never signed a petition, walked in a demonstration, or written a letter to my congressman to protest nuclear build-up."

At the *universal level,* she realized that she was accepting war as a strong possibility. While conflict and danger are universal and inherent in life, it is possible to work toward understanding of the people of other nations. On a practical level, she decided that she would begin to increase her knowledge and that of her children in people of other cultures with the intention of getting to know and like them.

This dream also gives us an opportunity to distinguish between literal and symbolic meanings of a dream. Literally, she might take the dream as suggesting she store away a year's supply of food. While some might feel storing rations is a good idea, others might see it as unrealistic. However, symbolically, her dream presents the threat of nuclear war as an issue to be dealt with. She might ask, for example, "What would it take to make my children and me safe in a nuclear age? What kind of nurturing is important for my children in a nuclear age? How can I express in my community and nation my concern for the safety of my children in a nuclear age?"

Dreamwork Technique 24
Metaphoric Processing

Procedure:

This technique is to be used with dreams that deal with multi-leveled issues. After basic dreamwork has been done on the dream, use the dream as a metaphor for processing some life experiences.

1. Ask how the dream is a metaphor for:
(a) my personal life and attitudes,
(b) my feelings and emotions,
(c) my relationships,
(d) my spiritual life,
(e) my community life,
(f) life worldwide.
It is not necessary to deal with all six levels of metaphoric meaning, nor is it necessary to limit the meaning to those six.

2. An alternative approach might be to ask: "How does my dream reflect my childhood, my sexuality, my attitude toward my physical body, etc.?"

3. It will be helpful, whenever possible, to make practical applications to waking life from the insights gained through metaphoric processing. (See Technique 15: Choosing Personality Tasks, and Technique 16: Choosing Outer Life Tasks.)

Metaphoric Processing and the Church

Symbolic and metaphoric processing is an ancient technique used not only with biblical dreams, but also with other scriptural passages. The Bible was presumed to contain many levels of meaning, and those who dealt only with the literal meaning missed much of the Bible's richness. Origen taught that Scripture had three levels of meaning—literal, moral, and mystical. Augustine, and John Cassian before him, distinguished two—the literal and the figurative—but the figurative could have many levels of meaning, they said, for example, the allegorical, moral, and eschatological. Thus, while literally a biblical passage might be dealing with the people of Israel, Augustine and Cassian might also see the events of the passage allegorically describing the Christian Church on earth, morally describing the human soul, and eschatologically describing the heavenly Jerusalem. While it might not be very practical to interpret one's night dreams on these early Christian categories or types, it does show that a traditional understanding of spiritual growth includes metaphoric processing. In fact, such metaphoric processing provided the fourfold structure (literal, allegorical, moral, eschatological) of a large number of sermons from the third to the twelfth centuries.[1]

Dreamwork Technique 25: Meditating on an Important Dream Symbol

The point of this dreamwork technique is to suggest how to spend meditative time with a dream symbol that seems to have a powerful effect. Especially in times of anxiety, insecurity, and difficulty, our meditative experience can help transform these situations, help us see them in a new light, and respond to them in new ways. Dream symbols often provide just the right catalyst for this transformation. Remember, a dream symbol need not be a visual image, such as a rug or door, though it most often is. A symbol may be a word, a phrase, a sound, a smell, an action, a face. For example, one woman in her dream heard the phrase, "in God's hands." During a meditation, she kept softly repeating the phrase. She explained:

I also listened for other ways it wanted to be said and I found myself saying phrases such as, "I place myself in God's hands," "I place my child in God's hands," "I place my husband in God's hands," "We are held in God's hands," and so on. It allowed me to believe there could be a new outpouring of love in our family.

The objective of this technique is to take the dream symbol consciously into a context where God and the soul are present and allow the symbol's energy to be felt in that context. It is a way, for example, to take concern for our own growth toward wholeness and put it actively into prayer through dream symbols.

Dreamwork Technique 25
Meditating on an Important Dream Symbol

Procedure:

1. Choose a powerful dream image, or other symbol from your dream.

2. Sit in a comfortable posture as you would for meditation. Place yourself in relation to God.

3. Close your eyes and let yourself grow relaxed, alert-relaxed. The point here is to create for yourself an inner space. Let all distractions be outside you.

4. Let the dream symbol present itself in your imagination, and simply look at it, as if you were a camera, not trying to control, manipulate or change the symbol in any way. Do this for at least five minutes, preferably more, as long as you can stay with the image.

5. Acknowledge God in the experience, and reflect upon what happened to you, how you felt during the meditation, and how you are feeling right now.

If you find it too difficult to stay simply focused on your dream image, here are some alternatives for step 4. First, do *symbol immersion* with it, that is, get to know the symbol, experience it, relate to it. Second, do *symbol association* with it, that is, picture each person, place, thing or event it reminds you of, one at a time. Third, *choose a word or phrase* that relates a waking-life concern of yours to the dream symbol—for example, if you need to make an important decision, you might say to the symbol, "Teach me your wisdom" or "I accept the gift you offer," and repeat it over and over until you grow deeply relaxed and at peace.

Note to Chapter 11
Energy and Symbols in Dreamwork
1. For a general study of the early Christian writers' use of typology see Jean Daniélou, *From Shadows to Reality: Studies in the Biblical Typology of the Fathers*, trans. Wulstan Hibbard (London, 1960). Also Barbara Kiefer Lewalski, *Protestant Poetics and the Seventeenth-Century Religious Lyric* (Princeton, 1979), Chapter IV.

Chapter 12

Dreamwork and Healing: Bringing Nightmares and Other Dreams to Resolution

◆

Saying Goodbye

When Jane was twelve years old, her favorite uncle died suddenly. She felt sad for weeks, and couldn't understand why. Finally, she realized that she was sad and hurt because her uncle had died without saying goodbye to her.

A short time later, Jane had a dream in which her uncle appeared, hugged her, and said goodbye. Jane woke from the dream feeling relieved.

How could her intense sadness end so simply after having a dream? How did the resolution come about?

The dream offered the possibility of resolution and closure. Jane was open to her dream being important and real on an inner level. After it, she could tell herself—and others—that her uncle had indeed said good-bye to her. And she did. The wound in the relationship with her uncle had been healed in the dream state, her sadness was resolved and left her. For her, resolution was an experience of letting go, of allowing death, of saying goodbye.

The Nature of Healing

What then is healing? How does it function? What is religious about the process? Why is healing an important concept in terms of dream-work?

The need for healing implies that there is a wound, a conflict, a brokenness, a separation, a being out of harmony with others and oneself. We need healing when our bodies are diseased, our minds are in turmoil, or our spirits are unable to function because they are tied up in guilt, fear, meaninglessness and inadequacies.

We can see the need for healing everywhere. Sickness, physical, spiritual and mental, happens to everyone. In our communities and in the world we see tremendous conflicts needing resolution, needing unity rather than war and violence, which destroys both sides.

Healing is a verb form which refers to an ongoing action. We experience the grace of healing as a continuous process. Healing may be defined as bringing resolution to conflict and woundedness. In its most positive sense, healing is a resolution of conflict and woundedness followed by the building of a new unity or wholeness. For example, the couple on the verge of divorce begin marriage counseling, where they are helped to face and deal with their conflicts. When resolution occurs, a stronger and more mature relationship is often the result. Similarly, certain unfortunate choices in our lives can put us out of relation with God; usually, then, the need for a healing resolution asserts itself. Our woundedness and the need for healing are frequently reflected in our dreams.

A characteristic of dreams is that they tend to be full of conflicts and unresolved situations: someone chases us, someone attacks, a conversation is interrupted, a path is taken which seems to lead nowhere, a religious figure appears but there is no gesture of relationship or response. These examples point to the fact that an important function of dreams is to present us with the full reality of our conflicts and issues, and to call us to heal and harmonize our lives.

From a dreamwork perspective, let us look at an example of a woman who had been wounded in her ability to trust, and how she was struggling toward healing.

A Woman Learning To Trust

The woman explained her problem and her dreamwork in the following way:

> I am most aware of being wounded in the area of trust. I experience it most in an inability to trust other people. Psychologically, I can understand my wound from having been abused and deprived as a child. I couldn't trust my parents, and I was unsure of my own lovability and trustworthiness. However, understanding my wound psychologically does not seem to make it go away. I still have a hard time trusting. I don't even know if it will ever heal. I may have to carry my wound with me all my life.
>
> Dreams and dreamwork make me conscious of the ways at present where I am most non-trusting—toward specific people, toward myself, and even toward God. So if I cannot have complete healing, at least I can bring about resolution in specific relationships.

This woman had the following dream.

> I am at sea on a beautiful yacht which I inherited from my father. A strong, intelligent and experienced captain and mate, who knew the vessel and the seas well, came as part of the inheritance. The dream ego is a beautiful and well-dressed blonde woman. She goes to the pilot house and says to the captain and the mate, "I can see that the sea is very stormy. We are going to be in for real trouble." The white bearded captain and alert mate stand at their posts, and their demeanor expresses competence, capability and strength.
>
> In another scene, I see a rocky shoreline off in the distance. Although the yacht is safely far from the shore, I am afraid. Even in the dream, I realize I have no reason to fear except for my own lack of trust.

This is a clear example of a dream's response to a major problem. From childhood, as she explained, she had learned to fear relationships and life itself; in her mind, the storms and conflicts of life would lead to hurt and destruction for her. Her response was to trust no one and to avoid conflict or confrontation at any cost. This was a learned response and an attitude developed during an abused childhood. What does the dream suggest can be done with this attitude in her present life? In a dreamwork dialogue she did with the captain and the mate, she told them of her concern for the rocky shoreline. They reassured her that they were well aware of it. She learned also from them that her life was being guided by a competent captain and first mate who lived within her, and that her task was to discover that these sides of herself were really trustworthy.

The dream invited her to trust that she was actually capable of handling the conflicts and rough seas of life. If at times she experienced a lack of self-trust, she could call upon the competence of the captain and the first mate within her, and feel the confidence to handle what she was afraid of. For her, resolution did not necessarily mean having her lack of trust disappear; rather, it meant being able to bring a strong part of herself into play, so that her fear might be transformed and the fearful challenge confronted.

In this example, we see how a dream brings up a central problem and includes within its imagery and action the potential for a healing resolution. Her dreamwork contributed to the resolution by making her conscious of her inner potential, and thus offering her a resource to use in dealing with future fear-evoking situations.

Healing the Nightmare

Nightmares, among the most dramatic of dreams, point out vividly the need for resolution. A nightmare may be defined as any dream from which we wake up because of fear. We leave the dream state for fear of being overwhelmed there. To escape the terrifying situation of the dream, however, is to abort the dream, which results naturally in a lack of resolution. A nightmare is almost always an incomplete dream. Typically, in nightmares people find themselves imprisoned, trapped, hunted, lost, falling; about to be killed, attacked, or somehow endangered; unable to run, escape, hide, communicate, or defend themselves.

Many nightmares are recurrent, that is, they may occur again and again with essentially the same imagery. When this happens, it is likely that the dream is attempting to mirror an inner conflict which is in need of healing; the inner conflict is probably being experienced in some form in outer life as well.

Usually recurrent dreams and nightmares have their origin in traumatic events or in situations of extreme stress. In such dreams, the urge for healing is quite strong, but so is the resistance, expressed by the ego which attempts to flee the situation out of fear of being overhelmed. It is likely that the more we flee or fear something, the more power we give to it. Dreamwork with nightmares and recurring dreams encourages us to work through the fear and to relate to the feared object in a context of divine healing.

In the Book of Job, it is said that Job underwent the worst disasters and misfortune possible, and still maintained his trust in God. Friends counseled Job to give up on God and live with his wounds in a kind of existential despair. He did not deny his wounds, but neither did he deny that healing was possible. Job not only accepted his suffering and suffered, he also insisted that God could heal his wounds and bring health, harmony, and fullness back to his life again. Job confronted the nightmare of his life and with God's help the nightmare was brought to resolution.

With certain dreams, especially conflictual and nightmarish ones, we are presented with our suffering as that which we would want to avoid. With many of these dreams, we are also presented with potentials for healing and new life.

Most nightmares and recurring dreams do not resolve themselves. For healing to occur, work needs to be done by the conscious and committed sides of ourselves. Choosing to work with our dreams in a healing context and allowing resolution to come to them, and through them to our waking lives, is in itself an experience of miracle. Let us now look at a man's nightmare and his subsequent dreamwork.

Healing a Nightmare Through Dreamwork

A Catholic priest came to one of the authors because he had a recurrent nightmare which concerned him greatly. The nightmare replayed a scene that had happened to him in waking life during the war. The dream was so powerful that once recently it even broke into his waking consciousness. The dream is told as follows.

> I am in Vietnam and hear the helicopters coming in with the wounded and dying at around two in the afternoon. I immediately go to the chapel to get the things I use in administering the sacrament of last rites to those who are dead or dying. I go down the corridor to the receiving room of the hospital where they bring in the wounded. But before I can enter the door, the dream stops and I wake up.

It had been ten years since this priest had been in the war zone, yet the dream continued to reoccur. The time it broke into his waking consciousness, he had been walking down the corridor of a building and had heard a helicopter outside nearby. He described this experience as "going into a trance completely beyond my control."

We decided to do a guided dream re-entry, a powerful technique for dealing with trauma revealed by nightmares. Together we closed our eyes and the priest was asked to see again the scene as it happened in his dream.

The scene replayed itself. He came to the receiving room door where the dream usually stopped and woke him up. As the dream re-entry guide, I asked him if he would like to go into the room this time and see what was there. Still in the meditative dream re-entry state, he entered the room, described the doctors and all the wounded soldiers lying about, and then he left.

His departure seemed too hasty to allow significant feelings to develop, so I asked him to enter the room again. "This time let your eyes focus on something."

He then saw a soldier lying on a gurney table, the top of his head all in bandages. The priest went over to the soldier and moved the bandage slightly to see who the soldier was. A doctor scolded him for touching the bandages, saying that the soldier's brains might fall out.

Nevertheless, in the dream re-entry, the priest had recognized the dying soldier as a Catholic young man he had met two weeks earlier in the camp. At that time, they had talked happily about how they were both going home within a month. The soldier had shown him a photo of his wife and young daughter. Now the priest realized that the soldier would never go home to his family or to life, and he gave the soldier the last sacraments.

This dream re-entry scene had filled the priest with strong feelings. "Why did this happen?" he asked. "This war seems utterly senseless."

I suggested to the priest that he could, still in his waking dream, go to the altar in his chapel and have a dialogue with God, where he might express anger or whatever emotions he found he had—which he did, privately. After the dream re-entry and his dialogue at the altar, he felt relief.

Afterward we had a long talk. The questions and feelings he had blocked because they seemed too horrible had been revealed and accepted. He said he could now accept that this senseless war and other evils of the world must somehow be included in God's plan. When in dialogue with God he had asked God, "How could you let this happen?" the answer was that *it did happen* and that God let it happen, or rather could not stop such things from happening. He also learned in his dialogue that humans, the priest included, could not stop things like this from happening. There always was and always will be tragedy to deal with on earth.

The recurring nightmare reminded him that the initial response he took of blocking the whole experience was, in the long run, not acceptable to him or to God. True, the enormity of the incident and the challenge to the priest's religious beliefs and practices made him block what seemed unbearable. But also true was the push for truth and healing called for by the recurrent nightmare, until finally the priest found a way to participate in healing. The immanence of God may be observed in the persistence of the dream demanding help. God's strongest calls to healing and wholeness often come through the voice of our suffering. The dreamer fled, perhaps had to flee, from the truth, and even from God in certain ways. But the dream kept coming back, indicating, if you choose to see it this way, that God did not desert this human being and wanted his healing.

In discussion, it turned out that because the priest had become afraid to dream this nightmare again, he had developed a pattern of light sleeping, getting up many times during the night to go to the bathroom. In the past few years he had also developed diabetes and wondered, after doing dreamwork, if he had not acquired his disease in order not to let himself sleep long enough to have a dream. But of course the traumatic nightmare came to him anyway and at last, with help, he dealt with it. Since the dreamwork, he reports sleeping well at night and having many dreams.

A Spiritual Perspective in Healing

We have included this powerful example to show the extent to which healing is possible with dreams and dreamwork. It also shows how closely spiritual issues and personality issues may be connected.

Most of the time a spiritual issue is involved in a recurring nightmare. Dreamwork is designed to make the spiritual issue conscious so that the dreamer may work at its resolution. The priest's nightmare brought up not only a personality issue, but a spiritual one as well.

In confronting his perception of God's role in the war as unacceptable, he had stepped into a question of destiny. Confronting the position he took on God's role in war invoked the largest or broadest perspective of his life: how he was living, or not living, in terms of his soul.

It was precisely his destiny to struggle with this theological issue and come to terms with it in his own life. He was tempted to deny or suppress his beliefs about God because the facts of the war did not fit into his religious picture of who God should be. But his dreams would not let him avoid the issue. The energy calling for its resolution disturbed his sleep as well as his waking life, and he was forced to deal with it. No ego, perhaps, is strong enough to deal with the great energies of life and death from within a purely personalistic view. His denial reopened the issue of his belief system. To explore his belief system was part of his present journey.

The nightmare was calling him to discover courage within to confront the task of dealing with the inadequacy of his belief system. For him, then, resolution had to take place on the personal level: recognizing and accepting how the particular psychological wound of the war experience affected him and his ability to function in waking life. Resolution also had to take place on the spiritual level of his soul, his relation to God, and the long-range purpose and direction of his life.

And while dreamwork will ask him to deal with the destiny question, "Why did this have to happen in my life?" dreamwork will also ask him to face spiritual and personality healing with other questions such as "What choices can I make to consciously experience the purpose of this event in my life?" and "What kind of spiritual perspective am I being asked to take in order to include even tragedies as part of the total web and purpose of my life within God's life?" Questions like these call for him not only to understand the issues involved but to integrate them consciously and actively into his life.

The Universal Need for Healing

While we cannot escape the fact that tragedies and deliberate evils happen, we cannot deny the fact that we who live on this earth can do much to cure ourselves and the world of certain woundednesses. In our dreams arise countless issues and conflicts needing resolution. (We can be deeply spiritual and committed persons, and yet there will be areas of our own beliefs and behavior which embarrass us or call into question our whole view of life and God.) Dreams and difficult life events do not come to embarrass us or cause us to feel completely inadequate. They bring with them also the potential for healing, for resolving conflicts, facing challenges, and creating new life and values. God is at work in every situation. We have the opportunity to cooperate in that work.

Dreamwork has been used effectively in aiding the resolution process. We know that it can work for many people, not only with daily issues and interpersonal conflicts, but also with destiny experiences such as trauma caused by war, accident, and crime. These things happen, but healing of even the worst situation is often possible.

Perhaps the major need today is for a strong commitment to bring healing and resolution into everything we do, as individuals, in community, with God, and in the world. What would it be like if the people of the world took as focus, not the maintaining of conflicts, the building of armaments, the fostering of hatred and differences, the maintaining of one's own position as the "right" position, but the working for unity and resolution, no matter how great the conflict seemed? We would not fear our neighbor. We would befriend our enemies. In dreams and dreamwork we learn to face our adversaries and establish new relationships with them. Can we afford to do less than this in the outer world?

Dreamwork Techniques That Help
Bring Resolution to a Major Issue

From time to time, people experience dreams which seem spontaneously to bring an important issue to a healing resolution. The woman's yacht dream, for example, suggested not only her major issue around trust, but also its possible resolution. In contrast, there are many other night dreams, such as the man's war nightmare, that remain conflictual and unresolved during sleep. Is it possible to find dreamwork techniques to deal with such unresolved dreams? The answer is yes.

The following four techniques—Choosing the Issue To Be Resolved, Dream Re-Entry, Carrying the Dream Forward, and Four Quadrants—are all useful in bringing resolution or fostering healing. Their main purpose is to foster the process of creating unity, harmony, and necessary change or rechanneling of energy in us and in our relationships. They are useful in working with nightmares, recurring dreams, and other major dreams.

Choosing the Issue To be Resolved and Four Quadrants are techniques that may be used by anyone. Dream Re-Entry and Carrying the Dream Forward, however, are recommended to be done alone only by those experienced in dreamwork or when facilitated by a therapist or spiritual director familiar with the techniques.

Rewriting an Unresolved Dream (Dreamwork Technique 18), which is often carried out after using Following the Dream Ego, is another resolution technique which may be used by anyone.

Resolution means not only the release of anger, pain, or any conflictual emotion, but a fundamental change in the underlying pattern causing the expression of that conflictual emotion. The major task in resolution through dreamwork, then, is to transform that conflictual and painful energy (emotion) into something useful, meaningful, valuable, joyful, peaceful, etc. Such a fundamental change can happen because through dreamwork we can learn to view the trauma or wound from the larger perspective of our destiny or purpose in life. In this way, we experience meaning, not just pain. Meaning allows the wound and its energy to be transformed into an integral part of our history; it allows the personality and the soul to own the wound as valuable, and to integrate it into who we are.

For example, many people feel anger toward their parents for the treatment they received during childhood. In therapy, they may learn to vent this anger in non-destructive ways. But when true resolution happens, they are able to view their parents from a new perspective, one that is not so personal. No longer is the issue simply "something that shouldn't have happened in my life, something I didn't deserve," but the wounds of the parents are somehow integrated into the destiny of the children.

Dreamwork Technique 26: Choosing the Issue To Be Resolved

Each dream has a potential for bringing about resolution, but since a dream usually presents a number of major or minor issues, it is important to decide which issues to focus on in any dreamwork involving resolution. Resolution is a process, and it also requires a commitment of time and energy. Selecting the issue and making a commitment are both functions of the waking ego, so this preparatory dreamwork technique is usually carried out in waking consciousness.

Dreamwork Technique 26
Choosing the Issue To Be Resolved

Procedure:
1. In the waking state, identify and list the major and minor issues that surfaced in the dream, then choose those you would like to work with. It is best to formulate questions or issues in the language of the dream itself. They should involve both the behavior of the dream ego and the major conflicts or lack of resolution in the dream itself.

2. Clarify your commitment, specifying how far you plan to go with the resolution process. For example, "Will I continue until some kind of resolution or breakthrough happens?" "Will I stop when I feel blocked or overwhelmed?" "Will I focus my effort on this particular aspect of the larger issue?" etc.

3. Make your commitment to the process, choosing your attitude toward the process, and the time you will spend on the process.

4. Follow this technique with one or other resolution technique, e.g., Dreamwork Techniques 18, 27, 28, 29.

Dreamwork Technique 27: Dream Re-Entry

A dream may be looked at as a drama made up of scenes happening in a certain order. If a drama is incomplete, the author may add a few more scenes to bring the plot to resolution. If the play's dramatic movement feels unsatisfactory or unresolved, the author may enter the drama somewhere in the middle, where things have not yet become blocked, and reconstruct the rest of the play in a completely new way. In Dream Re-Entry, we are like the author who reconstructs the play; we also play the parts of the actors who dramatize the new scenario.

In an earlier technique (No. 18), we suggested a redramatization of an unresolved dream by rewriting it. Here we ask you to *re-enter the dream material in a waking-dream state,* inviting the old dream to work itself to resolution in a new, healing way. This approach is more fluid and open than the rewriting process. Here are some suggestions to facilitate it.

In doing Dream Re-Entry, maintain a spiritual and religious perspective. Treat the technique as you would a period of prayer or meditation. Locate yourself in a quiet place that provides some sense of healing for you. Spend a few moments meditating, getting centered, writing in your dream journal, or doing some other ritual that would keep you aware of a spiritual presence.

Let your intention be clear and open-ended. Be open to any resolution that could be healing for you, not merely to one that you specifically want. Dream re-entry is not just an ego process. But the ego can do an important service by adopting an open attitude and allowing the dream re-entry to become an interaction between the dream ego, the inner self, and the soul. This technique's purpose is not to manufacture a happy ending to an otherwise scary dream, but to allow an authentic response to develop.

The dream ego is not meant to be helpless in Dream Re-Entry. We can't expect every dream to come out with a happy ending, but we can invite the dream ego to enter fully the dream's dynamics. In this process, which is a cooperative one rather than a controlling one, the waking ego and the dream ego, without trying to control what happens, clearly intend to take a more active, assertive, and focused part in the re-entry than they did in the original dream.

If the re-entry seems likely to be scary, then, at the place where you expect to encounter strong forces and feel inadequate to deal with them by yourself, *take some healing character, figure, or symbol with you in spirit as you re-enter the dream*—someone you know would be willing to be there with you. For example, children might take their parents with them, or someone they know and trust. Of course, you may always take with you some healing symbol such as a cross, a spiritual figure, a light, a stone, holy water, a lamp, etc.

Some people do dream re-entry while *listening quietly to some suitable music,* using its mood and its drama to foster the re-entry.

Some people prefer to do dream re-entry *with the assistance of a facilitator*—a therapist, spiritual director, or dreamwork partner—who would provide a supportive presence as they do a re-entry. Some choose to describe the re-entry process aloud to the facilitator as it is happening to them.

Dreamwork Technique 27
Dream Re-Entry

Procedure:

1. Keeping in mind the suggestions given above, take a reverential attitude in a quiet and restful place where you are not likely to be disturbed.

2. Close your eyes, breathe in a relaxed way, and let all distractions drift away. Then visualize the dream scene where you wish to begin. Get a feel for the characters and the setting. Focus on details. Go slowly. If your images are not clear, let them be what they are. Keep the story going the way it happened in the original dream.

3. When you come to the difficult place—where the most energy is or where the energy seems to be blocked—let your dream ego assert itself and interact fully with the dream figures. Be open to new imagery and action stimulated by the dream source, as the dream seeks to resolve itself.

4. Cooperate with the dream energy, trusting that it will bring you to a healing resolution. We trust because of the spiritual nature of the process.

5. When the new dream comes to some stopping place, acknowledge God for the experience, and journal it as if it were a new dream.

6. If resolution doesn't happen naturally, the experience is still valuable, for it helped you focus on dream content and realize the important issues.

For Facilitators of a Dream Re-Entry. We are assuming that you feel comfortable guiding someone else, because of your own training and spiritual work. As a facilitator, please do not try to make something happen for the person you are helping, even if you want to. Guiding means being with the person, asking questions from time to time to make things clear, and in moments of blockage and transition offering statements of possible alternative choices. You may also close your eyes with the person in order to visualize the process and receive intuitions about new possibilities.

Dreamwork Technique 28: Carrying the Dream Forward

This is a resolution technique most often applied to nightmares, which are essentially incomplete dreams. Whereas Dream Re-Entry is designed to redramatize a complete but unsatisfactory dream, Carrying the Dream Forward is designed to complete an unfinished dream. It answers the question: What happened after that?

In this technique, we enter the waking dream state to let the dream imagery continue forward, to add a new chapter, so to speak, to the original dream. It allows the energy of the original dream to play itself out and present potentials never realized in the original dream experience.

For example, perhaps in a night dream I find myself in a storm-tossed ship at sea, and wake up in fear of being blown overboard and drowned. In this technique, in an attitude of openness to what might happen next, I place myself back on the storm-tossed ship, with or without a protective figure, to wait out the storm and see where the ship might take me. Perhaps the ship is destroyed and I find myself swimming, and I deal with that. Or perhaps the storm gives wind to the sails and I arrive at a new port full of things I have never seen or done before. Whatever happens, I am *allowing my dream source to complete the action* by keeping myself fully present to the dream and even participating actively in it. This dreamwork technique may also be titled Completing a Nightmare.

Dreamwork Technique 28
Carrying the Dream Forward
(Completing a Nightmare)

Procedure:

1. Locate yourself in a quiet, healing setting, and let your intention be to be present to the unfinished dream and to allow it to come to a healing resolution.

2. In imagination, in a meditative state with eyes closed, allow the original dream to play out its drama in your imagination. Focus on details. Go slowly. Get in touch with the feelings that surfaced in the original dream.

3. When the dream comes to its overwhelming part, the part where you originally woke up, encourage the dream ego, perhaps accompanied by a healing symbol and a protective figure, to remain courageous and strong, and let the dream continue as a waking dream. (It is said that nightmares, when allowed to complete themselves, turn out to be either healing dreams or heroic dreams—where the dream ego expresses heroic capacities, healing capacities, or both.)

4. After the new dream reaches a suitable stopping place, you might say a word of gratitude to God, journal the new ending, and do dreamwork techniques that tend to foster healing.

Dreamwork Technique 29:
Four Quadrants

Four Quadrants has a number of advantages as a resolution technique. It may be used by beginners as well as more advanced dreamworkers. It is rather simple and takes relatively little time to do. It uses graphic presentation, which keeps the dreamwork at a symbolic level and makes it easier to grasp. It may be used as a preamble to Carrying the Dream Forward, because it effectively grasps the dream's essential points, issues, and movements. It gets right to the heart of the dream experience. It may also be used to deal with a night dream whose ending seems unsatisfactory, especially because of an unassertive dream ego.

Dreamwork Technique 29
Four Quadrants

Procedure:

1. On a large piece of paper draw lines to separate the page into four equal parts numbering them I, II, III, IV, to represent four stages or quadrants of a dream.

2. Review the drama and action of the night dream requiring resolution, and mentally divide it into *three* acts.

3. In Quadrant I sketch some symbols, figures, or characters that represent the energies and issues portrayed in the first act of your night dream. Do the same for the second and third quadrants.

4. Rest meditatively for a few minutes with what you have produced. At this point, it often helps to give a descriptive title to each of the three quadrants.

5. Next, allow yourself meditatively to focus on the empty fourth quadrant as if another act were needed to bring full resolution to the drama. Wait for symbols for the fourth quadrant to begin to appear in your imagination, then sketch those symbols as you did for the first three. Title your fourth quadrant, and reflect on the process for a few minutes. How does what you have done feel to you? What values and insights have surfaced?

6. You may want to do some basic dreamwork on the new material such as Key Questions or Following the Dream Ego (being sure to compare the dream ego's actions in all four quadrants).

7. Share your experience with others who are working on their dreams or using this technique. In sharing, it is important that no one comments on or interprets anyone else's dream or artwork.

I	II
III	IV

Part III

Relating to the Community Through Dreams and Dreamwork

◆

Chapter 13

Dreamwork and the Christian Community: Dreams and the Holy Spirit

◆

The Community Dimension of Dreamwork

Throughout Part II we explored the personal dimensions of dreams and dreamwork. There is also a community dimension to our life-stories and our journeys as revealed in dreams, and that is the focus of Part III.

As individuals each of us emerges into the world within a network of interrelationships. We come to understand the meaning and purpose of our journey in the context of community. We cannot take our journey except as part of the interrelated network of other individual journeyers. Thus, even in our journey each of us is an individual in a community. Every individual's journey is part of the community's journey.

In what sense do my dreams belong to the community and the community's dreams belong to me? Can I be involved in the community's dreamwork? Can the community be involved in mine? These and many other questions like them are important for Christians, whose vision and theology is fundamentally that of a community.

A Christian Perspective

For Christians, God's covenant and call is to a people, not only to individuals. We are called by God and toward God *always in relationship.* The Kingdom of God is to come about by the combined efforts of all those who are related in friendship and love. Living and working together causes the dynamics of growth in holiness and wholeness to happen to us, individually and in community.

Christianity is a religion of the Spirit. It teaches that the divine Spirit comes into us collectively and individually to enliven us, bond us together, and build us into a loving community. The divine Spirit's gifts may take the form of visions, inspirations, and experiences of the divine presence, but the most common way is through dreams.

Paul and the Holy Spirit

If we apply Paul the apostle's theology of gifts to our understanding of the dream as a gift of God, we can clearly see the community aspect of dreamwork. In writing to the Corinthians, Paul makes three simple points for dealing with gifts of the Holy Spirit (see 1 Cor 12:4–7).

Paul's first observation is that *all gifts, whether special or ordinary, come from the Holy Spirit.* For this reason, we treat all of our gifts, including our dreams, with reverence and gratitude, not belittling or stifling them.

Second, says Paul, *all gifts are given for the benefit of the community.* The Holy Spirit's task in the world is to build the human community into a mature, loving totality, which Paul calls the body of Christ. For us, to cooperate with God's Spirit is to use the energies and insights released in our dreams to nurture the community.

Looked at from an individual perspective, a dream may seem only to be helping us personally and individually, say, deal with a trust issue. Looked at from a community perspective, the same dream may be suggesting that our ability to trust ourselves and others is essential to building loving relationships with others.

For example, a woman dreamed she was being offered the gift of a spaniel puppy. Its owner told her, in the dream, that if she did not take the puppy, he would have to put it to sleep. Her dream ego was in a quandary. On the one hand, spaniels were not among her favorite pets and, besides, she didn't want the responsibility of caring for a puppy since it would probably hinder her present life style. On the other hand, she didn't want to see the puppy die.

When she looked at the dream from a social aspect, she realized that being offered the puppy ("man's best friend") symbolized an offer of friendship she had received the day before from a lonely person, and about which she had mixed feelings. The potential friend was, like the puppy, not attractive to her, yet she felt uncomfortable and selfish at the thought of rejecting the person.

When she looked at her dream from a larger community perspective, she realized that the puppy symbolized all the lonely and uncared for people in her community looking for friendship and care. The dream asked her to become conscious of her attitude toward the members of the community who "were not among her favorites."

Certain dreams call us to be aware of community needs such as poverty, hunger, crime, unemployment, discrimination, sickness, and other forms of social injustice.

Other dreams, like those of the Old Testament prophets, may speak of visions for the community, calling it to greater consciousness and responsibility. In our own day, Martin Luther King announced before his death that he had been to the mountain top and had received a dream. "I have a dream that all people will one day live as brothers and sisters in peace and harmony" was its visionary theme.

Third, Paul asserted that the value of *each special gift is to be judged by its usefulness to the community.* The more a gift helps build community, he said, the more valuable it is to the community. It is perhaps because of this community principle that most of the dreams and visions which have been preserved in the Bible contain wisdom that is useful and beneficial to the community. Through dreamwork we recognize and develop the gift of love, as well as the special gifts of prophecy, wisdom, and understanding that are given to us in dreams from God's Spirit.

A Dream's Value to Others

In this part of our book, we suggest how our dreams bring us into relation with other people, first with our families and friends, and then with the larger community.

We hope that people will keep in mind that the wisdom of their dreams may be of value to others. For example, again and again in workshops and seminars, after individuals have shared their dream and dreamwork, others in the group remark how insightful that dream had been for them.

History is full of anecdotes about dreams of scientists, artists, inventors, business people, which have transformed some part of our civilization and thus benefited the community. There are also the biblical dreams to which generations of Christians have returned in order to find new energy for their faith and life journey. We are frequently indebted to the dreams of strangers for the wisdom and growth we enjoy.

The Senoi Dream People

Psychologist-anthropologist Kilton Stewart researched the customs of a mountain people, living in the Malay Peninsula, called the Senoi, who for centuries have built their community life and culture around dreams and dreamwork.

According to Stewart, each morning all the members of a Senoi family would gather to share their dreams. Beginning with the youngest, each person would tell a night dream he or she had while the rest of the family listened; after the dream was told, the eldest in the family gave thanks for the dream, hinted at its meaning for the individual *and the community,* and assigned the dreamer a task to perform which usually involved other members of the community, or some service that would benefit the community. The energy expressed in each dream—whether it was angry or peaceful, customary or taboo, welcome or seemingly unwelcome—was interpreted positively as energy that could be used to build community. The community leaders would also gather each day to share their dreams, to gain wisdom for governing and serving their people.

Remarkably, the Senoi were living without any equivalent of jails or mental institutions; they reported that their community had been without mental illness or major crime for hundreds of years.

The Senoi secret is, of course, the integration of dreams and dreamwork into their daily life, and viewing the dream as gift bearing important energy to build community.

We have adapted a number of dreamwork principles attributed to the Senoi for use in Christian dreamwork. Primary among their principles is the importance of doing dreamwork daily. Another is the assigning of personality tasks and community tasks to utilize the energy released in a dream. A third underlines the value of using artistic media as a way of symbolizing and sharing the dream with others. It is also from the Senoi people that we clearly learned to identify nightmares as incomplete dreams and, when completed, gifting us with healing and heroic energies. Finally, it is to the Senoi that we can trace the idea of doing dreamwork with a supportive group of people.[1] All of these principles are "naturally" Christian and indeed complement the dreamwork techniques handed on to us in our own Christian tradition.

Dreamwork Technique 30
Looking for Social Dimensions of a Dream

Procedure:

If it is true that God gives dreams to benefit the community, we may explore our dreams for their social implications. Dreams often ask us to look at our lives in light of the larger community. The word "community" has a variety of meanings; it may refer to our relationships and family, school or work settings, neighborhood or congregation, or larger segments of society. This dreamwork technique may be applied to community in all of those meanings.

Looking for the social dimensions in a dream is appropriate after doing basic dreamwork on a personal level. Here are some questions to facilitate reflection on a dream from a social perspective. Choose one or more of them to respond to.

1. How can this dream be a gift to my family, my congregation, my community?

2. How does this dream call me to foster the growth of the community? To act responsibly in the community?

3. Is there some way through this dream that my family or community is asking something of me?

4. Have I recently experienced conflicts or confrontations in family or community settings? If so, how might this dream be putting me in touch with my social rights and responsibilities?

5. Have I recently received affirmations or signs of esteem for my talents from family or community members? If so, how might this dream be confirming the fact that I have been using my talents to benefit the community?

Sharing Ourselves with Others

Working on our dreams with others, for example, with a dream group of peers or with a dreamwork partner, allows us to experience ourselves in a supportive context; such a context is additionally enriching because we also learn what is happening to others in their dreams and dreamwork. In sharing dream material not only do we experience the way the voice of the Spirit reaches us, but we get to experience how the voice of the Spirit is enlivening the lives of our fellow dreamworkers.

Besides, we are more likely to do dreamwork if there is someone willing to hear about it and validate the experience with us.

Here are some of the comments dreamwork group members have made after working together over a period of time: "I began to see my life—and life in general—as more rich and varied." "I began to view tensions and conflicts in my life as interesting and challenging, rather than a burden." "I developed a great reverence for dreamwork, and the time we spent together was like a sacred time, a period of soul-sharing."

From another standpoint, dreamwork groups helped individuals develop a number of personal skills, which they were able to use in other areas of their lives. Among the skills reportedly developed were: learning to listen more actively; learning to formulate questions; learning to work together without taking over control of the group; getting practice in analytic thinking, creative thinking, choicemaking, and intuition; learning how to recognize and identify different kinds of energies; learning to suggest tasks that respond to existing energies; learning to tell stories; learning how to get meaning out of symbols; learning to confront people and challenge them; learning to accept and affirm people.

The following dreamwork techniques suggest ways to interact with a dreamwork partner or in a dreamwork group.

Dreamwork Technique 31: Working with a Dreamwork Partner

When choosing a dreamwork partner, look for someone who is:
- *readily available,* someone who has the time and is agreeable to using it with you in dreamwork.
- *willing to reciprocate,* someone who not only will help you search

for the meaning of your dream, but who wants you to do the same for him or her.

- *respectful of you,* someone who takes a reverential attitude toward your personality and your spiritual journey.

- *imaginative,* someone who will ask stimulating questions and suggest interesting personality, family, and community tasks.

- *trustworthy and trusting,* someone from whom you would welcome a task suggestion and by whom you would not feel judged.

- *a good visualizer,* someone who can picture your dream in their imagination as you tell it, and asks for clarification when it is needed.

- *creative and helpful,* someone who knows something about dreamwork (or is willing to learn) and is willing to suggest techniques that would help further your understanding of your dream.

- *sensitive,* someone who senses when to listen, when to ask a question, when to encourage, and when to make suggestions for dreamwork or outer-life tasks.

- *matched to you,* someone who is willing to work at your speed, geared to your level of commitment, and interested in dreamwork for some of the same reasons you are.

It often takes a while for partners to get used to each other's style, so there is value in a sustained dreamwork relationship. Familiarity with a number of your dreams also allows your partner to help make connections between current dreams and past ones.

We also recommend that dreamwork time be set aside and treated as if it were a time of shared prayer, which in a sense it is.

Dreamwork Technique 31
Working with a Dream Partner

Procedure:

1. When the two of you come together, recall your interest, enthusiasm, and reverence for the work you are about to do. You may choose to acknowledge God's presence and ask that the Holy Spirit bless and energize your dreamwork.

2. For sharing, choose one dream that occurred since the last time you met with your partner, and tell it to your partner as clearly as

you can, either by reading it from your journal or describing it spontaneously.

3. Your partner may ask clarifying questions, if necessary, to make sure that the dream images in your mind are the ones that are in his or hers. For example, if you said, "I stopped by the side of the road to pick up some hitchhikers," it may help to clarify how many hitchhikers there were, how they were dressed, how old they were, whether they were male and/or female, etc. It is surprising how often others presume they know exactly what you're describing when they really don't. And it would be helpful for the dreamer to be in touch with additional clarifying details. But do not get lost in details.

4. Share with your partner your general feelings about the dream and whatever dreamwork you may have already done with it.

5. Your partner may ask you which of the issues brought up by the dream you would like to deal with. When that has been clarified, your partner and you may suggest some of the dreamwork techniques you might try in order to deepen your understanding of the dream. While some of these techniques such as Dialoguing or Following the Dream Ego will be appropriate homework, others, such as Carrying the Symbol Forward or Key Questions, might be carried out during the session. Getting a partner's perspective is usually fresh and stimulating, for often a partner sees things you don't see. In addition to all the dreamwork techniques described in this book, your own creativity may generate others to use that are more appropriate to your dream and your personality.

6. When some further steps have been made toward understanding the meaning of your dream in light of your personality, your soul and the needs of the community, express gratitude to your partner, and change roles—becoming the listener while your partner articulates his or her chosen dream.

7. Close by acknowledging God's gift in your dreams and dreamwork.

8. Once your dream sharing sessions become regular, it is helpful to spend the first few minutes of each new session sharing dreamwork done since the last meeting. Partners are more likely to do their dreamwork if they know they will be asked to talk about it at the following session. Sharing dreamwork like this also helps maintain continuity in the process.

Some Suggestions for Dreamwork Partners

Be sure to allot an equal amount of shared dreamwork time to each partner, unless because of special circumstances you agree to spend most of the time together on one person's dream.

To underline the community nature of dreams, it is often helpful to ask your partner, just before you switch roles, "Does my dream have any symbolic meaning for your life? Do you relate to any of the issues or energies it brought up?" This final nuance in the dreamwork often brings up new material for both the dreamer and the listener.

To help a dreamwork partner (or partners in a dreamwork group) remain supportive, rather than dominating, a few requests are in order:

1. Try not to place *your* interpretation of another's dream or his or her personality onto that dream. You may have a sudden intuition about what another's dream means, but remember, that's your experience, not the dreamer's. Your task as a partner is to help that partner more fully experience his or her dream, rather than for you to give your interpretations of it.

2. If you do have intuitions or even projections about the meaning of others' dreams, don't announce your thoughts to them. Instead, turn them into questions ("Could this dream be asking you to look at issues between you and your spouse?"), or suggest them as possible tasks they might consider doing ("Would it be helpful for you to make a list of the things about which you and your spouse disagree?"). Then observe what feelings and reactions are evoked from them.

3. Do not judge the dreamwork of others as good or bad; instead, support them in working at resolving the issues their dreams bring up.

Dreamwork partners are often invaluable. Many times people have written a dream in their journal and commented, "I can't make any sense out of that dream." And then, when they began to articulate it to their dreamwork partner and the partner began to ask questions and suggest tasks, the significance of the dream began to dawn upon them.

Even some of the greatest dreamers and dream interpreters could not understand some of their own dreams, and had to seek help from another person.

Creating a Dreamwork Group

Dreamwork groups are meant to be supportive. Most people understand group sessions as places to offer and receive questions, task-suggestions, and alternatives for developing new points of view toward issues brought up by dreams.

We have found through experience that even in a dreamwork group of peers, someone needs to serve as group leader for each session. This task may be rotated among the group members, but someone needs to be responsible for managing the group's use of time during a session and seeing that the group work gets done.

The leader's role is primarily devoted to asking questions and suggesting tasks. Other group members may also ask questions, suggest tasks, and make affirmations, but it is the leader's responsibility to initiate this process and see that dreamwork tasks are suggested for each dream. It is the dreamer's responsibility to choose which task suggestions to work with. Tasks are merely suggested, not assigned, by others.

The leader's role is also to structure the group's response and participation, keeping it balanced and supportive. The leader stays aware of the time, making sure that each person scheduled to share a dream during that session has enough time to do so. Usually it is best to have each member share a dream during a session, even if there are only a few minutes for processing each dream.

The leader is also responsible for enacting the opening ritual or ceremony the group chooses to use to help each person leave outside activities behind and open up to a more meditative attitude suitable for sharing dreams and dreamwork. The leader keeps the group on the task of moving forward with the dreamwork.

It is important that a dream group not be too large: three or four is an ideal size; five or six is already getting large if you expect to have each person in the group work on a dream each session. It is not unusual for a dream group to be larger, especially when the leader is a professional or elder who tends simply to offer interpretations of the members' dreams. But, in our approach, where each person does his or her own dreamwork while the others support, question, affirm, and suggest tasks, it is good to allow twenty to thirty minutes to deal adequately with each person's dream. If you don't want your sessions to last longer than two or two and a half hours, work with a three or four member group. If there are six people interested in group dreamwork, either schedule sessions to last for three hours, or form two smaller groups.

Suggestions for choosing appropriate group members are the same as those for choosing a dream partner (see Dreamwork Technique 31).

Dreamwork Technique 32
Structuring a Dreamwork Group Session

Procedure:

1. The group leader facilitates the group's transition into an attitude of reverence and a sense of the sacred: from focus on the outer world to focus on the inner world. We suggest a few minutes of meditation with spiritual music followed by lighting a candle and a short, appropriate reading. In this way, the group would be acknowledging God's presence and their relation to the divine Source, affirming each person's dreams as a gift of God, and renewing the group's commitment to dreamwork and their bonding to each other.

2. Although the program of a dream group session may vary greatly, we suggest that, for the sake of continuity, the group spend the first part of the session, say fifteen to thirty minutes, on what has happened to group members during the past week as a result of dreams shared during the last session and dreamwork done in the meantime. Affirm and support each person's process and the work they are doing.

3. Next, in whatever order pleases the group, let people share, in turn, one new dream. Let one member at a time be focused upon, responding to questions other members ask to help objectify and clarify details of the dream, and receiving suggestions for more dreamwork and/or tasks to work on during the coming week. When that member is finished, let another become the center of attention.

4. When all have shared, the leader may acknowledge the energy that surfaced in their midst during the session, and recall how the members related to it, worked with it, and attempted to make it useful in their daily lives. Close the session by extinguishing the candle and inviting members into meditation or a spontaneous or formal prayer, perhaps while holding hands in a circle.

Celebrating Dreamwork

It is also helpful for an ongoing dreamwork group or partnership to schedule a few times each year an extended session. This might involve a half day, whole day, or a weekend during which each member of the group presents a special project reflecting and celebrating what has happened for them over the past months in their dreamwork and in their daily lives on important, personal issues. Some people may bring artwork, poetry, and music that relates their major dream themes. Some may be wearing clothing or jewelry that relates to their dreamwork. Others may read significant passages from their dream journals. Still others may choose to dance or dramatize for the group what has been happening to them. This kind of sharing in community adds a symbolic dimension to the personal celebration of spiritual growth.

Such a summary and celebratory session often has deep meaning for the participants, for it allows them to see and share significant changes in their personalities and spiritual lives occasioned by their dreams, their dreamwork, and their dreamwork partners. They are publicly affirming that they are bringing healing, resolution, and meaning into their lives and into their communities.

Note to Chapter 13
Dreamwork and the Christian Community
1. Kilton Stewart's original paper on the Senoi, "Dream Theory in Malaya," was reprinted conveniently in Charles T. Tart, ed., *Altered States of Consciousness* (New York: Wiley, 1969). Summary treatment of Senoi dreamwork principles may be found in Strephon Kaplan Williams' *Jungian-Senoi Dreamwork Manual*, pp. 281–284.

Chapter 14

Dreamwork and Holiness: The Spiritual Director's Perspective

◆

Spiritual Directors and the Spirit

The spiritual director knows that behind the forms and structures of the Church there is spirit—human spirit and divine spirit.

Where there is spirit, there is communion and relationship; energies manifest themselves, souls are shaped, and communities are built.

The spiritual director stands in close relation to the soul of the individual and to the soul of the community, helping one stay connected to the other. Individuals move from one phase of spiritual growth to another, always in the context of community. In helping individuals understand new experiences in the light of their destiny and adjust to their roles and responsibilities in the community, the spiritual director operates not primarily as a director but as a guide, a listener and a connector of spirits.

"Spiritual directors and gurus have always been listeners," writes Kenneth Leech in *Soul Friend,* "but the language to which they listen is the 'forgotten language' of myths and dreams and symbols, the language of fundamental human experience."[1]

From the time of the early Church theologians and the origins of monastic life, the great spiritual guides began to explore the unfathomable depths of the conscious and unconscious in the human person. It was recognized that from these depths, in the sea of the soul, the Holy Spirit comes to us and visits us. Within these depths the work of spiritual direction is carried on.

Dreams and Holiness

We do not intend in this book to define the role and enumerate the duties of a spiritual director. We simply propose some ways by which dreams and dreamwork can be used in spiritual direction to intensify spiritual growth, and thus foster the process of holiness and the eager acceptance of one's unfolding destiny.

Holiness is a focal word in this chapter, wholeness in the next. Although these terms have developed a separate meaning, probably because of differentiation in the training of psychological and spiritual service professionals, they find their etymological heritage in the same Anglo-Saxon stem or root. From the Anglo-Saxon word *hāl* arise the words (1) hale, heal, and health, (2) whole (and holistic), and (3) holy. Thus, to be *hāl* is at once to partake of health, wholeness, and holiness. It is a premise of this approach to dreamwork that both God and we want ourselves to be *hāl* physically, psychologically, spiritually, and in community.

The Religious Perspective

For us, dreams ultimately come from a source larger than our own ego, intellect, imagination, or reflective self-understanding. Although dreams happen in us, we are not their sole creators. They are given to us as a resource. Primarily, we prepare for and respond to dreams. The intentional methodological preparation and response we make to a dream is called dreamwork.

Although our ego, or choice-making capacity, initiates dreamwork, we also recognize that dreamwork tunes us in to other sources and resources than the ego. Dreamwork is not merely an intellectual enterprise; dreamwork is more than the ego simply carrying out process techniques from its own conscious point of view. Dreamwork, for us, is indeed a time of encounter with God. More precisely, in doing dreamwork techniques, the ego is responding to and evoking the original dream Source in order to have the dream come more fully present and produce some elements of its meaning and significance for understanding our destiny.

In the Old Testament Book of Daniel, for example, Daniel acknowledges not only that dreams come from God but also that the *meaning* of dreams is a gift of God. Daniel's ability to understand and interpret the dream comes from God. And when he is doing what we call dreamwork, he is in relationship to God.

In this book, we work with dreams in a spiritual and religious context. For us, dreamwork is indeed time spent in the presence of God. This allows us to develop a fuller meaning and significance of dreams than if we approached dreams simply from a psychological or personalistic point of view. We, of course, affirm that dreams and dreamwork reveal much about our personality. Dreams often mirror our behavior patterns, attitudes, traits, new potentials, life experiences, important issues, and areas of growth. Dreams indeed reflect the inner push toward what we call wholeness that is at work in our lives. What we also want to affirm is that, because dreams come from a Source greater than us, the very act of doing dreamwork requires a spiritual and religious perspective, for in dreams and dreamwork we are in touch with a transcendent energy urging us toward personal and social wholeness. This energy comes from God.

Maintaining a religious context in doing dreamwork means we keep acknowledging that the energy for wholeness and holiness is of God and comes from God, as a gift to ourselves and the community. Through our free choice, we can express this energy in realizing personal and social potentials in our daily lives.

Guiding the Spiritual Journey

From what we have learned thus far, it is clear that dreams and dreamwork could help consolidate and confirm other work a spiritual director does to help persons on their spiritual journey. Dreams share some of the key characteristics of your spiritual journey and that of your client. Every person's spiritual journey is *unique,* and so are our dreams. Every person's spiritual journey is *ongoing, evolving;* our dreams reflect our evolving journey every day, at every step along the way. And every person's spiritual journey is *full of surprises,* which often means struggles, challenges, and conflicts; and just as often traditional customs and teaching do not respond directly to our needs. Dreams are ready for any and all surprises, and offer wisdom and alternatives for dealing with difficult issues that have no ready-made solutions.

Realistically, because of human nature's weakness, the tendency of most individuals in the face of the deepest call to live their journey and their destiny is to avoid, evade, and escape in many ways. Yet our dreams continue to call us to consciousness of who we are and who we are called to be. The deepest calls to spiritual growth occur when our minds and hearts are in an open and undefensive place; during night dreams we are in our most undefensive state and let rise into spontaneous awareness what is truly important to us.

Dreamwork and Spiritual Direction

We acknowledge that spiritual directors today have a very complicated role; among other things, they are often expected to understand much about the psychological life of a person.

The methods of dreamwork presented here may be reassuring to the guide in this context because they allow a guide and client to have access to significant growth experiences. Insights produced by clients doing dreamwork often help integrate psychological and spiritual development.

There are other supports to the guide's task in direction provided by dreamwork. This dreamwork approach can bring hope and optimism into the guide-seeker relationship. The dream is viewed as an intervention from God. It is a gift of consciousness, that is, a possibility for insight plus the energy to act on insight. The dream speaks to the whole person and as such integrates the person's calls to holiness and wholeness. The very premise of dreamwork done from a Christian perspective says that God can be present to me; each night God sends me a dream that is meant to nurture my growth and reassure me of God's love for me. I am reminded that even dreams which provoke anxiety and fear are, at a deeper level, experiences calling me to healing and to explore unknown depths of energy in order successfully to deal with the conflicts and troublesome issues in my life.

When sincerely done, dreamwork generates enthusiasm for life and development. It is a daily reminder that both God and we are working together to achieve the purpose for which we have been given the gift of life.

Applying Dreamwork Techniques to Other Areas

Such an open and optimistic attitude can spill over into other matters of spiritual direction which may not surface directly in dreams and dreamwork, but are daily life issues brought into the counseling session such as impatience, anger, irresponsibility, defiance of authority, harshness, lying or other forms of dishonesty, sexual issues, rebellion, jealousy, and so on. Just as a guide learns to ask "What is the *gift* in this dream?" and "What energy is being released in this dream?" and "What is being asked of you by this dream?" the guide can also learn to ask the same positive-oriented questions regarding painful issues or situations of failure: "What is the *gift or teaching* in this experience?" and "What energy is being released in you through that issue?" and "What is being asked of you in this situation?"

Thus, rather than focusing on failure and guilt, this approach focuses on the forgiveness (notice the *gift* in forgive) coming from God and the self, and on the energy to act in new ways being revealed in the situation. Thus, the pattern causing destructive acts is changed, not only by insight and feelings of repentance, but also by action and acceptance.

For example, a parent confessed to her spiritual director that she treated her child harshly at certain times. He asked her if she could identify the times of day it usually happened. She could. Then he asked what the gift was in her telling him this and in the harsh treatment she gave to her child. At first she was taken aback by the question. She said it sounded to her like asking, "What are the benefits from sin?" The guide acknowledged that the two questions were similar, and encouraged her to struggle with his question. She did, and produced not one but two possibilities. First, the situation reminded her of a list she had made many years before of the qualities of a good parent. Second, since the gift was coming from God, she was also being reminded that her child had a unique destiny in life just as much as she, and she wanted to help him be ready for that destiny. By the time the guide asked: "What energies are being released in you in these situations?" she was ready with her insight. "When I am harsh with my child," she said, "I have strong feelings. I want him to know that I care. Yes, there is a strong energy flowing in those moments." And the director asked: "How can you best put that strong, connecting, caring energy to work when it surfaces between you and him?"

Together they worked out a plan of action. He made suggestions, some of which she liked. She made a list of possible tasks she could choose to do with the energy she discovered. "The tasks," she said, "had to be things for my son and me to do together because it is a connecting energy. They also had to be actions where we are engaged as we do them. And they need to contain moments when I communicate my concern for his destiny, moments when our souls touch."

She discovered they could read together, or play games together, or work together in the kitchen, or even take a walk or a drive together. They could look through old photos, or plan parties, or go visiting someone special.

In this way, she was able to grow far beyond the stage of simply feeling sorry for her sins or her "failure as a mother." She went beyond contrition to good works, a very traditional Christian practice.

Having practiced basic dreamwork techniques such as TTAQ and Key Questions had helped her to deal with the spiritual guide's questions very productively. She was able to become conscious of the energy being released in her and of concrete ways to translate that energy into tasks that related her to her family and her community.

The Effectiveness of Tasks

Another prominent benefit of dreamwork for the guide-seeker relationship is to orient the counseling session toward *tasks,* i.e., actions the client chooses to carry out in light of the work done and insights gotten during the session. The principle behind doing tasks is that insight alone rarely changes people. Action, a commitment to try living differently, often does.

Suggesting appropriate tasks is an art. It involves designing tasks that both effectively utilize the energies being released and attract the personality of the client. Tasks need to be reasonable, realistic, and able to be accomplished in a finite amount of time. Tasks that are too simple and easy for people will simply not sufficiently engage the energy released; tasks that are too difficult, or where success cannot be measured in some way, tend to overwhelm people and discourage them. It takes much skill and practice to suggest an attractive series of tasks requiring increasing involvement and energy, and even more skill to know when to let up, shift gears, or stop entirely. Suggesting Tasks is the dreamwork technique presented next.

A counselor who has studied our dreamwork techniques said they were quite useful even when applied to other than dream material. She found herself, for example, asking clients at the end of a counseling session to take a few minutes to do a TTAQ applied to the session they had just completed. "It is remarkable how much more growth can happen to an individual in a few focused moments," she said.

So while we do encourage guides to use dreams and dreamwork for their own and their clients' spiritual growth, presuming, of course, that both director and client are comfortable with the idea and willing to try it, we are suggesting that the techniques we offer throughout the book have a wider usefulness and applicability.

Dreamwork done from a Christian perspective allows the guide to begin making connections between the client and the community, whether it is the believing community or the larger community, preferably both. Just as the Holy Spirit gives grace and energy for personal sanctification, so God releases energy in the dream that is meant for building up the total Kingdom of God in loving community. A principle well known in family systems' theory says that when an individual changes the whole system is affected. As each of us attains more wholeness, the human community responds and changes.

How To Introduce Clients to Dreamwork

Here are some suggestions to spiritual directors for introducing and using dreams and dreamwork with your clients. For those just beginning, begin gently.

You might suggest they meditate on some biblical dreams (see Chapter 6 on Waking Dreams) *and practice some basic dreamwork techniques on the meditational material produced.* For example, they may write down the images and feelings of the meditation, do TTAQ, Key Questions, Dialoguing and Following the Dream Ego. To maintain a reverential attitude during dreamwork, suggest that it might be done in the spirit of private prayer.

One reason we suggest this indirect approach to dreams and dreamwork at the outset is that many clients, especially middle-aged or older, will be afraid to do dreamwork because they were probably told somewhere along the way that observing dreams was either superstitious, forbidden, useless, misleading, occult, or satanic. It is startling what misconceptions people have about dreams and how they can almost permanently close their minds because of something heard spoken in childhood by a parent or a Sunday school teacher. To clarify historically the role of dreams and dreamwork in the Judaeo-Christian tradition was why we wrote the first part of our book. It will certainly be helpful for your clients to be aware of this tradition.

We have written this book for lay people and professionals alike. Thus, it would be important for clients interested in spiritual growth through dreams to begin working with the techniques and using the book as a reference. The spiritually transformative power of the book's content and techniques cannot be fully understood or experienced simply by reading the text. As a spiritual director, you may wish to guide clients through the book, emphasizing certain sections of it to certain clients and referring to the book's description of the methods when you suggest using them. By making their way experientially through the book, clients discover that working with their dreams is a very possible, practical, and profitable spiritual discipline.

Usually, clients are surprised to hear of dreams described as "gifts from God" or "the language of the soul" or "more a question than an answer" or "containing energy" or "God's personal revelation to us" or "God's way of building a relationship with us." Yet, in a Christian approach to dreams and dreamwork, this is what the early Church writers and theologians seemed to be saying, and it is what we as authors are saying based on a number of years of personal experience—our own and that of the people with whom we have worked.

While some people who intuitively sense the importance of dreams for their souls will be relieved and delighted to hear you describing dreams in such affirmative terms, others may find these descriptions surprising, and even upsetting; for many they demand a complete reversal of attitudes toward the dream, the irrational, and the unconscious.

Have the client do dreamwork on a major dream from their own life. It may be a recent dream, one many years old, or even a childhood dream. Dreams long remembered are usually important. Invite the client to write out the dream and do the techniques of TTAQ, Key Questions, Dialoguing and Following the Dream Ego, at least. Even if the client takes more than one or two sessions to do the dreamwork, it may well be worth it. Such a remembered dream probably has to do with destiny and will undoubtedly, with sufficient dreamwork, bring up the key issues and themes of the client's life journey. Again, encourage them to treat dreamwork time as prayerful experience.

Choose a few past dreams from the client's personal journal on which to do dreamwork. You will sometimes find, as we often do at workshops, certain people who have been watching their dreams and keeping a dream journal (probably because one or other of the popular writers about dreams suggested it). However, many who have been recording their dreams are at a loss what to do next. No one has taught them any other dreamwork techniques. Ask such people to choose one or two (no more than that at first) dreams from their journal that they consider important. To help make the choice, you might ask them to favor the dreams that seemed most memorable and generated the strongest emotional reaction (a positive one at first). Then ask them to do some basic dreamwork techniques on the chosen dream.

Work on current dreams. Once a client has become comfortable and familiar with the basic dreamwork techniques, you may move toward more advanced techniques (such as those in Part II), and work with current dreams. Dreamwork may be carried on at home or, for shorter techniques or ones that are helped by having a facilitator, during the counseling session.

During the session, the guide's role regarding dreamwork will be to ask about the client's reaction to the dream and what was learned from the dreamwork on it, what issues, energies, and feelings were prominent in it, what questions the dream may be asking, and, if appropriate, where in life he or she feels the dream applies.

The guide can also suggest tasks to be done after the session that will foster spiritual growth; these may include more dreamwork tasks such as Dialoguing, Symbol Immersion, Personality Tasks and actions that involve healing of personal wounds, or community tasks which involve choices responding to community needs and/or relationship conflicts and issues.

Integrating Dreamwork into a Session

Some spiritual directors become concerned that dreamwork may begin to consume entire sessions. What actually happens, however, is that dreamwork becomes part of the overall counseling process. At times, there may be a particularly important dream. At other times, other spiritual practices will be the focus.

For a number of people, since dreams consistently bring to the surface most of the major growth issues in their lives, a guide can develop an adequate spiritual growth program around dreams and dreamwork. And when the energies released in the client in this way are channeled into personality tasks, spiritual tasks, and community tasks, the counseling session is likely to be actively productive, as well as insightful, for the client.

If you are already using dreamwork as an element of spiritual direction with clients, you may find some of the more advanced dreamwork techniques in Part II and Part III of value in working with difficult or long-standing issues.

Dreamwork Technique 33:
Suggesting Tasks

Suggesting appropriate tasks for oneself or others is both a skill (using logical and analytic capacities) and an art (using imagination and intuition). In taking an attitude toward dreamwork proposed in this book, it is essential for dreamwork partners, spiritual directors, and therapists to learn the skill of suggesting appropriate tasks.

A *task* is a commitment to doing a specific project within a specific amount of time. Tasks completed are the actualizations in life of potentials from dreams.

Some questions emerge. Who ultimately suggests the tasks? And by what authority? And to what purpose?

In a counseling session, a spiritual director is dealing with a number of realities: the client, the client's relationship to God, God, the dream, and everyone's—the client's, God's, the director's—relationship to the dream.

In a very obvious sense, the task suggestions come from the awareness of the director. And yet we have discovered that many effective tasks are those evoked from the client; to do this the director asks the client a question such as "What task would you give yourself?" From another viewpoint, it is the dream itself that suggests the tasks; the director and the client merely put them into words. And on the deepest level, the tasks are suggested by the giver of the dream, for the dream is the language of a voice that lives in the deepest levels of the inner world—the inner self and the soul, and most certainly God. Therefore, to be involved in suggesting tasks is to operate at the heart of the spiritual process. It is to step into a relationship between a human soul and God. It is to deal with sacred and numinous energies.

Having a guide suggesting tasks adds structure to the situation, which can aid the client in overcoming insecurity, inadequacy and resistance. The client has the responsibility in carrying out the tasks.

Often, as a person gets into the task, the experience and outcome change. This is often purposeful, for it shows the force of the Self at work in the process.

When as a director you make some task suggestions, it is wise to check them out, that is, see how the client reacts to them. In suggesting a certain task, you might say, "It seems as though the dream is suggesting that you do this task (or take this specific action). How does this feel to you? How might you carry it out?" Or, "Is this task something you will actually do during the coming week?" Or, "Have we gotten at the main issue with this task, the issue most important for you to work with?"

It often happens that in doing the task some new developments will occur, so that at the next counseling session the client will not report on the precise task agreed upon. However, it is likely there will be other significant work for the two of you to evaluate and apply to spiritual growth. For example, one client who agreed to do Symbol Immersion on a dream symbol found herself spontaneously doing Dialoguing with the symbol. The dialogue proved fruitful. Another client was planning to do Carrying the Symbol Forward but discovered that the symbol took her backward in time instead, which allowed her to get in touch with an issue that had been eluding her for months and bring it to resolution.

Dreamwork Technique 33
Suggesting Tasks

Procedure:

This technique may be used by spiritual directors, therapists, dreamwork partners, or members of a dream group.

1. Listen as the dreamer recounts the dream. Then ask questions to clarify the main issues, feelings, and energies released in the dream. The function of any task is to help the dream energy come alive in the waking world. Whatever tasks foster this transformation of energy from the dream into daily life are appropriate.

2. Here are some possibilities for suggesting tasks.

- Focus your task suggestions on issues or symbols which seem to evoke the most energy and emotional response in the dreamer.
- Have the person write down the various task suggestions as they are being offered or developed.
- Suggest tasks in the form of questions, propositions, alternatives. Say, "Do you think it might be helpful if you tried . . . ?" or "Does either this task or that one attract you more?" Remember, the commitment to carry out a task belongs ultimately to the dreamer.
- Suggest a broad range of tasks (even as many as ten) from which the dreamer may choose.
- Invite the dreamer to participate in developing task suggestions. The dreamer may also like to adapt or modify some of your suggestions.
- It is sometimes helpful to begin doing a task together during a session, leaving the client to finish it later.

- The task may suggest projects that involve either inner reality, outer reality, or both.
- Make task suggestions specific enough to be accomplished in a short time. Long-range tasks may always be subdivided into a series of smaller and simpler tasks.
- Make clear to the client the values and growth to be gained from a particular task.
- To keep the task grounded in the energy released by the dream, keep task suggestions specific to the dream. Even if doing the task takes the client away from the dream, it is all right as long as the task experience evokes response to the dream's energy and leads to new consciousness.
- Ask, "What task would you give yourself regarding this dream?"
- In a subsequent session, leave time for the client to share the results of dreamwork tasks. Such sharing may lead to other related and more productive tasks utilizing the same energy.

Note to Chapter 14
Dreamwork and Holiness
1. Kenneth Leech, *Soul Friend* (New York: Harper and Row, 1980), p. 134.

Chapter 15

Dreamwork and Wholeness: The Therapist's Perspective

◆

Working Toward Wholeness

While the spiritual director's domain includes spiritual issues and struggles over life's meaning, moral development, value choices, facing one's destiny, and relating to God, the therapist's focus is more on psychological issues such as personality problems, ego development, sexuality, personal relationships, conflicts, dependence, and meeting a host of needs that may be physical, emotional, intellectual, and social. Naturally, certain issues overlap. The healing work done by both spiritual director and therapist are meant to complement each other.

Some people begin their growth-journey through therapy and subsequently develop a spiritual perspective. Others begin their journey through religious involvement or spiritual discipline, but discover they can't adequately deal with psychological issues such as anger, assertiveness, interpersonal conflicts, and self-esteem, and so discover they need therapy. It is recognized that the need is not simply for spiritual growth nor simply for psychological growth but rather for an increase in both psychological and spiritual consciousness. The need to integrate the spiritual and psychological is acknowledged as part of the human developmental process.

Many spiritual directors today have also received training in psychological and clinical skills, and so are able to bring a holistic perspective to their counseling work. In a similar way, many therapists, sensitive to the central influence of spirit and faith on the personality, have learned meditation and other spiritual and transpersonal practices, and are now bringing a fuller perspective to their therapeutic work.

Therapists who have trained exclusively in psychological dynamics can use the dreamwork methods presented in this book to begin integrating the spiritual level into their work without a serious need to be trained in any school of dream interpretation or religious practice. Our methodology, though presented from a Christian perspective, is not directly dependent on any school of psychology or any religious tradition. Nevertheless, it is a methodology which, when fully used, goes deeply into psychological and religious issues. It responds to the needs of the human spirit as well as to those of the ego and personality.

Among those themes and energies that are chiefly associated with spiritual values and religious traditions are: questions of meaning, destiny, and truth; willpower, commitment, and discernment (how to identify what is my personal destiny or truth); mystery, wonder, and awe; compassion, forgiveness, and sacrifice; and many others. To begin thinking about these things and wanting to know about them mark the beginnings of spiritual growth. Most, if not all, of these themes naturally surface in dreams and dreamwork.

When Is a Therapist Needed?

Many people wonder if they need a therapist to help them with dreamwork. Our position is that for the most part they do not. Our feeling is that people who have learned to use the dreamwork techniques in this book will find that they have many inner and outer resources for dealing with their problems and their growth without having to seek out a therapist. In addition to their own conscious dreamwork, many have found inner guides with whom to dialogue.

Inner guides and wisdom sources may be found among the figures and characters of our dreams. Once such a character appears in our dreams, we may begin a long-term dialogue relationship, even if the character never appears in our dreams again. Such characters, often filled with insights and energy, function like inner therapists.

Other people in our lives, such as our dreamwork partners or dream group members, can also be therapeutically helpful by giving support, affirmation, and wisdom, and by responding to our dreams by suggesting appropriate dreamwork tasks.

However, at times of extreme confusion, crisis and transition, a professional therapist can provide valuable help and support, and even guide the dreamwork process when that is appropriate.

Other people, who are dealing with deep functional disorders or major psychological pain, will probably already be in a therapist's care. In such cases, dreamwork is best done or at least reviewed with the therapist.

Some people choose to have a therapist not because they are in psychological distress but because they want to develop themselves as fully and as quickly as possible under professional guidance—much as one would go to a swimming instructor or tennis pro in order to learn those skills as effectively as possible and in a professional way.

Choosing a Therapist

A first visit with any therapist is usually treated as an evaluation time. The therapist is checking out whether he or she would like to work with you, and you are evaluating the therapist.

You have the full responsibility for choosing a therapist with whom you feel comfortable, and the first visit provides an opportunity to discover if you and the therapist are in tune with each other. In addition to this intuitive sensing, you also can use the time to ask important questions. For example, you may ask the therapist: In what ways are you as a therapist open to the spiritual? Are you able to deal with my spiritual growth needs, as well as my psychological ones? What is your attitude toward prayer and spiritual practices? Will you respect the fact that I feel I have inner guides? Can I speak to you about the meaning of life and my destiny? Are you comfortable about me talking about having a call from God? Are you open to religious and spiritual experience, and can I comfortably bring it up with you? Will you help me work with my dreams? Will you respect the fact that I treat dreams as gifts from God?

A therapist likely to have a spiritual perspective is one who demonstrates openness on issues, who is ready to find meaning even in a negative context, and who believes in the possibility of healing, no matter how difficult the situation. Such therapists are also aware of many spiritual practices and are probably using some themselves. They are sensitive to the need for integrating the psychological and spiritual aspects of life.

An elderly couple recently in the charismatic renewal came to see a therapist because they had received "the gift of tongues" and were feeling "uncomfortable and a bit crazy."

"When we came home from the prayer meeting," they reported, "we felt disoriented, not knowing what was real and what was not. It was as though an unknown part of us was turned on, and we don't know what happened."

Obviously, a spiritual experience had happened to the couple. That was undeniable. What had not yet happened was the psychological integration of this fact into their self-image and their daily lives. They needed help in developing an ego to handle the numinous experience of speaking in tongues and an inner self to integrate it. They had to learn to deal with its effects on other parts of their personal lives, including its effect on other people. Spiritually, they were challenged to relate to the spiritual power that was released in them as well as the source of this gift. The couple needed help not in the psychological realm alone, nor in the spiritual realm alone, but in bringing the two dimensions together.

The Christian Client

As a therapist, what do I do when a Christian client shares a dream?

Most clients will be unaware of the Christian tradition of dreamwork, and so will need to be educated about the Christian understanding of dreams as the voice of the soul and as gifts of God given for our holiness and wholeness, themes that are developed in the introduction and early chapters of this book.

Our suggestion is that you and the client begin working together on some dream material doing basic techniques such as TTAQ and Key Questions. You may also suggest a few other dreamwork techniques as homework tasks.

You may encourage your client to record future dreams, do a few dreamwork techniques with them, and bring any dreamwork material that seems important to the next session.

You may also suggest that after this therapy session your client will dream and receive an important dream. You might say, "You've stirred up a lot of feelings and issues in this session, and it will probably reflect itself in your dreams tonight. It would be a good idea for you to record the dreams you may have tonight." By expressing such an attitude you honor your client's dreaming as a resource directed toward his or her wholeness and healing.

The dreamwork methods we propose in this book include certain values and orientations that are similar to those of most schools of therapy. This approach to dreamwork fosters the development of the whole person, it facilitates personal growth, it fosters ego-maturity, it facilitates a personal relation to the unconscious (the ego-Self relationship), it develops intentionality and consciousness, it is applicable to daily life, it helps people become more vital human beings.

Therapists sometimes complain to each other that they cannot seem to get their clients to face squarely a key therapeutic issue. Unconsciously, clients tend to avoid a key issue or defend themselves against dealing directly with it. Dreams offer material on which to focus that does not directly challenge the conscious ego, and dreamwork offers a way to confront a key issue symbolically, and often just as effectively and practically.

How a Therapist Might Use Dreamwork

One of the roles of a therapist is to work with clients on their life-situations, which usually include employment, school, family, and social life. Dreams will be affected by these life-situations and will often reflect what is going on in them, sometimes more accurately than the client is aware of. For example, many people feel they are acting ineffectively in life, at least some of the time. While some persons won't give themselves credit for what they actually do, the dream may give credit where credit is due.

For instance, one woman came to a therapy session saying, "I'm afraid I'm not treating my daughter very well. I'm not doing her any good. There is lots of conflict between us." She also brought to the session a dream in which the dream ego is hugging her daughter after having gone out of its way to do something helpful for the daughter. After doing Following the Dream Ego, the woman was asked if her conscious ego could identify with the dream ego's helpful behavior and affectionate feelings. She replied yes, which was a tip-off to the therapist, thanks to the dreamwork, that the negative self-image presented at the beginning of the session needed to be worked with. More dreamwork with the dream ego also generated a number of other alternative behaviors that she felt sure would enrich the relationship with her daughter.

While dreams present problems, conflicts, and issues that the personality needs to deal with, they almost always reveal potentials and positive aspects hidden beneath those problems. Dreamwork can be hopeful and healing. It can also help us focus more on health than on pathology. It has been found that the therapeutic emphasis—whether on health or pathology—conditions the outcome. Thus, by looking for signs of health we help generate health. In this perspective, dreams and dreamwork look for health by producing new and positive ways of perceiving the personality, new and constructive ways of acting in the outer world, new and creative energies for bringing conflicts to healing resolution.

For therapists, we stress using Following the Dream Ego I and II, since so many therapy issues come to light in its process. In fact, after clients have learned to do Following the Dream Ego with their night dreams, we have asked them to apply the technique to segments of their daily life, say an emotional encounter with a relative, or events the day before a big decision. It is a surprise to clients how much they can learn about themselves with this simple reflective technique. As they begin to spell out the nuances in the attitudes and emotions of their dream ego, they begin to see patterns underlying their behavior in waking life.

Dreamwork Technique 34: Researching Dreamwork

As a therapist, you may have the opportunity of watching a client grow and develop over an extended period of time. If your client has been keeping a dreamwork journal all the while, it is possible for the client or the two of you together to review the dreamwork in search of important patterns in attitudes and behaviors. You may focus the research on special issues, ego-attitudes, choice-making, assertiveness, sexuality, anger, relationship, or whatever personality patterns you are particularly interested in.

Dreamwork Technique 34
Researching Dreamwork

Procedure:
1. Working alone or together, select a sampling of the client's dream material that covers an extended period of time. One dream per week might be sufficient, though some clients may wish to review more.

2. *Researching emotions and affect,* you may simply ask the client to list in chronological order what has been marked down as Affect for the TTAQ work done on each dream, and look for a pattern. For a more detailed analysis on emotional issues, take the text of each dream report and underline all the words that express a feeling or emotion, and look for patterns.

3. *Researching ego-issues* such as assertiveness, choice-making, or decisiveness is best done when the client has completed Following the Dream Ego for a number of dreams. Since so many psychological problems are related to ego-functioning, it may be well to ask clients as a matter of course to do Following the Dream Ego for every dream they bring to a therapeutic session. Some ego issues are also reflected in the Theme part of the TTAQ technique, so a list of the Themes for each of the dreams being studied may provide some patterns for consideration.

4. *Unconscious processes* may be studied from the key symbols that clients may have been collecting in the back of their journals. You can also go through the dream texts underlining key symbols and looking for patterns. Dreamwork with symbols may be reviewed, looking for patterns. Or make a list of the Questions from the TTAQ technique done for each dream, and again look for patterns.

5. *Relational issues* may perhaps be best reviewed by studying the dreamwork dialogues the client has written.

6. One can, of course, also survey the *personality tasks and reality tasks* that were chosen and their outcome, again watching for patterns of behavior and response.

Chapter 16

Dreamwork with Unusual Dreams: Dreams and Prophecy

Uncommon Dreams

The dreamworld which stretches up to the edge of waking consciousness and tunnels down to the deepest depths of the unconscious may at times appear complex and confusing. It seems to reflect heavens and hells, and all the realms of spirit and energy in between. In the dreamworld where the strange and unusual are commonplace, how can we introduce the topic of strange and unusual dreams?

There are dreams which evoke wonder when we are told about them. These dreams may be called prophetic, telepathic, synchronous (when someone dreams of an event exactly as it is happening many miles away), or ones in which the presence of a powerful spirit is felt. There is no doubt that prophetic and other uncommon dreams are the ones which usually make the headlines or are memorable enough to be passed on from mouth to mouth, and even from generation to generation. The biblical people, like the people of today, were fascinated and impressed by dreams that predicted future happenings, especially when they concerned famous people.

Many Levels of Meaning

We do not presume to present all possible levels of reality that people can experience in the dream state. Most dreams, as we already know, usually have many levels of meaning. Who is to say how many levels there are or can be? In this book we have been working with dreams on two basic levels: toward growth and consciousness on the psychological plane, and toward guidance and destiny on the spiritual plane. The question we must deal with here, faced with various kinds of apparent psychic and prophetic dreams, is: How do we treat such dreams in the light of our quest for holiness and wholeness?

The first and most basic response we give to this question is this: *What is most important is how you relate to such dreams.*

Some people deny outright that any dreams can be psychic or prophetic and are simply closed to this kind of experience; others tend to see many of their dreams as psychic or foretelling. We do not take a position in defining such dreams, but rather suggest ways to work with them for meaning.

From our perspective, all dreams are given for our growth, no matter how paranormal their content may seem. The ultimate source of the dream is God and its purpose is ultimately to bring about healing and wholeness. In this light, then, we feel that every dream has meaning and that this meaning can come to be understood through appropriate dreamwork.

The present approach is to suggest that when we receive what seems like an unusual dream, we first relate to it as if it were an ordinary dream, that is, we do dreamwork on it as we would any other dream, but remain open to the possibility the dream may be more than an ordinary dream, that is, that it may also be speaking to another level of reality.

In doing dreamwork with non-ordinary dreams, we maintain our intention of working toward personal growth and consciousness. Dreamwork keeps us grounded in our own reality and in the everyday world. Such dreamwork prevents us from being absorbed in the possibility of a foreseen event, and keeps us focused on ourselves as choicemakers, and as persons who have unusual dream dynamics that need to be understood. If we understand our own biases and take them into account, then when a truly fore-knowing event occurs in a dream, we will be more likely to discern it for what it is and deal with it creatively. The goal is to keep ourselves grounded and yet still remain open to unusual realities.

Let us consider some specific kinds of unusual dream material in turn: dreams about events soon to happen to people we know, dreams about events soon to happen to people we do not know, dreams about events soon to happen to ourselves, and so-called demonic dreams.

Dreaming About People We Know

People reporting telepathic dreams about events in the lives of relatives and friends seem to receive information in the dream state about things soon to happen to them, or happening at the same time. These dreams may be concerned with personal major life events such as births and deaths, moments of danger or passion, or a great loss or gain.

For example, in April a woman dreamed that her sister-in-law was to deliver a baby in November. She thought no more of her dream, but when she met her sister-in-law at her home the following week, she recalled her dream and related it, thinking it would be an amusing anecdote at which they would both laugh. Instead the sister-in-law became startled. "How did you know? I haven't even told your brother yet." The verification of the dream startled the dreamer too, and the incident was a source of embarrassment to her, for she had been telling information which her sister-in-law was keeping secret.

In order to ground such a dream in everyday reality, three meaningful questions may be asked: (1) How does this dream reflect my waking feelings and perceptions toward the person or situation referred to in the dream? (2) How does this dream reflect what this person or situation is like in waking life? (3) What purpose might be behind my having this dream now?

In dealing with questions such as these, first make note of the question in your journal and then write quickly, without censoring, whatever response comes into your mind. Perhaps new information or insight regarding the dream will come, or you may find yourself listing your fears and concerns about this person or your own life. Such responses most likely reflect your own personality issues, and call you to make choices in light of these insights and your own needs.

Once these questions are dealt with, we are perhaps ready to ask the dreamwork questions: What am I going to do about the information the dream seemed to be revealing to me? How shall I validate it? Should I share it with others for further grounding? What shall I do with the energy and feelings the dream evoked in me?

Dreaming About People We Do Not Know

When we have predictive dreams about events soon to happen to people we don't know, e.g., famous people or someone publicly known, how are we to deal with such dreams?

The recommendation is that such a dream be related to, first, as an ordinary dream in which the famous person appears simply as a dream symbol. Once enough grounding in our personality has been done with basic dreamwork, we may then deal with the question: What do I do with the information that apparently is being revealed in this dream? Usually this is an issue only if the information seems to be of consequence, e.g., if the person's life, family, job, or financial security seems to be in danger.

For example, a middle-aged woman was planning to invest her life savings in a business venture which seemed to her to be very safe and lucrative. However, she had a dream about her prospective partners which focused on areas of the business of which she was unaware. As her dreamwork task, she chose to investigate the partners in the areas the dream had suggested and found they were indeed weak. She treated the dream as a clear sign that the proposed venture was not a sound one. She withdrew her offer of investment and saved her money.

The woman believed her dream to be a telepathic dream, but it could also be explained as basic inner wisdom suggesting that her ego do a bit of prudent investigating before it made a lifetime commitment.

That people are capable of telepathy in dreams or in the waking state has been tested and verified again and again in laboratory studies.[1] However, it is another thing to say that this specific dream is telepathic, or that the main purpose for being given the dream was to communicate a piece of information to someone. Dream research shows that psychic dreams are common, though as a rule they don't happen frequently to the same person. There is much we still have to learn about such dreams.

To begin using dreams and dreamwork as a kind of fortune-telling tool for the benefit of oneself or others is to begin misusing the gift of dreaming. As we mentioned in Chapter 4, one reason that dreamwork fell into disrepute in the Church throughout the Middle Ages and Renaissance was the popular tendency of people to use dreams as a fortune-telling tool in order to predict the future and conduct their secular life. For example, people were seeking in their dreams answers to such questions as "Where shall I place my money, or my loyalty?" "Who is going to die soon?" "How long am I going to live?" They were looking for comfort and security as the goal of their life. Theologians may have been wise to object to this practice as superstitious because it tended to foster a compulsive and controlling quality in the ego and an attempt to manipulate spiritual energies.

Working with Predictive Dreams

What about dreams that seem to predict what is going to happen in our own lives?

President Abraham Lincoln had a disturbing dream a short time before his assassination in which he saw a coffin lying in state in the White House. In the dream he asked a guard, "Who died?" and the guard replied, "The President."

Many people have had predictive dreams about accidents or other major events that actually happened to them. Were some of these dreams warnings? Or were they self-fulfilling prophecies where the people involved would compulsively carry out a comic or tragic fate?

We know that we sometimes dream of death or accidents, our own or others'. Usually such dreams are symbolic statements meant to teach us something important. How can we know when our predictive dreams are more than merely symbolic?

It is said that when people have a literally pre-cognitive dream of their death or that of another person *the dream is accompanied by an experience of deep knowing,* which is unmistakable. Dreamwork with such dreams can be helpful using key questions such as: How can I best prepare myself if such an event were to happen? What would I want to have done now if what the dream portrayed really would happen to me?

Here arises the interesting issue that if I know my fate ahead of time because a dream revealed the possibility of a tragedy, can I take steps to avoid the worst? In other words, "Did I have this warning dream to help me avert this tragedy, or prepare for it?"

There are examples of spiritually conscious people who knew when death was coming to them. It has been reported of the great religious evolutionary thinker Teilhard de Chardin that he expected to and did die on Easter.

Another example of predictive dreams is told in the account of the great ship Titanic which sank on its maiden voyage. At least two passengers had dreams beforehand about the sinking of this ship. One passenger followed his dream literally and canceled his passage. The other gave no importance to his dream and drowned when the Titanic struck an iceberg in the North Atlantic fog.

In general, it is unrealistic to treat dreams literally. Yet the passenger who chose to cancel his passage on the Titanic because of a dream avoided the disaster.

There seem to be no hard and fast rules for determining when a dream is to be taken literally. We can only remind ourselves that dreams can have many levels of meaning, and one of these possible levels is the literal meaning. However, by doing dreamwork at each level with a dream containing unwanted circumstances, we can learn to avert and/or transform negative potentials in our lives.

For example, a car crash and death in a dream could mean that the actual event is going to happen and that we should put our life and legal will in order. It could also mean symbolically that we are going too fast in certain areas of our life and that to continue rushing will precipitate a crash physically, financially, psychologically, or otherwise. Or such a dream could open us up to the need to really "let go" psychologically and spiritually in areas where we are overly possessive or compulsively controlling. The dream may be telling us that if we can choose to go through an experience of dying symbolically in the inner world, we may not have to act it out in the physical world.

The Dark Side of Dreaming

Some people are curious about the possibility and meaning of what are called demonic dreams, that is, dreams about which people report the presence or energy of the demonic, accompanied by a certainty that the dream image is really an autonomous spirit presence.

It was commonly taught during the period of the Church Fathers that while many dreams came from God, some could come from the devil. So far in our research, however, we have not come across any concrete example of a genuine demonic dream in the early Church writings. Of course, there are many dreams in which a satanic figure is imaged. But while such an image might scare a dreamer and make the dreamer think it was a dream coming from the devil—or the devil himself—it seems more likely that the dream Source was presenting the imagery as part of a symbolic communication.

Such dreams may be dealt with using ordinary dreamwork. If the dream feels unresolved, or the dreamer wakes up from it feeling overwhelmed, dreamwork techniques designed for healing and nightmares will be appropriate (see Chapter 12).

As persons begin to relate to and deal with adversary figures in dreams, they also become willing to deal with adversity and adversaries when they spring up in life.

For those people, however, who feel they have experienced a genuine demonic presence in their dream, we recommend that the dreamer do whatever dreamwork is necessary with a spiritual director or therapist who is open to belief in this kind of spiritual reality. With such a dream, we suggest not doing dreamwork alone because it is likely that the dreamwork will produce powerful energies, feelings, and images that require professional support and guidance in their transformation or containment. In any case, do not dismiss the dream but work with it under guidance.

There is a classic dream, complete with a Faustian pact with the devil, that might seem to be a demonic dream but which can be dealt with as a very creative dream.

One day the great Italian violinist, Guiseppe Tartini, started to write a composition in a burst of inspired creativity, but he was unable to finish it because his creative spark went out. He fell asleep exhausted and had a dream. In the dream, Tartini saw himself wandering aimlessly, desperate and dejected. But at a turn in the road, the devil appeared and offered to finish the sonata in exchange for Tartini's soul. Without hesitating, Tartini agreed to the offer. The devil produced a violin and played a magnificent finale to the unfinished sonata. Tartini awoke, jotted down the music he had heard in the dream, and that is the story of the origins of *The Devil's Sonata.*

What Tartini seemed to have done in the dream was re-establish the ego-inner self relationship. He had encountered what Jung called the Shadow, a hidden unconscious side of us that would be our ally, if we would let it. We all have a little devil in us, as the saying goes, and Tartini's devil also happened to be a very creative composer. His dreamwork task, writing out the music he heard in his dream, honored the relationship he had reaffirmed in his dream between his inner and outer worlds. In this sense the devil is something which we have not yet made conscious.

Dreams and Intuition

How shall we think about telepathic and extra-sensory-perception dreams? When we talk to people who are considered psychics and clairvoyants, they will often acknowledge that their telepathic or special perceptual capacities seem to be a part of the intuitive function which all people have to a greater or lesser degree. There are many highly intuitive people (they are much more numerous than psychics) who can often "sense" what is going on in a relationship or in a person's life without being told. Many such intuitives enter the psychological and counseling professions, and usually become successful therapists. They "just know" how to be empathetic and supportive; they somehow say "just the right thing" to facilitate the healing process. Such persons are valuable in the community. They have learned to trust their intuitions at an everyday level; they do not require of themselves that everything they do must be logically reasoned. If you ask them why they did something, they might say, "I don't know. I just knew it would work. It just felt right."

One area where intuition has a natural function is in dreams. One expression of intuitive dreaming might be the telepathic or ESP dream. Those who work consistently with such dreams are developing the intuitive function and putting confidence in it.

The telepathic dream can be perceived as a confirmation of our ability in dreams and through intuition to perceive aspects of non-physical reality. It affirms that a spiritual realm of relationships and energies moves within reality and is not limited by physical capacities.

Working with Telepathic Dreams

The following dreamwork techniques are not for producing telepathic dreams, but for working with them when they occur. We assume that truly telepathic dreams are a sign of latent psychic ability, and that dreamwork may be used to accept this ability as a gift from God to be used in deepening one's spiritual insight and direction in life. Dreamwork here is designed to help broaden the dreamer's life view and to develop tasks that use the ability to serve others in healing ways.

The ability to tune in to the feelings of others is an important intuitive power for someone in the community to possess, for example, to help people work through emotional blocks. Often when it might take hours and days to ferret out the roots of a problem in a family or community, an intuitive person can step in and almost immediately sense what is wrong in the situation. Intuition is a faculty for knowing the truth about things for ourselves; it is also useful for perceiving the potential for truth in others and in situations. As a spiritual gift, one of its purposes is that those who have it can increase their effectiveness for creatively developing the world's human potential in the service of God.

Intuition in its various forms seems to manifest itself more frequently in circumstances that are transitional, stressful, or unusual. Probably that's when it is most needed as a relational tool, i.e., for establishing deeper levels of relationship and feeling related. Some people are able to use their psychic and intuitive capacities in their Christian ministry in situations where deep spiritual knowing and helping can bring issues into awareness for healing and growth. It is with this orientation that we offer suggestions for working with dreams that reflect paranormal human capacities such as telepathy, ESP, synchronicity, prophecy, and the like.

Dreamwork Techniques 35 and 36: Working with Paranormal Dreams

A first task we have when receiving what seems like a predictive or paranormal dream about another person is to test whether it is indeed a paranormal dream. This is a basic test question: *Do I feel that the dream belongs more to the other person and was given for the benefit of the other person, or that it belongs more to me and was given for my benefit?*

For example, if a day before my daughter goes on vacation I dream about her being in an accident and I wake up frightened, is my dream actually a warning that needs to be communicated to my daughter, or is the dream simply making me conscious of how much I over-worry about things, or is it a sign of how important my daughter is to me? One mother in a South American country, because of a dream, took her daughter off a bus which shortly afterward blew up on a land mine, just as her dream predicted. To be in tune with multiple levels of reality, whether in a dream or otherwise, requires strong choice-making and responsiveness.

Sometimes the response to the test question is rather clear. In any case, we suggest doing dreamwork to clarify, verify, and confirm whatever response is given to the dream in the waking world.

Dreamwork Technique 35
Testing a Paranormal Dream

Procedure:
1. To discern whether a predictive dream about another person is meant to be taken literally as well as symbolically, ask yourself: Do I feel that the dream belongs more to the other person and was given for their benefit? Or do I feel that the dream is meant more for me and was given for my benefit? Sometimes your response to these

questions can be clear and immediate. If you view the dream as only symbolic, an appropriate response would be to do dreamwork with the dream material. If you see the dream also as literal, your response might include an outer life action that utilizes a literal interpretation of the dream.

2. Sometimes an appropriate response to the dream is not clear. What is usually clear to people, however, after an apparently important predictive dream is their *wish* to make a helpful and constructive response. This usually means either to view the dream drama literally (as well as symbolically) and take an outer life action—such as telling your warning dream to the person concerned—or to view the dream as only symbolic and take no action as if the dream were literal.* If you are unclear on how to act after a predictive dream, we suggest you consider all available data including your emotional state, your fears and possible projections, and spend some time searching for inner discernment and guidance. The following suggestions may help facilitate your discernment process.

3. Perhaps the most objective approach is to begin by treating the dream as if it belonged *both* to you and the other person. After you have opened yourself up to both possibilities, you may choose what to do and what not to do in the outer world.

4. One dreamwork technique to use for further clarity would be Key Questions. For example, ask yourself: What is my relationship to this dream? How might this dream be a metaphor of my life? What is the quality of my relationship to the figure of the other person in the dream?

---

*Note. There is a third possibility. A predictive dream may have both a symbolic and literal meaning and yet not be calling us to take outer life actions in response to it. In this case the dream is probably given to us as an informative gift to help prepare us for an event. For example, a woman dreamed that she saw a close friend of hers lying on his deathbed. She awoke from the dream startled and saddened but took no outer life action such as telling the man or his family about the dream. She was even more upset a few days later when the man suddenly died. She felt guilty for not having *done something* with the dream information. After doing dreamwork on the dream she realized a number of things. First, without the dream she would have been overwhelmed by the sudden loss of her friend; the dream in its own way had tried to prepare her for the loss. Second, she realized, after reflection, that any attempted intervention on her part would not have influenced the outcome. This observation seems to be borne out in the majority of predictive dreams. This dream experience underlines a major dilemma people typically feel when they have predictive dreams. "What is my responsibility?" The woman had indeed received true information concerning the man's imminent death but she had also to accept the limits to her responsibility, her helplessness, and her inability to control some events.

5. An additional technique to use would be Dialoguing. For example, write out a dialogue between the figure in the dream and yourself, asking appropriate questions. Working with the above dream, for example, the mother might ask the dream figure of her daughter, Why did you come to me in this dream? What relation do you have to my physical daughter? Do you have a message for me or for her? etc.

6. In certain situations, you may wish to check out your dream information in the physical world. In the given example, I could not ask my daughter if she is going to have an accident. However, I might relate my dream to her and get her reactions. Or I might just ask her how she feels about the trip she is planning to take.

7. If appropriate, you may observe future dreams for confirmation of your analysis or of action you took in response to the dream. (See the following Technique.)

8. After you have spent some time weighing the likely effects of your proposed action or non-action, make your choice, own the responsibility for making the choice, then trust that it is an appropriate choice, and let go of your concern about its rightness or wrongness.

   With suitable adaptation, this technique may be used with dreams predicting events happening to you personally.

Dreamwork Technique 36
Asking for Confirming Dreams

Procedure:
   There are two approaches to confirming dreams following a supposed extra-sensory-perception dream.

1. The first is to ask for a dream the following night to clarify whether your attitude toward the given dream as paranormal is correct or not. Then do dreamwork on the new dream, keeping your question in mind as you do.

2. The second approach may be used when you have made a choice about the unusual character of a given dream and have acted upon it. In the days following your action, observe your dreams for confirming signs from your inner self.

Confirming Major Choices

After doing dreamwork on a significant, predictive dream which depicts an accident, loss, or major change in our own lives, we sometimes make important decisions. The technique of Asking for Confirming Dreams may be adapted to test the results of such major decisions. Does our soul or dream Source like a difficult choice we have made?

A number of people who made important personal decisions have reported subsequent dreams in which their dream ego is re-enacting the outer life choice they have made—with positive results if the decision was seen as positive by the inner self, with negative results if it was seen as negative. Personality change may also be expressed in subsequent confirming dreams, showing the dream ego enacting the new behavior.

To receive a confirming dream can give us a strong sense of having made the right move. It is as if the soul is looking upon all that we do and sometimes challenges us and sometimes confirms us as we seek God's purposes in our lives.

Does Telepathy Cause Things to Happen?

Some people who have had telepathic or prophetic dreams, e.g., that someone was going to die, or that there would be a fire in a certain building, or that someone would be in an accident, wonder if their dreaming helped cause the tragedy, after they found out that the tragedy did indeed occur.

The question at issue here is this: "Because we perceive something, do we cause it?" Perception is not in itself causative. Action is. To take action we must not only intend something, but use energy to bring it about.

If you feel you are causing things to happen in your life or the lives of others over which you have little or no control, it would be best to seek professional help to deepen your awareness of how to handle such feelings.

Notes to Chapter 16
Dreamwork with Unusual Dreams
1. For an exciting study of laboratory research in telepathy see especially Montague Ullman's and Stanley Krippner's *Dream Telepathy* (New York: Macmillan, 1973).

Chapter 17

Toward a Theology of Dreams and Dreamwork: Transforming Ourselves and Our World

◆

What Is Theology?

Theology, concerned with the study of ultimate issues and values, is a body of coherent beliefs or ideas about the nature of God and the nature of our relation to God.

While theologians and certain other scholars make theology their professional field of study, theological thinking is appropriate for all who are committed to a life of faith and who reflect on their religious experience.

For some, the study of theology and doctrine is their principal way of knowing God. For others, religious knowledge comes primarily through direct experience. It would seem that both approaches are necessary for a complete understanding of our relation with God. This is why within the Church we find both doctrine and practice. Practices may include ritual, prayer, meditation, dreamwork, and good works whose purpose is to experience God's grace.

People have beliefs and attitudes about practically everything in life, whether they are conscious of them or not. For mature believers, reflecting and meditating on their beliefs is an essential part of religious practice. Formal theology's purpose is to make conscious and to conceptualize the beliefs of a particular religion.

Even though we are emphasizing religious experience in the practice of dreamwork, we are not de-emphasizing the need also to reflect upon other religious experience or upon our religious traditions or beliefs. Certain dreams, in fact, may relate to our religious traditions and beliefs. Dreamwork with such dreams can help us become more aware of and inspired by those traditions and beliefs.

Through dreams and dreamwork can also come new values and spiritual insights for personal transformation and community renewal.

It may be that God is speaking to us directly each day in dreams. The questions facing us are: Will we listen? Will we allow original material to enter our lives?

We affirm the importance of the Church's values, beliefs, and teachings. Nevertheless, they cannot be substituted for direct and living experience of the presence of God. Yet, we need tradition and values within which to share, build, and process our experience. Communities are bodies of shared values as well as of shared experience. There needs to be a balanced emphasis on both belief and experience.

Why Have a Theology of Dreams and Dreamwork?

We may feel overwhelmed by the large number of branches of theology there are. For example, there is a theology of the Church (ecclesiology), a theology of the sacraments, a theology of Christ (Christology), a theology of Mary, and many more. And now we are proposing a theology of dreams and dreamwork. How can we begin to think theologically about dreams and dreamwork?

All branches of theology seem to have this in common, that they all are replies to the fundamental question: *What is God doing (or trying to do) in the world through* .... ? (Fill in the blank with key words like Church, sacraments, etc.) The responses which people give to that fundamental question are theological reflections.

To begin developing a theology of dreams and dreamwork, then, we ask ourselves: *What is God trying to do in the world through dreams and dreamwork?*

To indicate that theological theories are not simply the products of theologians, we asked a group of people on the final day of a Dreamwork and Spiritual Growth seminar to respond to the above question. Here are some of their responses. Through dreams and dreamwork:

- God is trying to put us in touch with a tremendous source of energy that we might not otherwise notice.
- God is trying to help us integrate the conscious and unconscious parts of our lives.
- God is trying to give us gifts and insights to help us grow.
- God is trying to get us to use our innate creativity and our intuitive powers.
- God is calling us to put an end to meandering and to clearly get in touch with our life's meaning and purpose.
- God is trying to get us to relate to him personally and to become familiar with the symbolic language he uses to communicate.
- God is trying to get us to be more conscious in our cooperation with him in what he's doing in the world.
- God is trying to get us to realize that though we can't control a lot of what happens in the world, we can be conscious of our attitude and response to it.
- God is trying to get us to bring our anxiety and fear to the surface, so he can fill us with love, peace, and trust.
- God is calling us as individuals and as a community to risk confronting the "nightmares" in our waking lives as well as our dreams in order to release in us energies for healing and courage.

People who approach dreams and dreamwork with such attitudes as these are certainly very much in tune with some of the best in the Christian theological tradition.

Is God Really the Giver of the Dream?

And the giver of the dream's meaning?

If so, in what sense is the dream divine revelation? In what sense is it meant to guide the individual and the community? And what kind of authority does a dream possess?

In our century we are not used to thinking of a dream as revelatory material. The basic text of divine revelation for Christians is the Bible.

The deposit of faith is handed down from generation to generation through the scriptural writings and through the tradition of belief and scholarship, which helps us understand and interpret the Bible's meaning for us.

But for the ancient Hebrews, there was no written revelation from God before the commandments given to Moses. For the Old Testament patriarchs, the basic "text" of revelation was twofold: it consisted in their *inner experience* of dreams, visions, prophecies, inspirations, and other inner movements of the divine Spirit, and in *outer experience*, the events happening to individuals and communities of the people of God that shaped their journey and destiny. The early Hebrews shaped the stories of these inner and outer events into an oral tradition. Only in later centuries were they written down and the writing treated as sacred text.

As these ancient believers reflected on their experience, they gradually came to consciousness about what God was trying to do in the world through them. Not only did they feel a need to deal with their dreams and visions, but these inner events taught them how to connect their inner and outer worlds. For the Hebrews, the dream and visions were what brought about in them awareness of the relationship between the inner and outer worlds of consciousness and life. Dreams and visions also brought them into relationship with God and allowed them to be governed by God in a personal and direct way.

Although the early Christians had much of the Old Testament as their text of revelation, it soon became clear to them that God had plans for his new community that were not clearly spelled out in the Old Testament. Just about every major step that shaped the budding Christian community was guided by a breakthrough of the divine Spirit into the lives of the believers and their leaders. In the Book of Acts, dreams, visions, prophecies, and inspiration are greatly in evidence. God is very present to their spirits and souls, clearly guiding and directing them, becoming personally involved in their lives.

As we saw in our short study of the Church Fathers and dreams, the Christians of the next few centuries believed that God continued to be a God-with-us, guiding and inspiring the body of believers and their leaders through dreams and visions.

In our recent decades of Church renewal, we have witnessed a revival of this God-with-us perspective, not only in dreams but in many other ways. God and the Holy Spirit are seen as present to us, establishing personal relationship, healing us and growing us and guiding from within the evolving destiny of the Christian community.

The revival of a Christian perception of dreams and dreamwork presented in this book suggests that we might be open to new dimensions of divine revelation. Certain dreamwork techniques suggest we can add to the current methods we have for studying and interacting with biblical texts. Perhaps by admitting a religious significance to dreams and visions we are beginning to explore again an ancient primary "text": the dream and vision itself.

How Do Dreams Help Us Relate to God?

The problem in life is to find out who we really are; central to this process is to find out who God is in us and in our lives. Does relating to God really make a difference in who we are or how we live life?

For many people a split readily develops between their psychological and their spiritual selves. Some will emphasize self-growth but remain narcissistic because they are still ultimately self-centered. Others will be quite religious, showing great devotion to God, but miss out on developing or healing themselves. The way of wholeness and holiness is to integrate both these sides of ourselves.

Through working with dreams over a period of time we find out who we really are and how God is working in our lives. In the arena of dreamwork we enter into a creative process of self-revelation and God-revelation, always within an integrative context.

Dreams and dreamwork help us relate to God by bringing more of ourselves to the relationship, and by having God come really alive in our being and our lives. Dreamwork provides a highly personal relation to God. In the Synoptic Gospels, the most frequently used word for God by Jesus is "Abba," which means the personal father. Jesus personalized his relation to God and we can do likewise. Great transcendent experiences and ideas of God are not enough. We must develop and be changed by a personal relationship to God which is open to input from both sides. In dreams and dreamwork, God responds and we also respond, and meaning is achieved.

How Does God Appear in Dreams?

Where is God in the dream? If we can really find God in the dream and in our dreamwork, we can leave behind such questions as "Where does the dream come from?" or "Are all dreams from God?"

Certain characteristics which we might attribute to God seem to also be in dreams. Dreams often carry superior wisdom to our own personal knowledge. Dreams have a sense of possible wholeness and direction about them. Dreams can be felt as numinous or mystical experiences. Dreams re-enact many aspects of our lives, but often with a focus on greater truth and healing than we have yet perceived. Dreams comment on our own religious practices and seek to bring us more and more into relation with the will of God as the plan for wholeness and holiness in our lives. And then, certain dreams contain overtly powerful symbols which seem to reflect aspects of God very directly, as seen in the following excerpts from actual dreams.

> In a room at the end of a dark tunnel in the heart of Sacred Mountain, a golden liquid light hits me in the chest and drenches me, from which I go into feelings of spiritual anguish and conflict over surrender to the Divine.

God appearing as light within the heart of the Sacred Mountain caused deep spiritual feelings in a young man who was committed to spiritual growth. This dream became for him the prelude to a new consciousness and further steps in relation to the Divine. Another example:

> God was playing ball, bouncing it up and down, and he also was bouncing up and down in slow motion. I and my friends danced a ballet and God smiled.

This was a non-traditional image of God dreamed by a religious sister who responded creatively to God's creativity. We might also ask: When will the ball be thrown to her, the ball of her destiny, of her wholeness?

This next dream scene is from a young woman who was traveling to be with her father as he died of cancer. She had asked for a dream about death and this is what she received.

> I am camping on shore with my mom and dad and my sister. We have a campfire and it goes out as the sea gets rougher and rougher, with little rivulets of water seeping underneath the fire. Our rowboat is out on the water and big waves are about to engulf it. My dad goes out to save the boat. He looks strong and young. My mother swims out to follow him. I watch them get the boat, a wave goes over them, but they come up and finally come back to shore with the boat.

This dream was very moving to her. "Yes, the waters are rough," she explained. "The danger is great that mother and father will be overwhelmed, but they bring themselves and the boat ashore. Life, the campfire, goes out, but the soul remains in the boat brought to shore. A sense of eternality pervades the scene. The boat returned to shore seems to say that when father is dead his body will be placed in the boat and the boat will be released on the waters for its final journey." These are some of the thoughts which came out of this dreamer's working with her dream. There are theological implications in the fact that such a dream could come to her when she most needed it. And in the symbolism itself, she experienced the mystery of death and eternity.

Some of our most profound experiences of God come within the sanctuary of the church, either during a service or alone. And other profound experiences of God come to us in the sanctuary of the night. The following dream from a priest illustrates well the interconnections between one's inner and outer life which are possible in actively pursuing dreamwork.

> In my dream my mother was celebrating her first Mass as a priest. (My mother died four years ago.) My father was in the sanctuary doing the scriptural readings for the liturgy. I climbed to the choir loft to lead the offertory chant: its text was in Latin and its melody a Gregorian chant. Although I had not seen the music before, I sang confidently and joyfully. After singing, I went to the sanctuary and concelebrated the Mass with her. I returned to the choir loft after Mass to play my trumpet for the recessional.
> In the next scene, I found myself walking on a street near my parents' home where I met my Aunt Alice, my mother's youngest sister, who looked very young and youthful. I told her I had just come from church where my mother was celebrating her first Mass as a priest. Aunt Alice smiled and asked how it had gone. "Beautifully," I told her.

The priest's dreamwork comments follow:

> Even though the Church does not ordain women as priests, no one seemed surprised or uncomfortable at the liturgy. I was proud of my mother and happy to celebrate with her, sharing her priesthood. My mother had always been a devout woman, committed to the Church. It seemed quite appropriate that she should be offering prayers and sacrifice to God on behalf of the people.

In doing Following the Dream Ego, this dreamer had these insights. His image of himself in the dream was content to support and enhance the feminine figure which was very devout.

> Perhaps the dream is calling me to bring more of the feminine energies within me into my conscious life and work as a priest, to integrate the feeling level into my role as priest, and to be open to nurturing the feminine energies within the Church whenever I have a chance.

In drawing out theological issues possibly embedded in this dream, we would like to start with a major contrast, that is, the contrast between personal theology and the collective theology of an established religion.

In terms of personal theology, this priest is beginning to see the value of including more of the feminine within his role as priest. God is speaking to him directly about a major religious issue in his life and vocation, that to which he is called. If he did not have a sense of his inner world also being real, he would possibly completely extravert this dream and work to make it possible for women to become priests. This may, in fact, be a worthwhile value in terms of the Church of the future. But it is only one possible level of working with the dream. If this priest takes his dream primarily on the inner level, where he has the power to be effective, he will work on ways to change himself to being a more balanced person. He does not have to spend his life fighting for a cause which might not come about, and thus use up his life energy on other than that which would make him more whole as a person. He can also include a sense of presence of his mother and her qualities in his own life and work.

In effect, we are suggesting that this dream serves to increase consciousness on the personal level, the family level, and the religious level and in terms of the contemporary Church itself. The dream deepens the experience of religion by including aspects of self and life which might not be so included in the outer. Nor does the dream deny the value of present day Church practice since it is making a personal statement to this dreamer. However, if many religious men and women have dreams in which women are fulfilling the priestly role, then probably there is a major change occurring in the community before people are even aware of it. Thus, the new way is often seen in dreams before it becomes a reality in outer life.

What Is a Dream?

Each night we let go, we die symbolically, not to nothingness, but to the rich and sometimes terrifying tapestry of the inner world. How can we adequately approach what we see there? Throughout the book we have approached the dream as if by studying and analyzing and relating to it through dreamwork it would hand over its wisdom and meaning to us. Yet in the end, after all the dreamwork, must we not admit that the dream is still mystery?

One night the dream given to us is a great mystery; on another night it is a tiny jewel. Something special happens in the dark night, the interval between the days of creation. We are blessed by the creativity of our waking days. But are we not also blessed by the nights of dreams which are given to quicken and enliven our days with a higher meaning?

Perhaps God likes us most when we dream because then we are most receptive and responsive. God sometimes shocks us and sometimes consoles us. In dreams, God offers us a personal relationship and calls us to achieve wholeness, inner and outer.

Who is willing and able to look God straight in the eye, and for how long? And yet to be seen by God is to begin really to see ourselves. We must be seen in order to see. We are invited to look into the dark night and remember what we have seen. The dream is the potential, the beginning. In our devotion, we can make the eyes of God more real for ourselves and the world.

And still all is mystery!

Dreamwork Technique 37: Exploring the Mystery Level in Life Events

Mystery seems to come from many sources besides our dreams. Daily life events, such as chance but important meetings on the street, or an unexpected phone call at an opportune moment, may be looked upon as happenings that release an otherwise hidden, or almost mysterious, energy. When we view such events as laden with special energy for us, we acknowledge that our lives are being shaped by more than the decisions of our usual surface-conscious ego. We are open to seeing the graced undercurrents of our lives.

"I was quite late for the church service I usually attend," explained a man, "so I went to a neighboring church, a place I had never been to before. The Bible readings and the sermon I heard there struck me so deeply that it became an important turning point in my life."

To help us get more fully in touch with these mysterious movements in our lives, many dreamwork techniques may prove quite helpful. Instead of simply dismissing an unusual event by labeling it a mystery, coincidence, accident, chance, luck, or synchronicity, we can acknowledge the hidden energy present in the event, seek to understand it in light of our destiny, and welcome it. Dreamwork techniques applied to the event may release spiritual energy for our holistic growth and put us in touch with ways God is unsuspectingly working in our lives. For example, a woman said, "I went to the cocktail party unwillingly, only because the woman I work with insisted that I go. But it was there that I met the man I fell in love with and married."

What kinds of waking events can, upon reflection, prove fruitful for building awareness of self and God? To which such events may dreamwork techniques be productively applied?

In Chapter 6, we recommended using basic dreamwork techniques for reviewing and reflecting on meditation experiences, especially for clarifying our response to prayer and for designing tasks for personality development and community service based on the energy and gifts given to us during our prayer. These same techniques, including TTAQ, Key Questions, and working with symbols, may also be used to process our response to liturgical events, sacramental moments, homilies, scriptural readings, and other religious experiences.

Since God works not only in religious experience but also in the dynamics of daily life, these same dreamwork techniques may be helpful in finding deeper levels of meaning in events that happen to us in waking life.

People report that they have done TTAQ, Key Questions, Dialoguing, Following the Dream Ego, and symbol work in reflecting on the meaning and significance of events such as committee meetings, holiday dinners, birthday parties, visits to family or friends, workshops, concerts, vacations, etc. Others have done "dreamwork" on their reactions and responses to films, television dramas, novels, plays, even stories in magazines or newspapers that caught their attention. Whenever we engage in something toward which we feel a special energy or attraction, it has the potential for revealing God's hand in our lives.

A special area of experience that calls for dreamwork techniques to be applied are things that happen to us that are unwanted and unwelcome, such as accidents, illnesses, operations, deaths, delays, failures, disappointments, etc. In these instances, we may reflect upon the unwelcome event as if it were an unfinished dream; for example, we may ask Key Questions, look for the "gift" in the event, and find the transformative energies being called forth.

For Joseph of the Old Testament, being sold into slavery in Egypt by his brothers was an unwelcome experience. Yet, from the perspective of destiny, Joseph's presence in Egypt became an important turning point for him and his family. Similarly for Moses. Because of the edict of another Egyptian pharaoh, Moses' mother, to save her Hebrew child from death, was led to place him in a basket and set him adrift in a stream—-clearly an unfortunate situation for both mother and child. However, the child was discovered and lovingly raised by the pharaoh's daughter. For the Hebrews who reflected on this story, these happenings in Moses' life were not a series of coincidences, but the acts of a faithful God. For this reason, they referred to God as Emmanuel, which means God-with-us.

Not only may we reflect on life events using dreamwork techniques, but we may also ask for night dreams to help us understand the meaning of those life events in light of our destiny and call. Our dreams may comment upon our life events or bring up personal issues which may be worked with in relation to the event. Dreams may let us know how our inner world is being affected by what we do. In dreams we have, so to speak, a fairly independent observer inside us who also watches and comments on how we are or are not living life.

Dreamwork Technique 37
Exploring the Mystery Level in Life Events

Procedure:

Here are a few guidelines for relating dreamwork techniques to understanding life events at a deeper level.

1. Treat the life event as a dream. In your journal, describe the event as if it were a remembered dream. Give it a title, name its theme and affect, and let it ask you a question.

2. You may also ask other key questions. Whether the event evokes positive or negative feelings in you, you may ask: "What is the gift for me in this experience?" Reflect on these questions prayerfully.

3. At this point, if the event requires more processing for its understanding, try other appropriate dreamwork techniques such as Following the Dream Ego, or Dialoguing with a character from the event. You may also use Dream Re-Entry techniques, do Four Quadrants, use artwork, or work with the major symbols in the event.

4. Ask for night dreams to help you clarify the meaning and significance of the event for you at this time in your life.

A New Way of Looking at Life

One response to the presence of mystery and the divine is to tremble and quake at its awesomeness. But mystery also fascinates us. Our interest throughout this book has been to show how inviting and attractive the mystery of the dream can be, and to suggest ways to begin plunging into its depths.

In delving into dreamwork with faith and openness, we have seen that dreams can reveal to us a radically new way of looking at our inner life and can give us new perspectives on our outer life as well. Our intent in suggesting dreamwork techniques has been to nurture a new way of looking at mysterious things. In the dream world, we discovered a treasure full of opportunities to help us become more whole and holy. As we did dreamwork, however, we began to realize that every moment of life—awake and asleep—was full of grace and potential. For some of us, there came a breakthrough in consciousness of who we could become.

Maybe through dreams and dreamwork the tasks we give ourselves—or those which are given to us—that release energy for growth in the world are a part of the growing in consciousness that will bring about a new level of human awareness. From this new perspective may come the change on our planet that we are looking for and that we so desperately need.

Could it be that in exploring the primary mystery of existence, of which our dreams and the events of our lives partake, we may discover that all creation, conscious and unconscious, is ready and eager to live in peace and unity, working together in a holy communion vivified by the Holy Spirit?

The world of dreams is like a vessel full of precious things. There are three responses we might make to it: we can leave the vessel where we found it, the contents unexamined, and go on our way; second, we can look at the lovely things, acknowledge that they are indeed there, and go on our way; or, we can take out each object, one by one, examine it, discover its meaning and value, and put it to work in our lives, to transform ourselves and the world.

The choice is ours.

How will each of us respond?

Chapter 18

Summary

◆

Dreamwork and Life

For most readers, working with this book will be a journey into new territory in the spiritual life.

When we come to the close of dream'work courses and workshops, people often ask: "Now that I've been through the material, where do I go from here? How do I continue to develop the process?"

Dreams call us to consciousness. But consciousness is not complete when it only remains at the state of awareness; true consciousness is spelled out in appropriate action. From our religious perspective, we are all called to put spiritual energy and insight into action in our world. Through the activity of consciousness, the energy from dreams flows into our lives in transforming ways.

We have discovered how dreams and dreamwork can put us in touch with our personal journey, with the path we are traveling, as well as with our vision and quest, our destiny and fate. Our challenge is to use this awareness in a practical and methodical way so that the effects we desire may be achieved.

Working Individually

The book has been designed so that you can work with it individually as a learning manual. We suggest you review each of the techniques and try them out on your dreams or on biblical dreams and visions or Jesus' parables. At the end of this chapter is a list of some biblical passages we have found helpful. The list is not exhaustive.

When you try a technique on one of your own dreams or some biblical material, record your experience in your journal. It is surprising how much you can learn about yourself and your spiritual growth on your own when you write it down and review it.

It is often helpful to have a friend with whom you can share your dreamwork from time to time, better if your friend also has an interest in dreams, and best if your friend is also working with dreams the way you are.

If when doing dreamwork alone you begin to feel overwhelmed and feel you cannot handle it alone, stop working on the dream and seek professional therapeutic or religious help. Let your counselor or therapist know you have been doing dreamwork using this book. For most people, such overwhelming experience never occurs. They find dreamwork exciting, integrative, insightful and reassuring; they realize that through actively working with their dreams new meaning for their lives continues to reveal itself to them.

Working with a Dreamwork Partner

It often proves more supportive and meaningful to work on your dreams with someone who is also doing dreamwork. In proceeding through this book together, you may read and discuss chapters of the book, do dreamwork together, and share.

Partners can often only find time to work together once a week. During these meetings, we suggest you share the ongoing results, or at least the highlights, of the dreamwork you have been doing individually.

Having a dreamwork partner helps most people keep their commitment to dreamwork, and keeps a flow of energy and creativity going that is often hard to maintain without a partner.

Bringing your dreams and dreamwork to your therapist or spiritual director, who acts somewhat like a partner, usually helps deepen the growth work you are doing. Therapists and directors will want to be familiar with this book to be better in tune with your dreamwork process.

Working Within a Dreamwork Group

Since dreams and the help in discernment they provide can be a special gift to your family and community, we hope that many dream groups will spring up in homes, churches and spiritual centers.

One simple group format is for the members to meet each week to discuss a chapter of the book, try the suggested techniques on some dream material, and discuss the experience. Such a structure will undoubtedly help train people in using the dreamwork process. In less than six months, a weekly dreamwork group could process through most of the book and spend some extra time on the more central techniques.

The longer the group maintains their spirit and commitment, the more moving and self-awakening the dream experience becomes, each member using those techniques that seem most helpful.

In a group where everyone is working actively with reference to the book, no one member needs to be the expert or leader. In fact, we suggest that participants take turns leading the group meetings by helping the group to focus their attention, offering a short meditation, and facilitating the group discussion and sharing.

Sharing Dreams Within a Family

Within the family, a less formal structure is needed than with an ongoing dreamwork group. Families who do dreamwork together—we use the term "family" in a generic sense of people, related or not, who live and share together—report finding breakfast or dinner time, usually on weekends, the best times to share and work on their dreams together. It is important for parents to work on their own dreams, not merely to focus on their children's dream material.

Family and relationship issues are bound to surface through such dreamwork, and this will prove beneficial in the long run, for dreams tend to bring up in a safe and symbolic way the issues in a family that need healing and development. Remember always that in dreamwork the focus is on the dream itself and not on each other. Maintaining that focus encourages openness and non-defensiveness among the family. Dreams and dreamwork can provide a safe path for families to journey forward in life.

Lifestyle Benefits of Doing Dreamwork

Participants in our courses and workshops offer comments on the benefits this kind of dreamwork brings, whether done alone, with a partner, or in groups. Some of their responses are sampled here: Dreamwork

- helps point out my personality issues and fears.
- leads me to my sources of anxiety and to ways of dealing with stress in my life.
- fills me with creative ideas and new potential.
- offers me alternative ways of perceiving situations and alternative ways of acting in the world.
- points out my ego's style of choice-making.
- and my dreams inspire and entertain me.
- opens me to the magnificence of the cathedral of the inner world, which fills me with awe.
- offers me the opportunity of being a conscious participant in exploring the arena of the unconscious.
- keeps me from getting totally caught up in my outer life.
- is a technique of practicing new ways of being.
- helps me sort out what is essential and non-essential in my life.
- helps me articulate the journey.
- mirrors my soul and my inner world.
- offers a way of harmonizing my inner and outer worlds.
- has been my true ally at some of the great transitional moments of my life.
- has opened up a whole new window on what religious experience can be.

According to certain writers in contemporary spirituality, we are living in the era of self-awareness and self-responsibility, community-awareness and community-responsibility, awareness of the importance of the personal unconscious as well as of our collective human depths.

The dream is but one piece of data in creating a satisfying spirituality for our generation, but it is an important one. The dream's fullest value can only be tapped through consistent and integrative dreamwork. It is in the dreamwork that discernment can happen. It is through dreamwork

233

that the ego is presented with alternatives from which it can make its choices. Dreamwork invites us to follow a larger meaning and purpose in our lives than simply our own wants and thoughts.

Where Have We Come?

Historically, in Old Testament times we saw that dreams were viewed as a channel of direct contact with God, and that dreams and visions held an equal authority. In the New Testament we saw that from the Gospel according to Matthew to the Apocalypse, and especially in the Book of Acts, much guidance from God came to the nascent Church through dreams and visions. This spiritual practice of looking to dreams remained a tradition during the first centuries of Christianity, not only among the commonfolk, but among the most illustrious thinkers and teachers of the growing Church. We discussed the loss of dreamwork as a familiar tool of Christian spirituality somewhere around the time of St. Jerome in the fifth century, and noted its rediscovery and reintroduction to the Christian spiritual tradition during the twentieth century.

Psychologically, while we presented dreams and dreamwork as a way of relating to God, we also emphasized dreams and dreamwork as a way of relating to ourselves. We learned to look at dreams as questions rather than answers, and to see these questions as invitations to greater consciousness, holiness and wholeness. We became aware how the art of dreamwork could teach us to use the language of dreams in the service of interpersonal and intrapersonal healing. We came to understand the ego in its choice-making function, and discovered how dreamwork could help strengthen the ego in healthy ways and aid its cooperation with the soul and our deep inner wisdom.

Holistically, we are by nature spiritual beings as well as physical and mental, and dreamwork reminds us that it is as whole persons that we are called to fullest life in the Kingdom of God. This Kingdom is active not only in the physical world but within, where our dreams live and from where our inspiration for doing dreamwork and outer life tasks comes. We learn to honor the relationship to our spiritual development that dreams continue to evoke and nourish.

Dreams also reveal a community dimension. In the process of doing dreamwork, we learn to live out our intention of pursuing our spiritual growth, not merely for our own personal development, but also for the growth of the human community.

In the end, our hope is that through dreams and dreamwork we can lead our lives in light of our unique call from God. When enough of us begin doing dreamwork and putting our insights to use in our daily lives, we will be transforming the planet into a community of conscious people in harmony with each other and with all living things.

For further information and training in dreamwork and Jungian psychology please contact:

Strephon K. Williams
Jungian-Senoi Institute
Box 9036
Berkeley, California 94709

Offers training workshops and counseling in dreamwork and Jungian psychology from a spiritual perspective. Also publishes books and tapes under its Journey Press imprint.

Selected List of Important Biblical Dreams and Visions

From the Old Testament:

Abraham's dream-vision	Genesis 15:12–21
Jacob's dream	Genesis 28:10–22
Dreams in the life of Joseph	Genesis 37:5–11
	Genesis 40—41
Solomon's dream	1 Kings 3:5–15
Samuel's call	1 Samuel 3:3–14
Eliphaz's dream	Job 4:12–21
Isaiah's call	Isaiah 6:1–13
Ezekiel's call	Ezekiel 1:4—3:3
Ezekiel's vision	Ezekiel 37:1–14
Dreams in the life of Daniel	Daniel 2—4

From the New Testament:

Zechariah's vision	Luke 1:11–20
Joseph's dream to marry Mary	Matthew 1:20–21
Shepherds' vision	Luke 2:8–14
Joseph's other dreams	Matthew 2:13, 19–20, 22
Baptism of Jesus	Matthew 3:16–17
Transfiguration	Luke 9:28–36
Paul's conversion vision	Acts 9:3–9
Peter's dream-vision	Acts 10:3–21
Paul's night visions	Acts 16:9; 18:9; 23:11; 27:23

Many of Jesus' parables when experienced as waking dreams invite dreamwork. Here are some suggestions:

Parables:

Lamp of the Body	Matthew 6:22–23
Mustard Seed	Matthew 13:31–32
Yeast	Matthew 13:33
Pearl Merchant	Matthew 13:45–46

Seed Growing by Itself	Mark 4:26–29
Good Samaritan	Luke 10:29–37
The Master's Return	Luke 12:35–40
Barren Fig Tree	Luke 13:6–9
Lost Sheep	Luke 15:4–7
Prodigal Son	Luke 15:11–32
Importunate Widow	Luke 18:2–5
Good Shepherd	John 10:1–5

Dreamwork Techniques

1. The Dream Report
2. Title, Theme, Affect, Question (TTAQ)
3. Key Questions
4. Following the Dream Ego, I
5. Dialoguing with a Dream Figure
6. Symbol Immersion
7. Carrying the Symbol Forward
8. Carrying the Symbol Back in Time
9. Symbol Amplification
10. Symbol Association
11. The Waking Dream
12. Keeping a Dream Journal
13. Choosing Dreamwork Tasks
14. Honoring Dreamwork
15. Choosing Personality Tasks
16. Choosing Outer Life Tasks
17. Seeking a Dream (Incubation)
18. Rewriting an Unresolved Dream
19. Researching a Dream Theme
20. Resolving a Remembered Dream
21. Following the Dream Ego, II
22. Working on Personality Issues
23. Artwork with Dream Symbols
24. Metaphoric Processing
25. Meditating on an Important Dream Symbol
26. Choosing the Issue To Be Resolved
27. Dream Re-Entry
28. Carrying the Dream Forward (Completing a Nightmare)
29. Four Quadrants
30. Looking for Social Dimensions of a Dream

Bibliography

Books

Bergson, Henri. *The World of Dreams.* New York: Philosophical Library, 1958.

Brown, Raymond E. *The Birth of the Messiah: A Commentary on the Infancy Narratives in Matthew and Luke.* Garden City: Doubleday, 1977.

Daniélou, Jean. *From Shadows to Reality: Studies in the Biblical Typology of the Fathers.* Translated by Wulstan Hubbard. London, 1960.

Deikmann, Arthur. *The Observing Self.* Boston: Beacon Press, 1982.

Delaney, Gayle. *Living Your Dreams.* New York: Harper & Row, 1979.

Deloria, Vine. *God Is Red.* New York: Grosset and Dunlap, 1973.

Eliade, Mircea. *Myths, Dreams and Mysteries.* New York: Harper & Row, 1960.

Ellenberger, Henri. *The Discovery of the Unconscious.* New York: Basic Books, 1970.

Fedotov, G.P. *A Treasury of Russian Spirituality.* New York: Sheed and Ward, 1948.

Fitzgerald, Augustine. *The Essays and Hymns of Synesius of Cyrene.* London: Oxford, 1930.

Freud, Sigmund. *The Interpretation of Dreams* in *Basic Writings of Sigmund Freud.* New York: Basic Books, 1955.

———. *On Dreams.* New York: W.W. Norton, 1952.

Garfield, Patricia. *Creative Dreaming.* New York: Simon and Schuster, 1974.

Grunebaum, G.E. and Roger Callois. *The Dream and Human Societies.* Berkeley: University of California Press, 1966.

Hanna, Barbara. *Encounters with the Soul: Active Imagination as Developed by C.G. Jung.* New York: Signet, 1981.

Hartmann, E. *The Biology of Dreaming.* Springfield, Illinois: Thomas, 1967.

Hillman, James. *The Dream and the Underworld.* New York: Harper & Row, 1979.

Jaeger, Werner. *Early Christianity and Greek Paideia.* Cambridge: Harvard University Press, 1961.

———. *Paideia: The Ideals of Greek Culture.* Oxford: Oxford University Press, 1939–44.

Jung, C.G. *Archetypes and The Collective Unconscious.* Princeton: Bollingen Collected Works, 9, 1959.

———. *The Collected Works of C.G. Jung.* New York: Pantheon, 1958.
Writings with a special focus on dreams and dreamwork include: *Psychology and Religion, The Analysis of Dreams, The Practical Uses of Dream Analysis, On Psychic Energy, The Theory of Psychoanalysis, The Meaning of Psychology for Modern Man,* and *On the Nature of Dreams.*

———. *Man and His Symbols.* New York: Dell, 1968.

———. *Memories, Dream,, and Reflections.* New York: Random House, 1961.

Kelsey, Morton. *Dreams: A Way To Listen to God.* Ramsey, N.J.: Paulist Press, 1978.

———. *God, Dreams and Revelation.* Minneapolis: Augsburg, 1974.

Leech, Kenneth. *Soul Friend.* New York: Harper & Row, 1980.

Lewalski, Barbara Kiefer. *Protestant Poetics and The Seventeenth-Century Religious Lyric.* Princeton: Princeton University Press, 1979.

Linde, Shirley Motter and Louis M. Savary. *The Joy of Sleep.* New York: Harper & Row, 1980.

Lindskoog, Kathryn. *The Gift of Dreams: A Christian View.* New York: Harper & Row, 1979.

McLeester, Dick. *Welcome to the Magic Theater: A Handbook for Exploring Dreams.* Amherst, Massachusetts: Food for Thought Press, 1976.

Mattoon, Mary Ann. *Applied Dream Analysis: A Jungian Approach.* Washington, D.C.: Winston Wiley, 1978.

Mahoney, Maria. *The Meaning in Dreams and Dreaming.* New York: Citadel Press, 1966.

Meseguer, Pedro, S.J. *The Secret of Dreams.* Westminster, Md.: Newman Press, 1960.

Newhall, Daniel H. *Dreams and The Bible.* San Anselmo, San Francisco Theological Seminary, 1980. An unpublished doctoral dissertation.

Rader, Rosemary. "The Martyrdom of Perpetua: A Protest Account of Third-Century Christianity," in Patricia Wilson-Kastner, et al., A Lost Tradition: Women Writers of the Early Church. Washington, D.C.: University Press of America, 1981.

Reid, Clyde. The Return to Faith. New York: Harper & Row, 1974.

Sanford, John. Dreams and Healing. Ramsey, N.J.: Paulist Press, 1978.

———. Dreams: God's Forgotten Language. New York: Lippincott, 1968.

Singer, June. Boundaries of The Soul. Garden City: Anchor Books, 1973.
    See chapters on dreams and dreaming.

Speiser, E.A. Genesis: The Anchor Bible. New York: Doubleday, 1964.

Stewart, Kilton. Creative Psychology and Dream Education. New York: Stewart Foundation.

———. "Dream Theory in Malaya," in Charles T. Tart, editor, Altered States of Consciousness. New York: Wiley, 1969.

Taylor, Jeremy. Dream Work: Techniques for Discovering the Creative Power in Dreams. Ramsey, N.J.: Paulist Press, 1983. Extensive annotated bibliography on dream writings.

Ullman, Montague and Stanley Krippner. Dream Telepathy. New York: Macmillan, 1973.

——— and Nan Zimmerman. Working with Dreams. New York: Delacorte, 1979.

Vaughn, Frances. Awakening Intuition. Garden City: Doubleday, 1979.
    See chapter "Dreams and Intuition."

Watkins, Mary M. Waking Dreams. New York: Harper Colophon, 1977.

Welch, John. Spiritual Pilgrims: Carl Jung and Teresa of Avila. Ramsey, N.J.: Paulist Press, 1982.

White, Victor, O.P. God and the Unconscious. Cleveland: World Publishing, 1961.

———. Soul and Psyche: An Enquiry into the Relationship of Psychotherapy and Religion. London: Collins and Harvill, 1960.

Williams, Strephon Kaplan. Jungian-Senoi Dreamwork Manual. Berkeley: Journey Press, 1980.

Wink, Walter. The Bible in Human Transformation: Toward a New Paradigm for Biblical Study. Philadelphia: Fortress Press, 1973.

Woods, Ralph Louis, editor. The New World of Dreams. New York: Macmillan, 1974.

Articles

Barasch, Marc. "Dreamland: A Hands-On Guide to the New Dreamwork." New Age Journal (October 1983): 39–50.

Bianchi, Eugene. "Student Dreams: Perspectives on Spiritual Development." Religious Education 1979 74(6): 641–655.

Borelli, J. "Dreams, Myths, and Religious Symbolism." Thought (March 1975), 50: 56–66.

Brayer, Menachem M. "Psychosomatics, Hermetic Medicine, and Dream Interpretation in the Qumran Literature." Jewish Quarterly Review. Part I, 1969, 60(2): 112–127 and Part II, 1970, 60(3): 213–230.

Caldwell, J. "Dreams and Discernment." Sisters Today (May 1977), 48: 601–605.

———. "Paying Attention to Dreams." Sisters Today (January 1978), 49: 319–321.

Getsinger, S.H. "Dreaming, Religion and Health." Journal of Religion and Health 1978, 17(3): 199–209.

Gibson, Terrill L. "The Critical Dream Incident in Pastoral Psychotherapy." Pastoral Psychology 1979, 27(4): 260–267.

Gnuse, Robert. "Dreams and Their Theological Significance in the Biblical Tradition." Currents in Theology and Mission 1981, 8(3): 166–171.

Goldberg, M. "In Dreams Begin Responsibilities." Cross Currents (Winter 1976), 25: 451–455.

Gramlich, Miriam Louise. "The Questions of Jesus: Calls to Commitment." Review for Religious (March/April 1983), 42(2): 233–239.

Greene, Thayer A. "The Dream: Clinical Aid and Theological Catalyst." *Union Seminary Quarterly Review* 1969, 24(2): 171–180.

Hall, J.A. "Religious Images in Dreams." *Journal of Religion and Health* 1979, 18(4): 327–335.

Holloway, Marcella M., C.S.J. "Dreams Can Enrich Our Waking Hours." *Sisters Today* (February 1982), 53: 353–357.

Meany, J. "Dreams and the Counseling of Religious." *Sisters Today* (January 1971), 42: 265–268.

———. "The Role of Dreams in Religious Formation Groups." *Review for Religious* (January 1972), 31: 70–75.

Navone, John. "Dreams in the Bible." *Bible Today* (November 1975), 80: 515–518.

———. "Theologian as Interpreter of Dreams." *Spiritual Life* (Summer 1976), 22:115–124.

Warren, M. "Let Your Young Ones See Visions, Your Old Ones Dream Dreams." *Liturgy* (January/February 1979), 24: 11–13.

Zeitlin, Solomon. "Dreams and Their Interpretation from the Biblical Period to the Tannaitic Time: An Historical Survey." *Jewish Quarterly Review* 1975, 66(1): 1–18.